THE GOSPEL IN THE STARS

THE GOSPEL IN THE STARS

JOSEPH A. SEISS

kregel
PUBLICATIONS

Grand Rapids, MI 49501

The Gospel in the Stars
by Joseph A. Seiss

Originally published under the title *The Gospel in the Stars: or, Primeval Astronomy* in 1882 by E. Claxton & Company, Philadelphia, Pennsylvania.

Published in 1972 by Kregel Publications, a division of Kregel, Inc., P.O. Box 2607, Grand Rapids, MI 49501. Kregel Publications provides trusted, biblical publications for Christian growth and service. Your comments and suggestions are valued.

For more information about Kregel Publications, visit our web site at: www.kregel.com

Library of Congress Catalog Card Number: 72-86676

ISBN 0-8254-3796-2

10 11 12 13 14 / 04 03 02 01 00

Printed in the United States of America

PREFACE

It may seem adventurous to propose to read the Gospel of Christ from what Herschel calls "those uncouth figures and outlines of men and monsters usually scribbled over celestial globes and maps." So it once would have seemed to the writer. But a just estimate of the case cannot be formed without a close survey of what these figures are, what relations they bear to each other, whence they originated, and what meaning was attached to them by the most ancient peoples from whom they have been transmitted to us. Such a survey the author of this volume has endeavored to make. From an extended induction he has also reached conclusions which lead him to think he may do good service by giving publicity to the results of his examinations.

The current explanations of the origin and meaning of the constellations certainly are not such as should satisfy those in search of positive truth. Herschel characterizes them as "puerile and absurd." They are nowhere to be found outside of Greece and Rome and modern works which have thence derived them. They are part of the staple in the theories and arguments of infidelity. The more ancient and more knowing peoples never so explained these celestial signs, but uniformly regarded them as divine in source and sacred in significance. Even Greece and Rome never could separate them from their worship, their gods, and their hopes of futurity, whilst some of their best authors devoutly referred to them as divine. The theory that they have come from natural observations of the seasons and man's occupations in different parts of the year is but a rationalistic conjecture, unsupported by facts or analogy. It is the mere guess of men pressed by the presence of a great and masterly system marked on the heavens for which they knew not how to account —a guess which will not stand the test of its own assumptions or common sense, much less the light now in the world's possession respecting the remoter antiquities of man. That some Greek and Roman authors, who never understood any of these things,* should indulge in such unfounded suppositions is not remarkable; but that people of learning and science, jealous of building on anything but solid grounds, should still entertain and reiterate them for ascertained verities, is very surprising. And if men are constrained thus to accept and repeat them from sheer inability otherwise to solve the problem, it should convince them that they have not yet risen to the true character and dignity of these ancient records, and dispose them to a fresh and searching re-examination of the whole subject, to which this book is meant to furnish some humble aid.

The first suspicion that the original constellations may perhaps have come from a divine or prophetic source was impressed upon the writer's mind in connection with his studies of the marvellous wisdom embodied in the Great Pyramid of Gizeh. But it came only in the shape of an inference, which needed to be tested on its own independent grounds before

* See Grote's *History of Greece*, vol. i. pp. 394-444.

it could be reasonably accepted. That inference, however, was so direct, and the subject seemed so worthy of being investigated, that a course of special study was instituted to ascertain, apart from all pyramid-theories, whether the facts and probabilities in the case would warrant a conclusion of so much moment.

A new field of inquiry thus opened, for the exploration of which but few helps beyond the ordinary books on astronomy could be found. Something, however, had been done by Bailly in his *History of Astronomy*, Dupuis in his *L'Origines des Cultus*, Volney in *Les Ruines*, and some other writers of the same class. To throw contempt on Christianity as a mere accommodation of certain old mythic ideas common to all primitive peoples, these men adduced a large amount of traditional and astronomic lore, proving the great antiquity of the constellations, and showing a striking correspondence between them and the subsequent scriptural story of Christ and salvation. Able theologians like Roberts and Faber, in making replies to these French skeptics, were obliged to admit the strong array of facts alleged, and could only surmise a variety of explanations to do away with the intended conclusion as a *non sequitur*. The argument of these infidels is indeed fatally defective, especially in assuming that the old astronomy throughout, and all the myths and worships associated with it, have come solely from the natural observation and imagination of man, apart from all supernatural light, revelation, or inspiration. With this starting-point unproven and incapable of verification, and with the positive assertions of all the primeval world and all the indications directly to the contrary, the whole argument necessarily breaks down. Like all the efforts of unbelief, it signally fails. But though the argument, as such, is false and worthless, it does not follow that the materials collected to build it are the same. For the most part, they are solid enough in themselves, and the gathering of them was a valuable contribution to a better cause. The showings made of the close likeness between the old constellations and the Gospel are well founded, and can now be illustrated to a much greater and more minute extent. But, instead of proving Christianity a mere revival of old mythologies, they give powerful impulse toward the conclusion that the constellations and their associated myths and traditions are themselves, in their original, from the very same prophetic Spirit whence the Sacred Scriptures have come, and that they are of a piece with the biblical records in the system of God's universal enunciations of the Christ.

Gale, in his *Court of the Gentiles*, Faber, *On Pagan Idolatry*, Roberts, in his *Letters to Volney*, Haslam, on *The Cross and the Serpent*, and the author of *Primeval Man Unveiled*, have slightly touched upon the subject, and furnish some materials in the direction of the same conclusions.

Sir William Drummond, in his *Origines*, C. Piazzi Smyth, in his *Life and Work*, and J. T. Goodsir, *On Ethnic Inspiration*, also present some important facts and considerations relating to the general inquiry.

A more valuable aid to the study of the subject as treated in this volume is Frances Rolleston's *Mazzaroth ; or, The Constellations*—a book from an authoress of great linguistic and general literary attainments, whom Providence rarely favored for the collection of important facts and materials, particularly as respects the ancient stellar nomenclature. The tables drawn up by Ulugh Beigh, the Tartar prince and astronomer, about A. D. 1420, giving Arabian astronomy as it had come down to his time, with the ancient Coptic and Egyptian names, likewise the much earlier presentations, made about A. D. 850 by Albumazer, the great Arab astronomer of the Caliphs of Grenada, and Aben Ezra's commentaries on the same, are, to a considerable extent, reproduced in her book. Fac-similes of the Dendera and Esne Zodiacs are also given in the last edition (1875) of her work. And from her tables and references the writer of these Lectures was helped to some of his best information, without which this book could hardly have become what it is.

If any others have treated directly, or even incidentally, of what is sought to be shown in this volume, its author has not discovered their records or their names.

With but little, therefore, but the star-maps and descriptions as given by astronomers, and such notices of the constellations as are to be found in the remains of antiquity and general literature, he had to make his way as best he could. With what success he has done his work, and in how far his conclusions are entitled to credit or respect, he now submits to the decision of a candid and intelligent public.

CONTENTS

I

THE STARRY WORLDS

And God said, Let there be lights in the firmament of the heavens to divide the day from the night; and let them be for signs, and for seasons, and for days, and for years.   —Genesis 1:14

THE sublimest visible objects of human contemplation are the Starry Heavens. The beholder is awed at every thoughtful look upon them. And when viewed in the light of astronomical science the mind is overwhelmed and lost amid the vastness and magnificence of worlds and systems which roll and shine above, around and beneath us.

THE SUN

The most conspicuous, to us, of these wonderful orbs is the Sun. Seemingly, it is not as large as the wheel of a wagon, but when we learn that we see it only at the distance of more than ninety-one millions of miles, and consider how the apparent size of objects diminishes in proportion to their remoteness, we justly conclude that it must be of enormous magnitude to be so conspicuous across a gulf so vast. Our earth is a large body; it takes long and toilsome journeying for a man to make his way around it. But the Sun fills more than a million times the cubic space filled by the earth. A railway-train running

thirty miles an hour, and never stopping, could not go around it in less than eleven years, nor run the distance from the earth to the Sun in less than three hundred and sixty years. If we were to take a string long enough to reach the moon, and draw a circle with it at its utmost stretch, the Sun would still be six times larger than that circle. Belonging to the system of which it is the centre there are eight primary planets, some of them more than a thousand times larger than our earth, besides eighty-five asteroids, twenty-one satellites or moons, and several hundred comets. But the Sun itself is six hundred times greater than all these planets and their satellites put together. The greatest of them might be thrown into it, and would be to it no more than a drop to a bucket, a bird-shot to a cannon-ball, or an infant's handful to a bushel measure.

THE VASTNESS OF THE UNIVERSE

But, great and glorious as the Sun is, and seemingly so much greater than every other

9

object in the sky, it is really only a tiny fragment, a mere speck, in the magnificent starry empire of which it is a part. It is less to the material universe at large than a globule to our globe. With all its retinue of ponderous orbs, it is only one of innumerable hosts of such suns and systems. There are myriads of stars in space immeasurably greater than it. They look very diminutive in comparison with it, but they are hundreds of thousands of times farther off. A ball shot from a cannon and moving at the rate of five hundred miles an hour could not reach the nearest of them in less than thirteen millions of years. Light is the rapidest of known travellers. A ray from the Sun reaches us in about eight and a quarter minutes. But there are some stars in these heavens known to be so remote that if a ray of light had started from them direct for our world when Adam drew his first breath, it would hardly yet have reached the earth. Sirius alone gives out nearly four hundred times as much light as the Sun, and yet Sirius is a star of moderate size among the stars. The Sun is no more to many other stars than one of our smaller planets is to it. We know that the Sun turns on its axis as the earth turns, and that it is ever moving on a journey around some transcendently greater centre, just as the earth and other planets revolve around it as their centre. It takes the earth one year to complete its revolution around the Sun, but it takes the Sun eighteen millions of our years to make its revolution around the centre which it obeys.

We are amazed and overwhelmed in the contemplation of worlds and systems so vast. But there is solid reason for believing that all these tremendous systems, in which uncounted suns take the place of planets, are themselves but satellites of still immeasurably sublimer orbs, and thus on upward, through systems on systems, to some supreme physical Omnipotent, where the unsearchable JEHOVAH has His throne, and whence He gives forth His invincible laws to the immensity of His glorious realm.

These are the "lights," light-bearers, or luminaries to which the text refers, and which the potent creative Word has brought into being and placed in the firmament of the heaven.

OBJECTS OF THESE MATERIAL CREATIONS

Such wonderful creations of almighty power and wisdom were not without a purpose. It was the will of the eternal God to be known —to have creatures to understand and enjoy His glory — to provide for them suitable homes—to acquaint them with His intelligence, power, and perfections—to fill them with a sense of the existence and potent presence of an infinite creative Mind, from which all things proceed and on which all creatures depend.

All the purposes of creation we cannot begin to fathom or comprehend. No plummet-line of human understanding can reach the bottom of such depths. We stand on solid ground, however, when we say and believe that the intent of the physical universe is *to declare and display the majesty and glory of its Creator.* Hence the apostolic assertion: "The invisible things of Him from the creation of the world are clearly seen, being understood by the things that are made, even His eternal power and Godhead." But the particular ends and objects included in this grand purpose are as multitudinous and diverse as the things themselves. Among the rest, there is one specially expressed and emphasized in the text. When God created these heavenly worlds He said, "*And let them be for* SIGNS."

THE STARS AS SIGNS

A *sign* is something arbitrarily selected and appointed to represent some other thing. The letters of the alphabet are "signs"—signs of sounds and numbers. The notes on a clef of musical writing are "signs"—signs of the pitch and value of certain tones of voice or instrument. There is no relation whatever between these "signs" and the things they signify, except that men have agreed to employ them for these purposes. Their whole meaning as "signs" is purely conventional and arbitrary—something quite beyond and above what pertains to their nature. And so with all "signs."

When Moses said that the swarm of flies

should be a "sign" to the Egyptians, there was nothing in the nature of the thing to show what was thereby signified. When the prophet told Hezekiah that the going back of the shadow on the dial should be a "sign" that he would recover from his sickness, live yet fifteen years, and see Jerusalem delivered out of the hand of the Syrian invader, there was nothing in the nature of the thing to express this gracious meaning. Isaiah's walking barefoot had no natural connection with the Syrian conquest of Egypt, and yet this was "for a sign" of that fact. And thus when God said of the celestial luminaries, "*and let them be for signs*," He meant that they should be used to signify something beyond and additional to what they evidence and express in their nature and natural offices. Nor can any sense be attached to the words, consistent with the dignity of the record, without admitting that God intended from the beginning that these orbs of light should be made to bear, express, record, and convey some special teaching different from what is naturally deducible from them.

What the stars were thus meant to *signify*, over and above what is evidenced by their own nature, interpreters have been at a loss to tell us. And yet there should not be such a total blank on the subject. Light has been at hand all the while. For ages this whole field has been almost entirely left to a superstitious and idolatrous astrology, which has befouled a noble and divine science and done immeasurable damage to the souls of men. But we here find it claimed to be a sacred domain laid out of God in the original intent of creation itself. And when I look at the deep and almost universal hold which a spurious and wicked treatment of this field has so long had upon mankind, I have been the more led to suspect the existence of some original, true, and sacred thing back of it, out of which all this false science and base superstition has grown, and of which it is the perversion. There is no potent system of credulity in the world which has not had some great truth at the root of it. Evil is always perverted good, as dirt is simply matter out of place. It is the spoliation of some better thing going be-

fore it. And so there is reason to think that there is, after all, some great, original, divine science connected with the stars, which astrology has prostituted to its own base ends, and which it is our duty to search out and turn to its proper evangelic use.

"As from the oldest times the suns and other worlds have been arranged into groups, is it not allowable to inquire whether there was not a unity of purpose and connected meaning in them, though these grotesque figures are represented as hieroglyphs which we trace to the Chaldeans and Phœnicians?" is a question which Ingemann, the distinguished Danish author, puts, and who was by far more persuaded of their probable reference to divine revelations than of their origin as more commonly explained.

Richer, a French writer, has repeatedly asserted that the whole primitive revelation may be traced in the constellations.

Albumazer describes the various constellations as known over all the world from the beginning, and says, "Many attributed to them a divine and prophetic virtue."

Cicero, in translating the account of the constellations by Aratus, says, "The signs are measured out, that in so many descriptions divine wisdom might appear."

Roberts, in his *Letters to Volney*, accepts it as a truth that the emblems in the stars refer to the primeval promise of the Messiah and His work of conquering the Serpent through His sufferings, and traces out some of the particular instances.

Dupuis, in *L'Origine des Cultus*, has collected a vast number of traditions prevalent in all nations of a divine person, born of a woman, suffering in conflict with a serpent, but triumphing over him at last, and finds the same reflected in the figures of the ancient constellations.

Dr. Adam Clarke says of the ancient Egyptians that they held the stars to be symbols of sacred things. Lucian and Dupuis assert the same, and say that "astronomy was the soul of the Egyptian religious system." The same is equally true of the Chaldeans and Assyrians.

Smith and Sayce, in *The Chaldean Account*

of Genesis, say : " It is evident, from the opening of the inscription on the first tablet of the great Chaldean work on astrology and astronomy, that the functions of the stars were, according to the Babylonians, to act not only as regulators of the seasons of the year, but also *used as signs;* for in those ages it was generally believed that the heavenly bodies gave, by their appearance and positions, *signs of events which were coming on the earth."*

The learned G. Stanley Faber admits the connection between the starry emblems and the myths and mysteries of the ancients. He thinks " the forms of men and women, beasts and birds, monsters and reptiles, with which the whole face of heaven has been disguised, are *not without their signification,"* and allows that the reference, in parts at least, is to the Seed of the woman, and His bruising of the Serpent.

It is furthermore a matter of inspired New-Testament record that certain wise men from among the Gentile peoples not only looked to the stars as by some means made to refer to and represent a coming Saviour, even the Lord Jesus himself, but were so moved and persuaded by their observations of the stars, from what they saw there signified, that they set out under the guidance of those starry indications to find Him whom they thus perceived to have been born in Judea, in order that they might greet Him as their Lord and honor Him by their adoration and their gifts (Matt. 2 : 1–11). All that entered into this case we may not now be able to determine, but the fact remains that these wise men of the Gentiles did actually come to Jerusalem, and thence to Bethlehem, to find and worship the new-born Saviour, moved and led *by astronomic signs*, which they never could have understood as they did if there had not been associated with the stars some definite evangelic prophecies and promises which they could read, and believed to be from God.

And since these starry emblems are invariably connected with the most striking and sublime appearances in the visible creation, seen in all climates, accompanying the out-wandering tribes of man in all their migrations, why should we not expect to find among the names and figures annexed to them some memorial of great and universal importance to the whole human race? Certainly, if we could find connected with every constellation and each remarkable star some divine truth, some prophetic annunciation, some important revelation or fact, there would be opened to us a field of grand contemplations and of sublime memorializations which we may well suppose the infinite Mind of God would neither overlook nor leave unutilized.

For my own part, having investigated the subject with such aids as have been within my reach, I am quite convinced, as much from the internal evidences as the external, that the learned authoress of *Mazzaroth* was correct in saying that from the latent significance of the names and emblems of the ancient astronomy " we may learn the all-important fact that God has spoken—that He gave to the earliest of mankind a revelation, equally important to the latest, even of those very truths afterward written for our admonition on whom the ends of the world are come." Taken along with the myths and traditions which have been lodged among all the nations, I am quite sure that we have here a glorious record of primeval faith and hope, furnishing a sublime testimony to the anticipations of the first believers, and at the same time an invincible attestation to the blessed Gospel on which our expectations of eternal life are built. Not to the being and attributes of an eternal Creator alone, but, above all, to the specific and peculiar work of our redemption, and to Him in whom standeth our salvation, are these " lights in the firmament " the witnesses and " signs "

THE GLORY OF GOD

One of the sublimest of the Psalms, which celebrates the twofold world of Nature and Revelation, begins with the ever-memorable assertion, " *The heavens declare the glory of God."* What the heavens are thus said to declare certainly includes more than the celestial bodies naturally tell concerning their Creator. Their showing forth of His " handi work," His wisdom and power, is the subject of a separate and distinct part of the grand sentence.

The chief "glory of God" cannot be learned from Nature alone, simply as Nature. The *moral attributes* of Deity, and His manifestations in moral government, are pre-eminently His glory. In the sending, incarnation, person, revelations, offices, and achievements of Jesus Christ, above all, has God shown forth His glory. We are told in so many words that Christ is "the image and glory of God;" nay, "the brightness—the very outbeaming—of His glory." The glory of God is "in the face of Jesus Christ." There can therefore be no full and right declaring of "the glory of God" which does not reach and embrace Christ, and the story of redemption through Him. But the starry worlds, simply as such, do not and cannot declare or show forth Christ as the Redeemer, or the glory of God in Him. If they do it at all, they must do it as "signs," arbitrarily used for that purpose. Yet the Psalmist affirms that these heavens do "declare the glory of God." Are we not therefore to infer that the story of Christ and redemption is somehow expressed by the stars? David may or may not have so understood it, but the Holy Ghost, speaking through him, knew the implication of the words, which, in such a case, must not be stinted, but accepted in the fullest sense they will bear. And as it is certain that God meant and ordained a use of the heavenly bodies in which they should "be *for signs*," and as we are here assured that what they have been arranged to signify is "*the glory of God*," there would seem to be ample scriptural warrant for believing that, by special divine order and appointment, the illustration of God's moral government, particularly as embraced in the story of sin, and redemption by Jesus Christ, is to be found in the stars, according to some primordial and sacred system of astronomy.

Thus, by way of the Bible itself, we reach the idea of THE GOSPEL IN THE STARS, which it is my purpose, with the help of God, to identify, illustrate, and prove.

THE GOSPEL STORY

The Gospel is chiefly made up of the story of the Serpent and the Cross—the doctrine of the fall and depravity of man through the subtlety of "the Dragon, that old Serpent, called the Devil and Satan, which deceiveth the whole world," and the recovery of fallen man through a still mightier One, who comes from heaven, assumes human nature, and by suffering, death, and exaltation to the right hand of supreme dominion, vanquishes the Dragon and becomes the Author of eternal salvation. The preaching of this is the preaching of *the Gospel*, and the earnest and hopeful belief of this is the belief of the Gospel, according to the Scriptures and all the accepted Creeds of the Church from the days of the apostles till now.

The same was also known and believed from the earliest periods of human existence. The Bible is particular to tell us, in its very first chapters, of a subtle and evil spirit, contemplated and named as "the Serpent," through whose agency Eve was beguiled, and the human race, then consisting of but two persons, brought into sin, condemnation and death. It is equally particular to tell us in the same chapter that while Adam was yet in Paradise, though guilty and about to be driven out into an adverse world, the Lord pronounced a sentence on the Serpent, in which He gave forth the comprehensive primordial Gospel promise, with all the fundamental elements of the true and only evangelic faith: "*And the Lord said unto the serpent, Because thou hast done this, thou art cursed. . . . And I will put enmity between thee and the woman, and between her Seed and thy seed; it (He) shall bruise thy head, and thou shalt bruise His heel*" (Gen. 3 : 14, 15).

From the most sacred and authoritative of records we thus find the original of all legends and myths of the Serpent and his Destroyer, of the conflict with the Dragon, and the ultimate slaying of him by that mighty One to be born of woman; who would have to toil and suffer indeed, but would not give over till His victory should be complete. In that one pregnant text we identify the Serpent and the Cross—the Prince of Evil and the Prince of Peace—the Dragon-Deceiver and the suffering Redeemer—the deadly malignity of the one and the self-sacrificing beneficence of the other—an irreconcilable feud between them, with a promised crushing out of the Destroyer by the wounded Saviour. In other words, we thus, from the very beginning of human history, come upon and identify the one great master-theme of both Testaments, the chief substance of all prophecy and promise, and the sum of all evangelic preaching, faith, and hope, from the foundation of the world. And what I propose to show in this series of Lectures is, that this very story, in all its length and breadth, stands written upon the stars, put there in the original framing of astronomy as an everlasting witness of God's gracious purposes toward our race, and that the heavens do verily declare the highest glory of God.

How the Stars are Made to Speak

To those who have never looked into the science of astronomy, its truths, predictions, and revelations necessarily appear very mysterious and surprising. Looking out upon the multitude of stars that shine in the nocturnal heavens, they seem to be so scattered, so entirely without order, so confusedly spread over the face of the sky, that the untutored mind may well despair of reading anything intelligible there. And when, by the aid of the telescope, thousands are multiplied to millions, and suns, systems, and universes rise to view, and the eye sweeps outward to distances which no figures of our arithmetic can express, and into unfathomable gulfs of space all filled up with an endless profusion of innumerable worlds, any understanding of them, especially the deciphering of great evangelic truths from them, would seem to be the height of impossibility. And if now, for the first time, man had to grapple with the problem, with nothing going before to assist him, vain indeed would be our poor short-lived efforts to master such a tremendous field.

But we have not now for the first time, or with only our weak and unaided powers, to make the commencement of this study. Men who lived almost a thousand years—men who lived almost a thousand years—men with powers of vision that lasted undimmed through nearly a decade of centuries—men with minds in much closer communion than ours with the infinite and eternal Intelligence — have employed themselves, helped as they were by the great Maker's Spirit, in observing, classifying, grouping, and designating these starry worlds, assigning them their names, marking their courses, and making them the bearers of wisdom the dearest and most precious ever made known to man. In their hands and to their peering scrutiny this wilderness of stellar glories took order, shape, and readable meaning which the depravities of the after ages have not been able to set aside, and which, by the scientific enlightenment of our times, we may retrace, and bring our minds into communion with their own.

Star-Groups

Any one attentively observing the starry heavens will see that some of the stars are brighter than others, "for one star differeth from another star in glory." Some hold their places from age to age with variations so slight as scarcely to be observable in thousands of years. Some of them are "wandering stars," changing places continually, going and returning at fixed intervals. Some of them are nestled together in particular groups, or stand alone in their special glories so as to be easily distinguished. By means of these facts maps of the heavens can be made as well as maps of the earth; and by the long and careful observation and study of them it has come to be known how these heavenly configurations stood and will stand at any particular period of time.

The starry heavens, therefore, are not mere unmeaning and incomprehensible show—not a boundless and trackless wilderness of luminous orbs. There are paths which we can thread, sometimes dark and rugged, and often leading into depths through which it is hard to follow them, but still not untraceable. As men can find a way through the most intricate musical composition, through a great poem, through a sublime oration, and through the plans and ideas of the most complicated specimen of mechanism or architecture, so may we find our way through the starry heavens, and mostly tell where we are, what we are contemplating, what relation part bears to part, and read from these glorious luminaries as we would read from the face of a clock or from the placements of the letters of the alphabet. And as most of these star-groups retain almost precisely the same places and relations for thousands on thousands of years, if any one cognizant of the facts, and setting himself for the first time to describe them, had wished to record certain great ideas for unchanged perpetuation to the most distant ages, among all the objects of Nature he could have selected none so appropriate to his purpose or so permanently enduring as these stellar groups and configurations. Naming them, and connecting them with certain symbols of the ideas he wished to convey, and transmitting and explaining to his posterity those names and figures thus conjoined with the stars, he would link with his astronomy a whole system of thoughts and hopes as clear as the stars themselves, and utterly imperishable as long as that astronomy should remain in the knowledge of men.

And this, as I hope to make manifest, is exactly what has been done.

FIGURES OF THE STAR-GROUPS

Somewhere in the earliest ages of human existence the stars were named and arranged into groups by some one thoroughly familiar with the great facts of astronomy. Those names and groupings were at the same time included in certain *figures*, natural or imaginary, but intensely symbolic and significant. These names and figures have thence been perpetuated in all the astronomic records of all the ages and nations since. They are founded on indisputable astronomic truth, and hence form the groundwork of all maps and designations of the celestial presentations. They are in all the planispheres, celestial globes, and star-charts among all people, from one end of the earth to the other. Astronomers growl at them, consider them arbitrary and unnatural, and sometimes denounce them as cumbrous, puerile, and confusing, but have never been able to brush them off, or to substi-

tute anything better or more convenient in their place. They are part of the common and universal language of astronomical science. They have place and representation in all the almanacs of all enlightened peoples. They are in all the books and records devoted to descriptions of the heavens. Faith and skepticism, piety and irreligion, alike adopt and use them. Revelation and pagan superstition both recognize them. Heathen, Mohammedans, and Christians, the oldest with the latest, disagreeing in so many things, yet agree in adopting and honoring these primitive notations of the stars. Even those who have the most fault to find with them still employ them, and cannot get on without them. And in and from these the showing is, that all the great doctrines of the Christian faith were known, believed, cherished, and recorded from the earliest generations of our race, proving that God has spoken to man, and verily given him a revelation of truths and hopes precisely as written in our Scriptures, and so fondly cherished by all Christian believers.

The announcement may sound strange, and the undertaking to trace it may be deemed adventurous and fanciful; but if those who hear me will go with me into the investigation, and look at and weigh the facts, I am sure that we shall come out of the study all the more satisfied with the certainty of our Christian hopes, and all the more filled with admiration of the goodness and wisdom of the eternal Creator of all things.

I ask no preliminary scientific knowledge of astronomy in order to follow what I have to say, as that will not be needed. If a star-map, celestial chart, or globe of the heavens were consulted to familiarize the mind with the figures denoting the principal constellations, it would aid in appreciating the discussion; but if my hearers will favor me with their attention, and follow me with their sympathetic and earnest interest, it will be enough to secure a reasonable impression of the subject, and to enable them to see and judge of these star-pictures, whether they do not grandly set forth great religious truths, past, present, and to come.*

* See inside covers for such a map.

2

THE SACRED CONSTELLATIONS

By His Spirit He hath garnished the heavens; His hand hath formed the crooked Serpent. —Job 26:13

THE Gospel story, as written on the stars, like much of the sacred Scriptures, is *pictorial*. The record is accompanied with important explanatory materials, but the chief substance is given in pictures.

THE CONSTELLATIONS

Every atlas of the heavens is filled up with figures and outlines of men, women, animals, monsters, and other objects, each including a certain set of stars. These stars, as thus designated and embraced, constitute so many separate clusters or groups called the *Constellations*, and these asterisms or constellations cover all the principal stars visible to the naked eye.

In the primeval astronomy the number of these figures or star-groups was forty-eight. In imitation of them, dozens more have been added, mostly by modern philosophers. Among these additions are the Sextant, the Giraffe, the Fox and Goose, the Horned Horse, the Fly, the Greyhounds, the Lynx, the Bird of Paradise, Noah's Dove, the Clock, the Sculptor's Workshop, the Painter's Easel, the Air-Pump, Sobieski's Shield, the Brandenburg Sceptre, and such like; which may serve to designate the groups of inferior stars to which they have been assigned, but which are otherwise totally meaningless, and utterly unworthy of the associations into which they have been thrust. Having no connection whatever with the primitive constellations, except as poor and impertinent imitations, they must of course be thrown out and cast quite aside from the inquiry now in hand. They are no part of the original writing upon the stars, as proposed for our present reading.

The primary and chief series of the old forty-eight constellations is formed on the line which the Sun seems to mark in the progress of the year, called the *Ecliptic*. That line is really the path of the earth around the Sun, in the course of which the Sun seems to move thirty degrees every month, and at the end of the twelfth month appears again where it started at the beginning of the first month. The moon and planets follow apparently much the same path, and are always seen within eight or nine degrees of the line of the Sun's course. We thus have a Nature-indicated belt, about sixteen degrees wide, extending around the entire circuit of the heavens, half the year north and half the year south of the equator of the earth extended into the sky.

THE ZODIAC

Whilst the sun is thus making its annual course from west to east through the centre of this belt or zone, the moon makes twelve complete revolutions around the earth, suggesting the division of this belt into twelve parts, or sections, of thirty degrees each; for twelve times thirty degrees complete the circle. We thus note twelve equal steps or stages in the Sun's path as it makes its annual circuit through the heavens. And this belt or zone, with these twelve moons or months for its steps or stages, is called the *Zodiac*, from the primitive root *zoad*, a walk, way, or going by steps, like Jacob's ladder.

THE TWELVE SIGNS

So, again, each of these steps, stages, or sections includes a certain number of fixed stars, making up a group or constellation, which has its own particular figure, picture, or "sign" to designate it, and after which it is called. Hence the *Twelve Signs of the Zodiac*, which are given in all the regular almanacs, and to which people have generally had much regard in timing their industries and undertakings. These signs are:

I. VIRGO, the Virgin: the figure of a young woman lying prostrate, with an ear of wheat in one hand and a branch in the other.

II. LIBRA, the Scales: the figure of a pair of balances, with one end of the beam up and the other down, as in the act of weighing. In some of the old planispheres a hand, or a woman, appears holding the scales.

III. SCORPIO, the Scorpion: the figure of a gigantic, noxious, and deadly insect, with its tail and sting uplifted in anger, as if striking.

IV. SAGITTARIUS, the Bowman: the figure of a horse with the body, arms, and head of a man—a centaur—with a drawn bow and arrow pointed at the Scorpion.

V. CAPRICORNUS, the Goat: the figure of a goat sinking down as in death, with the hinder part of its body terminating in the vigorous tail of a fish.

VI. AQUARIUS, tne Waterman: the figure of a man with a large urn, the contents of which he is in the act of pouring out in a great stream from the sky.

VII. PISCES, the Fishes: the figures of two large fishes in the act of swimming, one to the northward, the other with the ecliptic.

VIII. ARIES, the Ram, by some nations called the Lamb: the figure of a strong sheep, with powerful curved horns, lying down in easy composure, and looking out in conscious strength over the field around it.

IX. TAURUS, the Bull: the figure of the shoulders, neck, head, horns, and front feet of a powerful bull, in the attitude of rushing and pushing forward with great energy.

X. GEMINI, the Twins, or a man and woman sometimes called Adam and Eve: usually, two human figures closely united, and seated together in endeared affection. In some of the older representations the figure of this constellation consists of two goats, or kids.

XI. CANCER, the Crab: the figure of a crab, in the act of taking and holding on with its strong pincer claws. In Egyptian astronomy the scarabæus beetle, grasping and holding on to the ball in which its eggs are deposited, takes the place of the crab.

XII. LEO, the Lion: the figure of a great rampant lion, leaping forth to rend, with his feet over the writhing body of Hydra, the Serpent, which is in the act of fleeing.

These twelve cardinal signs cover a large part of the visible heavens, and extend entirely around the earth, making and marking the Solar Zodiac.

THE MANSIONS OF THE MOON

But ancient astronomy gives a further subdivision of these twelve signs into twenty-eight, called *the Mansions of the Moon*, or the Lunar Zodiac. The moon makes its revolution around the earth in about twenty-eight days, and so suggests the division of its course through the heavens into twenty-eight sections, or steps, one for each day. Two and a third of these sections or Mansions are embraced in each sign of the Solar Zodiac, and

each mansion is marked with its own particular name and smaller group of stars. Some
Oriental nations also had particular and separate sets of figures for the designation of these
Lunar Mansions, though not uniformly the
same. It is rather from the names of these
Mansions, and of the stars in them, than from
the figures connected with them, that the significations are to be learned, the main theme
being most commandingly given in the twelve
cardinal signs of which they are parts.

THE THIRTY-SIX DECANS

But these twelve great signs do not stand
alone. Each one of them has conjoined with
it, either on the north or south side of the Zodiacal belt, three other conspicuous constellations, called *Decans*, from the Shemitic *dek*, a
"part" or "piece."

Albumazer—sometimes called *Abu Masher*
—a great Arab physician and astronomer who
lived about a thousand years ago, and whose
minute and learned writings on the subject
have been commented on by Aben Ezra as
of the highest authority, refers to "*the Decans
and their houses according to the Persians,
Babylonians, and Egyptians,*" and says: "Here
follow *the Decans*, which the Arabs in their
language call *faces*. They are three to each
sign of the *Way*." He says that the Indians
also had these Decans to each sign. And
Aben Ezra says: "According to Albumazer,
none of these forms from their first invention
have varied in coming down to us, nor one of
their words [names] changed, not a point
added or removed." Southey (in *The Doctor*,
vol. iii. p. 115) remarks that "in Egypt every
month was supposed to be under the care of
three *Decans*, or directors, for the import
of the word must be found in the neighboring language of the Hebrews and Syrians.*
There were thirty-six of these, each superin-
tending ten days; and these Decans were believed to exercise the most extensive influence. Astrological squares calculated upon
this mythology are still in existence." These

* This word is evidently from the Noetic or Shemitic *Decah, to break*.
Hence *Decan*, a "piece," a "division." Thus we have *dek* in Dan.
2 : 45, to denote a fragment or piece. And thus we still have in
English the word *deck*, to denote a part of a ship—*the face of a ship*,
as the Arabs also called these Decans *faces*.

Decans can, for the most part, be distinguished by the fact that those belonging to
any one particular sign come upon the meridian, or close along the meridian-line, at the
same time with the sign to which they belong.
Originally, they perhaps were all on the meridian along with the signs to which they pertain.

Albumazer's enumeration of them is fully
credited by the Jewish Aben Ezra, himself a
learned astronomer, Orientalist, and scholar,
who wrote a commentary on Albumazer's
work. And after the closest scrutiny, those
who have most thoroughly examined and mas-
tered the subject in its various relations entirely agree with the same enumeration, which I
therefore accept and adopt for the present
inquiries into this starry lore, sure that the
particular examination of each sign, with the
Decans thus assigned to it, will furnish ample
internal proof that this enumeration is correct according to the original intention.

I. THE DECANS OF VIRGO

1. *Coma*, the Infant, the Branch, the Desired One (erroneously, *Berenice's Hair*);
2. *Centaurus*, a centaur, with dart piercing
a victim;
3. *Boötes*, or Arcturus, the great Shepherd
and Harvester, holding a rod and sickle, and
walking forth before his flocks (erroneously
called *Bears*).

II. THE DECANS OF LIBRA

1. *The Cross*, over which Centaur is advancing, called the Southern Cross;
2. *Victim of Centaur*, slain, pierced to death;
3. *The Crown*, which the Serpent aims to
take, called the Northern Crown.

III. THE DECANS OF SCORPIO

1. *The Serpent*, struggling with Ophiuchus;
2. *Ophiuchus*, wrestling with the Serpent,
stung in one heel by the Scorpion, and crushing it with the other;
3. *Hercules*, wounded in his heel, the other
foot over the Dragon's head, holding in one
hand the Golden Apples and the three-headed
Dog of hell, and in the other the uplifted club.

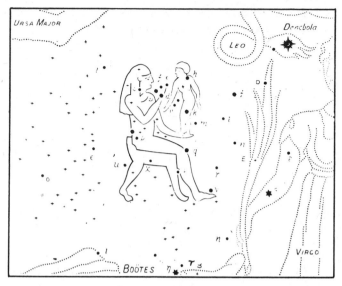

COMA, THE DESIRED

IV. The Decans of Sagittarius

1. *Lyra*, an Eagle holding the Lyre, as in triumphant gladness;

2. *Ara*, the Altar, with consuming fires, burning downward;

3. *Draco*, the Dragon, the old Serpent, winding himself about the Pole in horrid links and contortions.

V. The Decans of Capricornus

1. *Sagitta*, the Arrow, or killing dart sent forth, the naked shaft of death;

2. *Aquila*, the Eagle, pierced and falling;

3. *Delphinus*, the Dolphin, springing up, raised out of the sea.

VI. The Decans of Aquarius

1. *The Southern Fish*, drinking in the stream;

2. *Pegasus*, a white horse, winged and speeding, as with good tidings;

3. *Cygnus*, the Swan on the wing, going and returning, bearing the sign of the cross.

VII. The Decans of Pisces

1. *The Band*, holding up the Fishes, and held by the Lamb, its doubled end fast to the neck of Cetus, the Sea-Monster;

2. *Cepheus*, a crowned king, holding a band and sceptre, with his foot planted on the pole-star as the great Victor and Lord;

3. *Andromeda*, a woman in chains, and threatened by the serpents of Medusa's head.

VIII. The Decans of Aries

1. *Cassiopeia*, the woman enthroned;

2. *Cetus*, the Sea-Monster, closely and strongly bound by the Lamb;

3. *Perseus*, an armed and mighty man with winged feet, who is carrying away in triumph the cut-off head of a monster full of writhing serpents, and holding aloft a great sword in his right hand.

IX. The Decans of Taurus

1. *Orion*, a glorious Prince, with a sword girded on his side, and his foot on the head of the Hare or Serpent;

2. *Eridanus*, the tortuous River, accounted as belonging to Orion;

3. *Auriga*, the Wagoner, rather the Shepherd, carrying a she-goat and two little goats on his left arm, and holding cords or bands in his right hand.

X. The Decans of Gemini

1. *Lepus*, the Hare, in some nations a serpent, the mad enemy under Orion's feet;

2. *Canis Major*, *Sirius*, the Great Dog, the Prince coming;

3. *Canis Minor, Procyon*, the Second Dog, following after Sirius and Orion.

XI. THE DECANS OF CANCER

1. *Ursa Minor*, anciently the Lesser Sheepfold, close to and including the Pole ;

2. *Ursa Major*, anciently the Greater Sheepfold, in connection with Arcturus, the guardian and keeper of the flock ;

3. *Argo*, the Ship, the company of travellers under the bright Canopus, their Prince, the Argonauts returned with the Golden Fleece.

XII. THE DECANS OF LEO

1. *Hydra*, the fleeing Serpent, trodden under foot by the Crab and Lion ;

2. *Crater*, the Cup or Bowl of Wrath on the Serpent ;

3. *Corvus*, the Raven or Crow, the bird of doom, tearing the Serpent.

This ends up the main story. And the mere naming of these significant pictures casts a light over the intelligent Christian mind, which makes it feel at once that it is in the midst of the most precious symbols and ideas connected with our faith, as they are everywhere set out in the Holy Scriptures.

THE PLANETS

A further and very conspicuous marking among the heavenly bodies appears in the difference between the fixed stars and those more brilliant orbs which are continually changing their places. In reality, none of the stars are absolutely fixed. Nearly all of them have been observed to be in motion, shifting their relative places, but moving so very slowly that the changes are quite imperceptible except when hundreds of years are taken into the observation. But it is very different with some four, five, or more of the most brilliant of the heavenly luminaries. Though seeming to go around the earth like all the other stars, their behavior is eccentric, and their periods and motions are uneven. Two of them make their rounds in less than a year, and three others take two, twelve, and thirty years. They do not keep at the same distances from each other, nor their places among the more fixed stars. They are called *Planets*, or *Wanderers*. The names of these five old planets, as known to our astronomy, are, Mercury, Venus, Mars, Jupiter, and Saturn. There are other planets, but they are not recognizable to the naked eye. And to these five wanderers, hence called *planets*, the ancients added the Sun and Moon, making the seven most renowned of all the celestial bodies. The path of each of them lies within the limits of the Zodiacal belt or zone ; and the Twelve Signs of the Zodiac themselves were mostly regarded as the Twelve Mansions of these conspicuous travellers, which the old idolaters glorified as the seven great gods.

THE CONSTELLATIONS DIVINE

In these several markings, groupings, and designations of the heavenly hosts we have all the most conspicuous elements and notations of the primeval astronomy. And these pre-eminently are what the text refers to as the *garnish* of the heavens, of which "the crooked," or rather "*fleeing*, Serpent" is here named as a specific part.

There are but three things with which to identify this "fleeing Serpent." It has been justly said, "It is not likely that this inspired writer should in an instant descend from the garnishing of the heavens to the formation of a reptile." The discourse is of the starry heavens, and "the Serpent" must necessarily pertain to the heavens. Barnes says: "There can be no doubt that Job refers here to the constellations," and that "the *sense* in the passage is, that the greatness and glory of God are seen by forming the beautiful and glorious constellations that adorn the sky." But if the reference is to a sky-serpent, it must be either the Zodiac itself, often painted on the ancient spheres in the form of a serpent bent into a circle, with its tail in its mouth, or to *Draco*, or to *Hydra*, which is the longest figure in the sky, stretching through an entire night, and trailing along as if in flight from the point of the Scales, beneath the Virgin and the Lion, to the point where the feet of the Crab and the Lion press down its snaky head. All things duly considered, I take it as referring to *Hydra*, just as Leviathan (in Job 41 : 1) refers to *Cetus*, the Sea-monster. The Dragon does not so well answer to the description of "*the fleeing Serpent*," nor yet the sphere in the figure of a serpent. *Hydra* is in every respect "*the fleeing Serpent*," as distinguished from all other astronomic serpents. It does nothing but flee. It flees from the triumphing Lion, with the Bowl of Wrath on it and the bird of doom tearing it, whilst the holders of the precious possession trample its head beneath their feet. But, in either case, there is here a distinct recognition of the constellations and their figures, and the same noted as the particular garnishing of the heavens to which we are referred to see and read the transcendent glory of Jehovah.

Who Job was we do not precisely know. That he lived before the Hebrew Exodus, before the destruction of Sodom and Gomorrah, and hence before Abraham, is evidenced from the character, style, contents, and non-contents of his sublime book, which is at once the oldest, broadest, most original, most scientific in all the Bible. From repeated astronomical allusions contained in this book, with which uninformed translators have had much trouble and done some very unworthy work, different mathematicians have calculated that Job lived and wrote somewhere about twenty-one hundred and fifty years before Christ, which carries us back more than one thousand years before Homer and the Greeks, and a millennium and a half before Thales, the first of the Greek philosophers. And yet, already in the time of Job the heavens were astronomically laid out and arranged in the manner just described, with the Zodiac formed, the constellations named, the figures of them drawn and recorded, and the same accepted and celebrated by God's people as the particular adornment of the sky in which to read the Almighty's glory.

Very significant also is this word, "*garnished*," here employed by our translators. Its main sense is that of ornament, decoration, something added for embellishment; but it has the further meaning of summons and warning. And by these adornings God hath summoned the heavens and filled them with proclamations and warnings of His great purposes. Perhaps it would be hard to find another word to fit so truly to the facts or to the original for which it stands. It falls in precisely with the whole idea of the celestial luminaries being used "for signs," of the Gospel being written in the stars, and of the adornment and beaming of the heavens with this brightness of all sacred brightnesses. And when we come to the direct analysis of these frescoes on the sky, as I propose in my next Lecture, we will find the diction of the Bible from end to end most thoroughly conformed to these beautiful constellations.

But more remarkable and important is the positive testimony here given to *the divine origin* of these embellishments and significant frescoes. All interpreters agree that the text refers to the heavenly constellations. This is made the more certain by the designation of the Serpent in the second part of the parallelism. That "fleeing Serpent" must mean either *Draco*, the Zodiac, or *Hydra*. And the affirmation is clear and pointed that the thing referred to is divine in its formation. Of the Almighty and His wisdom and power Job is speaking; and of that Almighty it is declared, "By His Spirit *He* hath garnished the heavens," and "*His hand* formed the fleeing Serpent." If the frescoing of the sky with the constellations is meant, then *He* caused it to be done "*by His Spirit*"—by impulse and inspiration from His own almightiness. If the Zodiac is meant, then His own hand bent and formed it. And if the constellation of the Dragon, or *Hydra*, is meant, then He himself is the Author of it, and, by implication, the Author of the whole system of the constellations of which *Draco*, or *Hydra*, is a part. We may wonder and stand amazed and confounded at the assertion; but here, from the Book of God, is the unalterable voucher for it, that these astronomic figures, in their original integrity and meaning, are *from God*, and as truly inspired as the Bible itself. And many are the facts which combine to prove that such is verily the truth.

Who, of all the sons of men, can point out any other origin of these remarkable denotations of the starry heavens? Who can tell us when, where, or by whom else the Zodiac was invented, its signs determined, and the attendant constellations fixed? Historical astronomy is totally at a loss to give us any other information on the subject. Here is the Solar Zoad, with its twelve signs and their thirty-six Decans; here is the Lunar Zoad, with its twenty-eight Mansions, each with its own particular stars, and each with its very expressive name; and here are the noted seven Chiefs, playing a part in the traditions, sciences, theologies, and superstitions of earth, as brilliant as their splendid display on the face of the sky; but whence and how they were framed into these systems or came to place so conspicuous, acceptation so universal, and life so commanding and imperishable, even the science which handles them most is quite unable to explain. As seven cities claimed to be the birthplace of Homer, who most likely was born in neither, so men in their uncertainty have referred to names and widely different countries, times, and ages for the source and authorship of the primeval astronomy, with about equal reason for each, and no solid reason for either. The world has looked in vain for the origin of these inventions on this side of the Flood, or anywhere short of those inspired patriarchs and prophets who illumined the first periods of the race with their superior wisdom and exalted piety.

Age of the Constellations

One great and commanding fact in the case is that, as far back as we have any records of astronomy, these sidereal embellishments and notations existed and are included. We know from the Scriptures that they are older than any one of the books which make up the Christian and Jewish Bible. We have monumental evidence in the Great Pyramid of Gizeh that they were known and noted when that mighty science-structure was built, twenty-one hundred and seventy years before the birth of Christ and a thousand years before Homer, who also refers to them. The learned Dr. Seyffarth, than whom there is not a more competent witness living, affirms that

we have the most conclusive proofs that our Zodiac goes back among the Romans as far as seven hundred and fifty-two years before Christ, among the Greeks seven hundred and seventy-eight years before Christ, among the Egyptians twenty-seven hundred and eighty-one years before Christ, and among the Oriental peoples as far as thirty-four hundred and forty-seven years before Christ—even to within the lifetime of Adam himself. Riccioli affirms that it appears from the Arab astronomy that it is as old as Adam's time, and that the names preserved by it are antediluvian. Bailly and others have given it as their conclusion that astronomy must have had its beginning when the summer solstice was in the first degree of Virgo, and that the Solar and Lunar Zodiacs are as old as that time, which could only be about four thousand years before Christ. Professor Mitchell says: "We delight to honor the names of Kepler, Galileo, and Newton; but we must go beyond the epoch of the Deluge, and seek our first discoveries among those sages whom God permitted to count their age by centuries, and there learn the order in which the secrets of the starry world yielded themselves up." According to Drummond, "Origen tells us that it was asserted in the Book of Enoch (quoted by the apostle Jude) that in the time of that patriarch the constellations were already named and divided." Albumazer attributes the invention of both Zodiacs to Hermes; and Hermes, according to the Arab and Egyptian authorities, was the patriarch Enoch. Josephus and the Jewish rabbis affirm that the "starry lore" had its origin with the antediluvian patriarchs, Seth and Enoch.

The Sabbatic Week and the Stars

It is generally claimed that the Sabbath, and the week of seven days which it marks, date back to the beginning of the race, to the institution of God himself at the completion of the great creation-work. But that system of the seven days is essentially bound up with these selfsame astronomical notations. We find among all the ancient nations—Chaldeans, Persians, Hindoos, Chinese, and Egyptians—that the seven days of the week were in universal use; and, what is far more remarkable, each of these nations named the days of the week, as we still do, after the seven planets, numbering the Sun and Moon among them. Hence we say *Sun*-day, *Moon*-day, *Tuisco* or *Tuves'*-day (Tuisco being the Anglo-Saxon name for Mars), *Woden's*-day (Woden being the same as Mercury), *Thor's*-day (Thor being the same as Jupiter), *Friga*-day (Friga or Freiya being the same as Venus), and lastly, *Saturn*-day, anciently the most sacred of the seven. The order is not that of the distance, velocity, or brilliancy of the orbs named, neither does the first day of the week always coincide among the different nations; but the succession, no matter with which of the days begun, is everywhere the same. It is impossible to suppose this mere accident or chance; and the fact forces the conclusion that the devising and naming of the seven days of the week dates back to some primitive representatives of the race, from whom the tradition has thus generally descended, and who at the same time knew and had regard to the seven planets as enumerated in the primeval astronomy.

The Alphabet and the Stars

It is now mostly admitted that alphabetic writing is as old as the human family—that Adam knew how to write as well as we, and that he did write. There certainly were books or writings before the Flood, for the New Testament quotes from one of them, which it ascribes to Enoch, and Adam still lived more than three hundred years after Enoch was born. All the known primitive alphabets had the same number of letters, including seven vowels, and all began, as now, with A, B, C, and ended with S, T, U. But whilst we are using the alphabet every day in almost everything, how few have ever thought to remark why the letters appear in the one fixed order of succession, and why the vowels are so irregularly distributed among the consonants! Yet in the simple every-day *a, b, c's* we have the evidence of the knowledge and actual record of the seven planets in connection with the Zodiac, dating back to the year 3447 before Christ. If we refer the twenty-five let-

ters of the primitive alphabet to the twelve signs of the Zodiac, placing the first two letters in Gemini as the first sign, and take the seven vowels in their places as representing the seven planets, *a* for the Moon, *e* for Venus, the two additional sounds of *e** for the Sun and Mercury, *i* for Mars, *o* for Jupiter, and *u* for Saturn, as Sanchoniathon and various of the ancients say they are to be taken, the result is that we find the Moon in the first half of Gemini, Venus in the first half of Leo, the Sun in the latter half of Virgo, Mercury in the first half of Libra, Mars in the latter half of Scorpio, Jupiter in the latter half of Aquarius, and Saturn in the first half of Gemini; which, according to Dr. Seyffarth, is an exact notation of the actual condition of the heavens at an ascertainable date, which can occur but once in many thousands of years, and that date is the seventh day of September, 3447 before Christ!

It would be very absurd to say that this was mere accident. But, if it was not accident, it proves what the Arab and Jewish writers affirm, that the alphabet was in existence before the Flood, and demonstrates that astronomy is coeval with the formation of the alphabet.

Other facts, equally striking, but rather complex for ready popular statement, exist, to some of which we may have occasion to refer, all going to show and prove that the notations of the heavens so fully recorded in all antiquity do unmistakably date back beyond the Flood; that they came into being by no long-forming induction of man; that the whole system appeared full and complete from the start, like Pallas from the brain of Jove; and that the only true answer to the question of its origin is the one given in the text, which unequivocally ascribes it to the inspiration of God, who by His Spirit garnished the heavens and with His own hand bent the traditional ring of their goings.

It thus appears that in treating of these starry groupings and pictures we are dealing with something very different from the inventions of paganism and mythology—with some-

---

* $\grave{E}$ and $\acute{E}$, with place next to the Hebrew *Cheth* and the Latin *h*.

thing as sacred in origin, as venerable in age, and as edifying in import as anything known to man. Corrupt religion and classic fable have interfered to obscure and pervert their meaning, and scientific self-will has crowded them with impertinent and unmeaning additions; but, in reality, they constitute the primeval Bible—a divine record of the true faith and hope of man, the oldest in human possession. With solemn and jealous veneration does it become us to regard them, and with devout earnestness to study them, that we may get from them what God meant they should be to His children upon the earth,— sure that what, by His Spirit, He caused to be written on the sky is of one piece with what, by the same Spirit, He has caused to be written in His Word.

> Field of glories! spacious field,
> And worthy of the Master: He whose hand
> With hieroglyphics, elder than the Nile,
> Inscribed the mystic tablet; hung on high
> To public gaze, and said, Adore, O man!
> The finger of thy God.

3

THE DESIRE OF NATIONS

Behold, a virgin shall conceive, and bear a son, and shall call his name Immanuel. Isaiah 7:14

THE learned George Stanley Faber, rector of Long-Newton, concedes to the showings of certain French skeptics what has often been noticed and remarked by the students of antiquity, that an extraordinary and very particular resemblance exists between the facts and doctrines of the Christian faith and the various theologies and mythologies of ancient paganism.

THE ETHNIC MYTHS

Gathering up and combining in one view what appears in the various modifications of ancient heathenism, we find it taught and believed, in one system or another, that eternal Godhead, or some direct emanation of eternal Godhead, was to become incarnate, to be born of a virgin mother, to spend his infancy and childhood among herds and flocks, whose life should be sought by a huge serpent or dragon, which was even to slay him, but which he was destined to conquer and crush; that he came, or was to come, from heaven for the purpose of reforming and delivering mankind; that he was mild, contemplative, and good, but still the god of vengeance, with power to destroy his enemies; that he was a priest, a prophet, and a king, the sacrificer of himself, and the parent, husband, and son of the great Mother, denoted often by a floating ark; that he was the creator of worlds and æons, previous to which he moved on boundless waters; that when slain he was entombed, descended into the hidden world, but rose to life again, ascended the top of a lofty mountain, and thence was translated to heaven.

The likeness of these particulars to the scriptural teachings concerning Christ is obvious. How to account for them among heathen peoples who never possessed our Scriptures, and lived before our Scriptures were written, is a very interesting and important question.

AN INFIDEL ARGUMENT

That the correspondence is not accidental must be admitted. Volney has attempted to draw an argument from it to prove that Christ never existed, and is only a mythic character, embodying the various old fancies afloat in the imaginations of mankind long before the time in which the Gospel records allege that He was born. The argument is, that, of the two presentations, one must necessarily be borrowed from the other; that the old myths could not be borrowed from Christianity, as they antedate the Christian times; and hence that Christianity must needs be borrowed from these old myths and traditions, which it has arrayed in a Jewish dress and palmed upon the world for the founding of a new religious sect.

But this alleged borrowing and accommodation is mere assumption, incapable of proof. Faber has shown that the antediluvian histories, including particularly that of Noah, furnished so many types of Christian facts that from them alone could have been deduced many of the ideas in the ethnic theologies which so remarkably accord with the doctrines of Christianity. Volney himself, and others of his school, with much labor and erudition have further shown that there is an astronomic record, dating back to the times of Noah and beyond, which really gives the story of the incarnation and history of Christ, just as Christianity attests. It accordingly devolves upon these men adequately to account for that record before they can justly use it against Christianity. To account for Christianity by means of that record, which they rightfully claim to be universal, and yet to leave that record itself unaccounted for, is really a mere begging of the question.

From the nature of the showings on the subject we claim that the substance of that record must needs have been a matter of divine revelation, a thing of inspiration, fixed in the earliest ages of the race. If we are right in this, it would fully account for all the old fables, notions, myths, and ideas so near akin to Christianity, and at the same time do away with all need, occasion, or right to infer that it must have been borrowed and accommodated from them. Tracing this record back to the first ages, as these men do, and finding in it the story of the Serpent and the Cross as contained in the Gospel, we thus have a demonstration of the early existence of what the Bible gives as a divine promise and proph-

ecy, and the same dating from the time to which the Bible assigns it. That story, thus embodied and set afloat from the beginning, would necessarily descend with the multiplication and division of the race into all nations, and give rise and support to just such sacred myths and anticipations as we find confusedly given in the traditions and beliefs of all the ancient peoples. The strong presumption, therefore, the rather is, that Christianity, instead of having been borrowed and accommodated from those myths, was in contemplation in that which gave rise to them, and was the real spring of them, as it is the fulfilment and realization of them.

THE INTENTION TRACEABLE

Of course this record has been much distorted, perverted, misused, and overlaid by the superstitions, apostasies, and idolatries of men; but the showings of Bailly, Dupuis, Volney, and more modern antiquarians are that it can still be traced, and its main features unmistakably identified.

Some years ago I was in the great church of St. Sophia in Constantinople, built by the first Christian emperor, but now possessed by the Mohammedan Turks. Among the rest of its wonderful mosaics is a gigantic figure of the Saviour on the wall over the altar-place. That picture was of course very distasteful to the followers of the false Prophet of Arabia; but, not willing to spoil the glorious edifice by digging it out of the wall, they covered it over with whitewash and paint. Nevertheless, in spite of all attempted obliterations, the original picture still shone through the covering, and could be distinctly perceived and identified. And just so it is with these mosaics upon the stars. With all the obscurations which the ages of apostasy and heathenism have imposed upon them, they still shine through, to tell of the faith which put them there, and to declare that very glory of God which received its sublimest expression in the imperishable truths of our Gospel. Even astrology, Sabaism, the abominations of idolatry, and skepticism itself, have been overruled to preserve to us what God, by His Spirit, thus caused to be recorded on the face

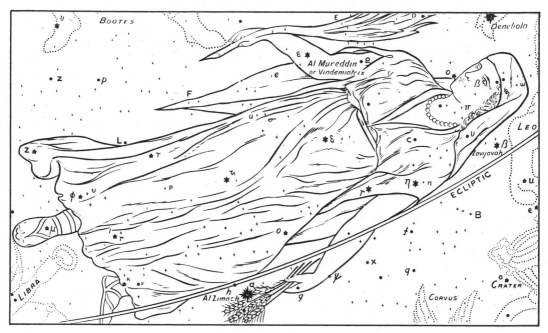

VIRGO, THE VIRGIN

of the sky from the very beginning of the world. And to the analysis and interpretation of this record we now come.

THE SIGN OF VIRGO

I begin with VIRGO, which I take to be the first sign in the Zodiac, according to its original intent and reading. The Zodiac of Esne begins with this sign. The story has no right starting-point, continuity, or end except as we commence with this constellation. I also have the statement from the best authorities that the custom was universal among the ancients to reckon from *Virgo* round to *Leo*. And in this sign of *Virgo*, if anywhere among the starry groups, we find the primary idea in the evangelic presentations.

The foundation-doctrine of all religion— the existence of an eternal and almighty God, the Originator, Preserver, and great Father of all things—is assumed as belonging to the natural intuitions of a right man. The presence of the universe is the invincible demonstration of eternal power and Godhead, so that those are without excuse who fail to see that there is a God or do not glorify Him as

God. Revelation is something superadded to Nature, which Nature itself cannot reach. Assuming the majesty of God and the sinfulness of man as things evident to natural reason and observation, its main subject is *the way of salvation through Jesus Christ*, the Gospel of the grace of God through His only-begotten Son. This is the one great theme of the Bible and of the primeval astronomy.

As Christians, we believe in a virgin-born Saviour. We confess and hold that our Lord Jesus Christ "was conceived by the Holy Ghost, born of the Virgin Mary." So He was preannounced in the text, and so the evangelists testify of the facts concerning Him. To deny this is to deny the fundamental features of the whole Christian system and to disable the whole doctrine of human salvation. It stands in the front of all the Gospel presentations. It is the foundation and beginning of the whole structure on which our redemption hangs.

It is therefore not a little striking that the very first sign which comes before us as we enter the grand gallery of the ancient constellations is the form and figure of a virgin.

The initiative sign of the Zodiac is called *Virgo*, THE VIRGIN. All the traditions, names, and mytholgies connected with it recognize and emphasize the virginity of this woman. Astrea* and Athene of Greek story identify with her. In Hebrew and Syriac she is *Bethulah*, the maiden. In Arabic she is *Adarah*, the pure virgin. In Greek she is *Parthenos*, the maid of virgin pureness. Nor is there any authority in the world for regarding her as anything but a virgin.

THE VIRGIN'S SON

But the greater wonder is, that *motherhood* attends this virginity, in the sign the same as in the text, and in the whole teaching of the Scriptures respecting the maternity of our Saviour. Krishna, the divine incarnation of the Hindoo mythology, was born of a virgin. A hundred years before Christ an altar was found in Gaul with this inscription: "*To the virgin who is to bring forth.*" And this maiden in the sign is the holder and bringer of an illustrious *Seed*. In her hand is the *spica*, the ear of wheat, the best of seed, and that *spica* indicated by the brightest star in the whole constellation. He who was to bruise the Serpent's head was to be peculiarly "the Seed of the woman," involving virgin-motherhood, and hence one born of miracle, one begotten of divine power, the Son of God. And such is the exhibit in this first sign of the Zodiac. She is a virgin, and yet she produces and holds forth a Seed contemplated as far greater than herself. That seed of wheat Christ appropriates as a symbol of himself. When certain Greeks came to Philip wishing to see Jesus, He referred to himself as the corn, or seed, of wheat, which needed to fall and die in order to its proper fruitfulness (John 12 :

21–24). Thus, according to the starry sign, as according to the Gospel, out of the seed of wheat, the good seed of the Virgin, the blessed harvest of salvation comes.

A very significant figure of Christ, much employed by the prophets, was the branch, bough, or sprout of a plant or root. Hence He is described as the Rod from the stem of Jesse and the Branch out of his roots (Isa. 11 : 1), the Branch of Righteousness, the Branch of the Lord, God's servant THE BRANCH (Isa. 4 : 2 ; Jer. 23 : 5 ; Zech. 3 : 8 ; 6 : 12). And so this sign holds forth the Virgin's Seed as *The Branch*. In addition to the *spica* in one hand, she bears a branch in the other. The ancient names of the stars in this constellation emphasize this showing, along with that of the Seed. Al Zimach, Al Azal, and Subilon mean the shoot, the branch, the ear of wheat. The language of the prophecies is thus identical with the symbols in this sign.

It is a doctrine of our religion that without Christ, and the redemption wrought by Him, all humanity is fallen and helpless in sin. There is none other name given among men whereby we can be saved. Even Mary herself needed the mediatorial achievements of her more glorious Son to lift her up to hope and standing before God. And this, too, is here signified. This woman of the Zodiac lies prostrate. She is fallen, and cannot of herself stand upright. Christ alone can lift up to spiritual life and standing. This woman accordingly holds forth the goodly Seed, the illustrious Branch, as the great embodiment of her hope and trust, the only adequate hope and trust of prostrate and fallen humanity.

And what is thus vividly signified in this constellation is still further expressed and defined by the Decans, or side-pieces, which go along with it.

COMA

Albumazer, who was not a Christian, says: "There arises in the first Decan, as the Persians, Chaldeans, and Egyptians, and the two Hermes and Ascalius, teach, *a young woman*, whose Persian name denotes a pure virgin, sitting on a throne, *nourishing an infant boy*, said boy having a Hebrew name, by some

---

* *Astrea* was regarded as the star-bright, good, and just goddess, the last to leave the earth as the Golden Age faded out, and then took her place among the stars. The four ages of Gold, Silver, Brass, and Iron were the periods of time in which the equinoctial point successively passed through so many signs of the Zodiac, each sign requiring about twenty-one hundred and forty-six years to pass. If the summer solstice was in Virgo in the first or Golden Age, her withdrawal over that point as the equinoxes proceeded would have been very slow, and everything else characteristic of that age would have passed away before she passed. The myth would hence well fit to the astronomical facts. Since passing that point she has never returned to her former place, and cannot until about twenty-five thousand years from the time she left it.

nations call *Ihesu*, with the signification *Ieza*, which in Greek is called *Christ*." The celebrated Zodiac of Dendera, brought by the French *savants* to Paris under the older Napoleon, contains a Decan of *Virgo*, which also gives the picture of *a woman holding an infant*, which she is contemplating and admiring. The woman in Virgo and the woman in this first Decan of Virgo are one and the same; and the infant here is everywhere identified with the Seed and the Branch there.

It is said of the infant Christ that " the child grew, and waxed strong in spirit, filled with wisdom, and the grace of God was upon him" (Luke 2 : 40); so here He is pictured as supported and nourished by what the Greeks made the virgin-goddess of wisdom, righteousness, and all good arts and human thrift.

The prophets are also very emphatic in describing the promised Saviour as the Desired One, " the Desire of women," " the Desire of all nations." So the name of this first Decan of Virgo is *Coma*, which in Hebrew and Oriental dialects means *the desired, the longed-for* —the very word which Haggai uses where he speaks of Christ as " *the Desire* of all nations." The ancient Egyptians called it *Shes-nu*, the desired son. The Greeks knew not how to translate it, and hence took *Coma* in the sense of their own language, and called it *hair*— *Berenice's Hair*. The story is, that that princess gave her hair, the color of gold, as a votive offering for the safety of her brother;

which hair disappeared. The matter was explained by the assurance that it was taken to heaven to shine in the constellation of *Coma*. Hence we have a bundle of woman's hair in the place of " the Desire of all nations."

Shakespeare understood the matter better, for he speaks of the shooting of an arrow up " to the good boy in Virgo's lap." Isis and other Egyptian goddesses figured holding the divine Infant, the Coming One, refer to this constellation of Coma, and hence unwittingly to Christ, born of a woman and nurtured on a virgin-mother's breast.

The next Decan of Virgo explains more fully concerning the Virgin's Seed.

The Double Nature

It is part of the faith, and a very vital part, that the Seed of the woman is the true and only-begotten Son of God, true God and true man in one and the same person. " For the right faith is, that we believe and confess that our Lord Jesus Christ, the Son of God, is God and man; God, of the substance of the Father, begotten before the worlds, and man, of the substance of His mother, born in the world: perfect God and perfect man." It is a great mystery, but so the Scriptures teach, and so the whole orthodox Church believes. In other words, we teach and hold that Christ, our Saviour, possessed a double nature, " not by conversion of the Godhead into flesh, but by taking the manhood into God," in the unity of one

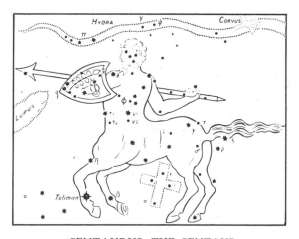

CENTAURUS, THE CENTAUR

Person, who accordingly is *Immanuel*, God with us, the Christ, who suffered for our salvation. And all this is signified in the constellation of *Centaurus*.

Very curious are the pagan myths concerning the centaurs. Fable represents them as the great bull-killers. They are said to have been heaven-begotten, born of the clouds, sons of God, but hated and abhorred by both gods and men, combated, driven to the mountains, and finally exterminated. Their form in the most ancient art is a composite of man and horse—man from the head down to the front feet, and the rest horse. There was no beauty or comeliness, that any should desire them. Some classical scholars have tried to account for the grotesque conception by imagining a race of Thessalian mountaineers who rode on horses, whom the neighboring tribes viewed with horror, supposing each horse and his rider to be one being. The conceit is without the slightest foundation in fact. The ancient Egyptians had the figure of the centaur long before the times of the Greeks.

The most noted of the centaurs of classic fable is *Cheiron*. To him are ascribed great wisdom and righteousness. "He was renowned for his skill in hunting, medicine, music, gymnastics, and the art of prophecy. All the most distinguished heroes in Grecian story are, like Achilles, described as his pupils in these arts." He was the friend of the Argonauts on their voyage, and the friend of Hercules, though he died from one of the poisoned arrows of this divine hero whilst engaged in a struggle with the Erymanthean boar. He was immortal, but he voluntarily agreed to die, and transferred his immortality to Prometheus; whereupon the great God took him up and placed him among the stars.

It is easy to see how this whole idea of the centaurs, particularly of Cheiron, connects with the primeval astronomy and related traditions. Strikingly also does it set forth the nature and earthly career of the divine Seed of the woman, as narrated in the Scriptures.

Christ had two natures in one person; and such was the figure of the centaur. Christ was a wise, just, good, and powerful Healer, Instructor, and Prophet; and such is the character everywhere ascribed to the chief centaur. Christ came to destroy the works of the Devil, and spent His energies in relieving men's ills, combating the powers of evil, teaching the ways of truth and righteousness, and driving away afflictions, as the centaurs hunted and destroyed the wild bulls and the wild boars, and as Cheiron helped and taught the Grecian heroes, minstrels, and sages. Nevertheless, He was despised and rejected of men, hated, persecuted, and deemed unfit to live, just as fabled of the centaurs. Cheiron was fatally wounded whilst engaged in his good work—wounded by a poisoned arrow from heaven not intended for him. And, though immortal in himself, he chose to die from that wound, that another might live. And so it was with Christ in His conflict with the Destroyer. And a vivid picture of the same appears in the figure of this constellation, which is also one of the very lowest and farthest down of all the signs belonging to the ancient astronomy.

Here is a double-natured being, to men repulsive and hateful, yet really great, powerful, and beneficent, pushing with his lance at the heart of some victim, and moving the while right over the constellation of the Cross.

The name of this Decan in Arabic and Hebrew means *the despised*. The brightest star in it the Greeks called *Cheiron*, a word which has a Hebrew root signifying *the pierced;* also *Pholas*, likewise from a Hebrew root signifying the making of prayer, *the mediation*. Sir John Herschel has observed that this star is growing brighter, and so belongs to the class of changeable stars. Ulugh Beigh gives its name as *Toliman*, which means *the heretofore and the hereafter*—brighter once, and to be brighter again, as the divine glory of Christ was much hidden during His earthly life, in which He made himself of no reputation, even lower than the angels, for the suffering of death, but was again glorified with the glory which He had with the Father before the world was. Thus, this sign, and the traditions and names connected with it, strikingly accord with the facts of Christ's earthly life and fate, and set forth some of the high-

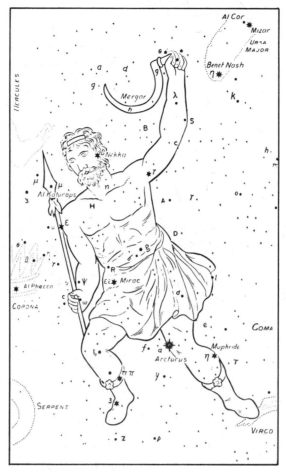

BOÖTES, THE COMING ONE

est mysteries of His Person, character, and mediatorial work.

BOÖTES.

The third Decan of this sign still further expresses and defines the marvellous story.

One of the most common, constant, and expressive figures under which Christ is presented in the Scriptures is that of the Oriental shepherd. Isaiah fore-announced Him as He who "shall feed His flock like a shepherd." Peter describes Him as the Shepherd and Bishop of our souls. He says of himself, "I am the good Shepherd that giveth His life for the sheep;" "I am the good Shepherd, and know my sheep, and am known of mine;" "My sheep hear my voice, and I know them,

and they follow me; and I give unto them eternal life; and they shall never perish, neither shall any man pluck them out of my hand." And this feature of what pertains to the Virgin's Son is the particular topic of this Decan.

We here have the figure of a strong man, whom the Greeks named *Boötes*, the ploughman. But he and the so-called plough are set in opposite directions. Neither does a man plough with uplifted hand in the attitude of this figure. The name thus transformed into Greek has in it a Hebrew and Oriental root, *Bo*, which means *coming*; hence, the coming One or the One that was to come. The Greeks, failing to hold on consistently to their idea of a ploughman, also called this man *Arcturus,* the watcher, guardian, or keeper of *Arktos,* the adjoining constellation, which in all the more ancient representations is *the flock, the sheepfold.* Boötes is not a ploughman at all, but the guardian and shepherd of the flocks represented by what are now ordinarily called the Great and Lesser *Bears;* though they both have long tails, which bears never have. The brightest star in the constellation of Boötes is also called *Arcturus,* the guardian or keeper of *Arktos,* a word which in its Oriental elements connects with the idea of enclosure, the ascending, the happy, the going up upon the mountains. According to Ulugh Beigh, the ancient Egyptians called Boötes *Smat,* who rules, subdues, governs; and sometimes *Bau,* or *Bo,* the coming One. *Al Katurops,* the star on the right side or arm of Boötes, means the Branch, the Rod, and is often connected with the figure of a staff, the shepherd's crook, the traditional emblem of the pastoral office.

There can, therefore, be no doubt that we have here not a Greek ploughman, but the far more ancient Oriental *shepherd,* the keeper, guardian, ruler, and protector of the flocks; and that shepherd identical with the Seed of the Virgin, the Promised One, He who was to come, even "the Desire of all nations," "that great Shepherd of the sheep" whom the God of peace brought up again from the dead (Heb 13 : 20). He also bears a sickle, which shows Him as the great Harvester; and the harvest He gathers is the harvest of souls, as where He directs his disciples to pray God to send forth laborers into His harvest. And the harvesting of souls is the gathering and keeping of the Lord's flock. The sickle and the crook thus go together as significant of one and the same idea, and show that Boötes is not the keeper of dogs and hunter of bears, but that promised Saviour who was to come to gather in the harvest of souls and "feed His flock like a shepherd."

Summary on Virgo

It is no part of my design in these Lectures to enter upon the exposition of all that is implied and expressed in the various symbols applied to Christ, except so far as necessary to show that what is written in the Scriptures is likewise written on the stars. And in so far as this first sign and its Decans are concerned, I think it must be admitted that the result is very marvellous. Ill must be the mind and dull the apprehension which cannot detect identity between God's sign in the text and this sign in the heavens. Are they not of a piece with each other, and hence from one and the same divine source? Here is the woman whose Seed was to bruise the Serpent's head. Here is the great Virgin-born, the divine Child, whose name is Wonderful, Counsellor, The mighty God, The everlasting Father, The Prince of Peace, of the increase of whose government and peace there is to be no end. Here is the prostrate one, deceived by Satan into sin and condemnation, but holding hopefully to the promised Seed, the most illustrious in the sphere of humanity, the vigorous, beautiful, and goodly Branch, as the particular joy and consolation of fallen man. Here is the Desire of all nations, the great Coming One, reseating the fallen who cherish and joy in Him. Here is His double nature in singleness of person, the "*God with us*" held forth in holy prophecy, the Seed of the woman, who is the Son of God. Here is the Rod, the Branch, on whom was to rest the Spirit of wisdom and understanding, the Spirit of counsel and might, the Spirit of knowledge and of the fear of the Lord, who should judge the poor with righteousness and reprove with equity, and smite the earth with the rod of His mouth, and slay the wicked with the breath of His lips. Here is the God-begotten Healer, Teacher, Prophet, the heroic Destroyer of the destroyers, yet despised and rejected of men, stricken, smitten, and afflicted, consenting to yield up his life that others might have immortality, and thereupon reappearing on high, clad in power and majesty, as the strong and everlasting Ruler, Guardian, and Shepherd of his flocks.

These are among the most essential and most precious things of our faith. The Gospel is nothing without them. Yet this is but one of twelve such signs, each equally full, vivid, and to the point. God never does things by halves. What He once begins He always completes. We have seen the first of these signs. It bears with it the internal as well as the external evidences of what Maimonides says the ancient Fathers affirmed, to wit: that it has come from the Spirit of prophecy. And if God inspired the framing of these signs, we may expect to find the rest as rich and telling as this opening of the series, each amplifying the other, till all the sublime wonders of redemption stand revealed upon the sky.

Meanwhile, let us believe and hold fast to the fact, so joyously fore-announced by the prophet, and so vividly inscribed upon the stars as the hope and trust of man, that a virgin has conceived and brought forth a Son, who verily is what Eve supposed she had when she embraced her first-born—even "a man, the Lord," *Immanuel*, God with us. Let us rejoice and be glad that unto us a Child is given, even that Seed of the woman appointed to bruise the Serpent's head and be the everlasting Shepherd and Guardian of His people. Let us see in Jesus the great Healer, Teacher, and Prophet, even God in humanity, who was to come, and who, though despised and rejected of men, hated, condemned, and pierced, still lives in immortal glory and power as the true *Arcturus*, to give repentance, remission of sins, and eternal life to as many as accept Him as their Lord and Saviour. And, in this faith established, let us be all the more quickened in our interest and attention in tracing the whole story as it shines upon us in our darkness from God's everlasting stars. Even the heathen bard, contemplating what was thus fore-signified, and deeming the time of fulfilment come, broke forth in the song:

> " Saturnian times
> Roll round again, and mighty years, begun
> From their first orb, in radiant circles run.
> The base, degenerate iron offspring ends;
> A golden progeny from heaven descends.
> O chaste Lucinda! speed the mother's pains,
> And haste the glorious birth! thy own Apollo reigns!
> The lovely boy, with his auspicious face,
> Shall Pollo's consulship and triumph grace;
> Majestic months set out with him to their appointed race.
> The father banished virtue shall restore,
> And crimes shall threat the guilty world no more.
> The son shall lead the life of gods, and be
> By gods and heroes seen, and gods and heroes see.
> The jarring nations he in peace shall bind,
> And with paternal virtues rule mankind."

4

THE SUFFERING REDEEMER

And they sung a new song, saying, Thou art worthy, . . . for thou wast slain, and hast redeemed us to God by thy blood.   —Revelation 5:9

REDEMPTION, the price of redemption, and the heavenly honor of Him who brings redemption, are the topics which come to view in this text. And what was thus exhibited to the enraptured Apocalyptist as he stood within the heavenly portals gazing upon the throne of the thrice-holy Lord God Almighty, observing the Lamb as it had been slain, and listening to the songs of the adoring living ones and elders, is the same to which the second sign in the Zodiac introduces us. Let us look at it with that devout reverence which becomes a subject so sacred, so solemn, and so mysterious.

THE SIGN OF LIBRA

There would seem to be little or nothing to arrest our attention or to illuminate our faith in a matter so ordinary and unpoetical as a p̶ balances for weighing commodities. homely, secular, and every-day figure hard to find, but a more expressive more profoundly significant of the ths that concern the hopes of still harder to select when con-

sidered in the relations in which we here find this figure. The arms of that tilting beam, with its attached bowls, reach out into eternities. The positions of that beam, which a feather's weight may change, indicate the fortunes of worlds, the destinies of ages, the estates of immortality. The equipoise of that beam marks the adjustment of a vast and mighty feud and the effectual bridging over of a chasm as deep as hell.

And the whole instrument together, in use, bespeaks the eternal justice which presides over all the boundless universe. In the Persian sphere a man or woman lifts these scales in one hand, and grasps a lamb with the other, the lamb being the form of the ancient weight. Nor can we be mistaken when we here read the divine determination of the wages of sin and the price of redemption.

The figure of the Scales, or Balances, is found in all the Eastern and most ancient Zodiacs, the down side invariably toward the deadly Scorpion. In some instances the bowl on the low side was held by the Scorpion's claws, whence, in some of the Western spheres,

Chelæ, the Claws, occasionally occupied the place of the Scales. Among the Jews it was denoted by the last letter of the Hebrew alphabet, T, or *Tau*, originally written as we still write it, and as written in nearly all the ancient alphabets, in the form of a cross, which signified the end, the boundary, the limit, the completion; as the Saviour when about to give up the ghost on the cross said, "*It is finished*," the last letter in the history of His humiliation having been reached.

The names of this sign indicate the range of meaning attaching to it. In Hebrew it is *Mozanaim, the scales, weighing*, as where God is said to weigh the mountains in scales and the hills in a balance. In Arabic, it is *Al Zubena, purchase, redemption, gain*. In Coptic, *Lambadia, station or house of propitiation*. In the Arab tongue, *Lam* is graciousness, and *badia* is branch—the atoning grace of the Branch. In Greek it is called *Zugos*, the cross-bar by which two oxen or horses draw, the yoke, pulling against each other, thwarts joining the opposite sides of a ship, the cross-strap of a sandal, the balance-beam in weighing. The name of the first star in Libra is Zuben al Genubi, *the price deficient*. Other names are: Zuben al Shemali, *the price which covers;* Al Gubi, *heaped up high;* Zuben Akrabi, *the price of the conflict*.

The figure in this sign is largely associated with the ethical impersonations of Astrea and Athene of the Greek and Roman mythology, who were the patrons of righteousness, justice, order, government, and the institutions and powers of the state, by which rights were protected, justice administered, and the general good secured. The same figure still connects with houses where courts are held, where causes are tried, where accusations and disputes are settled, and the awards of justice declared and given.

All this clearly settles, as near as may be, that this sign of the Zodiac has reference to some great divine adjudications and adjustments relating to defaults, defects, and accusations, involving penalties, prices, payments. And with these ideas applied to the continuation of the story of the Seed of the woman, the divine Son of the Virgin, promised and appointed to lift up the fallen, recover from the Serpent's power, and bring men to the pasturages on the heavenly hillsides, we are at once brought face to face with eternal justice weighing the demerits and awards of sin on the one hand, and the price of redemption rendered and paid for it on the other.

THE COMMERCIAL IDEA IN CHRISTIANITY.

There are some to whom this commercial element in the system of our salvation is very distasteful and repulsive. The natural heart is prone to be offended with it, and to reject it altogether. Rationalism proudly asserts

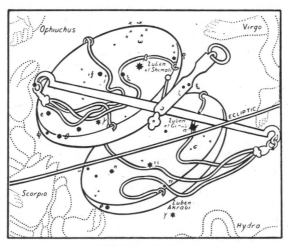

LIBRA, THE SCALES

that sin is personal and intransferable; that the action or merit of one cannot be the action or merit of another; and that there can be no such thing as a vicarious atonement, or the release and justification from the penalties of sin by the substitution of the work, sufferings, or merit of a second party. Physically considered, this may be true. The action of one is necessarily the action of that one. But there are spheres in which the action and force of one may and does go to the account, or the determination of the estate, of another. It depends upon the relations of the parties how far the doings of the one may accrue to the good or ill condition of another. In the case of a husband and wife, a father and child, a king and his subjects, an army and the country for which it acts, the qualities and activities, good or ill, on the one side most certainly redound to the other side as well. Sin is of the nature of a debt, and debt may be as completely discharged by a friend of the debtor as by the debtor himself. Sin is of the nature of bondage, and release from bondage is a negotiable matter, and may be procured at a valuation or price, which may be equally paid by the bondman himself or by some one else kind enough to pay it for him. Many crimes and misdemeanors in human law have penalties dischargeable in money consideration, which any friend of the criminal may as truly satisfy as the convicted one, and as may not be in the power of the convict to do. Crimes depend on law, for where there is no law there is no transgression; and law is the will of government. If the government condemns in righteousness, in the same righteousness it can adjudge and accept equivalent for the penalty, and there is nothing to say nay to it. The notions of men cannot bind the Supreme.

Remission of penalty is likewise something entirely distinct from the moral estate of the criminal. The justification or pardon of the guilty one is another matter from his sanctification or personal goodness. The one is a thing of price; the other is a thing of power. The one may be procured by a friend, mediator, or surety; the other must be wrought into the experiences, affections, and impulses of the man himself. The vicariousness of redemption relates to justification, the keeping of the law satisfied by an adequate and accepted consideration, the holding back of all the powers to hurt or condemn, and to these only; whilst another administration between the Redeemer and the one for whom He answers takes charge of the inward fitting of the absolved for the enjoyment of his freedom and his training for the kingdom of the redeemed. And if the just and righteous Sovereign of the universe, supreme in all His perfections and rights, is agreed and content to accept a certain price or equivalent for releasing the culprit to the sanctifying and reforming administration of his friend or surety on the payment of the price to governmental justice, where is the wrong, or what is there in the universe to question the rightfulness of the proceeding? Let the Redeemer be found to pay the required ransom and to fill the place of such an advocate, surety, and Lord, and neither men, angels, nor devils have any right on any ground to except to the proceeding if the great Supreme is satisfied and pleased, and says, So be it.

The only question to be decided is, whether God in His word sets forth to our belief that such is the arrangement in fact. We affirm that such is the clear and unequivocal teaching of the Scriptures from end to end. In all the old prophecies, in all the ritual observances connected with them, in all the New-Testament promises, facts, teachings, and institutes, and in all the visions of the final consummation,— everywhere we find the doctrine of salvation through the sacrifice of Christ as our Substitute, Surety, and Propitiation. And this is precisely what is signified by this sign of Libra and its Decans.

In the place of the woman and her Seed we have here a pair of balances suspended in the sky, in which is signalled to us the inexorable justice of the Almighty, in which the deficiency and condemnation on the part of man, and the all-sufficiency of the ransom paid on the part of his Redeemer, are alike indicated. One of the scales is up, which says to universal man, "Thou art weighed in the balances, and art found wanting." The name of the

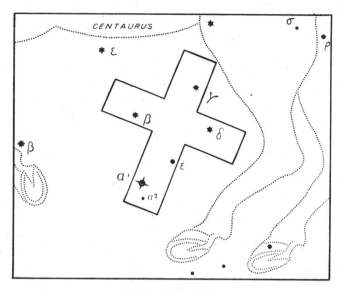

CRUX, THE CROSS

star which marks it records the verdict—*"The price deficient."* But the other side is borne down, and with it the star named *"The price that covers."* Of what that accepted price was to consist is more fully told in the accompanying Decans.

The Southern Cross

Strikingly enough, we here come upon a figure stationed in the darkest section of the heavens, in the very lowest part of the sphere, and outlined by the stars themselves so as to be readily recognized by every beholder—a figure of the shameful instrument on which the blessed Saviour died, even the Cross. Our latitude is too far to the northward for this constellation to be visible to us, but it is clear, distinct, and specially noticeable to those dwelling near or south of the equator. Humboldt speaks with enthusiasm of this cross set in stars of the southern sky. It was one of the reveries of his youth, he tells us, to be able to gaze upon that celestial wonder, and that it was painful to him to think of letting go the hope of some time beholding it. Such was his enthusiasm on the subject that he says he could not raise his eyes toward the starry vault without thinking of the Cross of the South. And when he afterward saw it, it was with deep personal emotion, warmly shared

by such of the crew as had lived in those southern regions; and the more on their part because religiously attached, as Humboldt himself was not, to a constellation "the form of which recalls the sign of the faith planted by their ancestors in the deserts of the New World." He describes this Cross as standing perpendicular at the moment when it passes the meridian. Up to that moment it leans one way, and after that moment it begins to lean the other way. It is therefore a most convenient and marked timepiece, which the people universally observe as such. "How often," says this philosopher and traveller, "have we heard our guides exclaim in the savannas of Venezuela or in the desert of Lima, 'Midnight is past; the Cross begins to bend'!"

Formerly this constellation was visible in our latitudes; but in the gradual shifting of the heavens it has long since sunk away to the southward. It was last seen in the horizon of Jerusalem about the time that Christ was crucified. It consists of four bright stars placed in the form of a cross, and is by far the most conspicuous star-group in the southern heavens. Standing directly in the path of the second Decan of Virgo, the double-natured Seed of the woman, and connecting with Libra and the price of redemption, it takes the same place in the celestial symbology which the Cross of Calvary holds in the Christian system.

THE SIGN OF THE CROSS

Ever since Christ Jesus "suffered for our sins" the cross has been a sacred and most significant emblem to all Christian believers. Paul would glory in nothing but "in the cross of our Lord Jesus Christ." It was a sacred symbol long before Christ was born. We find it in the most sacred connections, edifices, feasts, and signs of the ancient Egyptians, Persians, Assyrians, Hindoos, Chinese, Kamtschatkans, Mexicans, Peruvians, Scandinavians, Gauls, and Celts. The mystic *Tau*, the wonder-working caduceus, the invincible arrows, the holy cakes, all had their fabled virtues in connection with the form of the cross which they bore. But that sign has received a far more definite and certain consecration by the death of Christ upon it. Its original ancient meaning had reference to the Seed of the woman, the divine Son who was to suffer on it, to conquer by it, and to give eternal life through it. We cannot adequately account for it except as belonging to the original prophecy and revelation concerning Him and the price He was to pay for our redemption, conquering through suffering, and giving life through death. And in all the ideas connected with it by the ancient peoples we can readily trace the application of it, the same as in the arrangement of the constellations.

Aben Ezra gives its Hebrew name, *Adom*, which means *cutting off*, as the angel told Daniel of the *cutting off* of the Messiah. And Christ was cut off by being condemned and crucified.

In the Zodiac of Dendera this constellation is marked by the figure of a lion, with his head turned backward, and his tongue hanging out of his mouth as if in consuming thirst. It is the same idea. Christ is "the Lion of the tribe of Judah," and one of the few expressions made by Him as he died on the cross was that of His consuming thirst. Strong and divine as He was, His life was there parched out of Him. "Jesus, knowing that all things were now accomplished, that the Scripture might be fulfilled, saith, *I thirst;* and they filled a sponge with vinegar and put it upon hyssop, and put it to his mouth. When, therefore, he had received the vinegar, he said, It is finished: and he bowed his head, and gave up the ghost." The hieroglyphic name attached means *pouring water;* and David, impersonating the Messiah, exclaims, "I am poured out like water, all my bones are out of joint; my heart is like wax; it is melted in the midst of my bowels. My strength is dried up like a potsherd; and my tongue cleaveth to my jaws; and thou hast brought me into the dust of death" (Ps. 22 : 13–18). It is simply wonderful how the facts in the sign correspond with the showings of the Scriptures, and how all the old myths embody the same showings.

In the triad of the three great Egyptian gods each holds the sacred *Tau*, or the cross, as the symbol of life and immortality; but only the second, the Son, the Conqueror and Deliverer, extends the cross, thus pictorially expressing the offering of life and immortality through the Cross.

In the divine triad of Brahmanic deities the second, the Son, the One who became incarnate in the man-god Krishna, sits upon his throne cross-legged, holding the cross in his right hand; and he is the god of deliverance from dangers and serpents. The same is otherwise represented as the ruler of the elements, the stiller of tempests, the good genius in all earthly affairs. But in all these relations and offices he always wears a cross on his breast. It is the same story of deliverance and salvation through the Cross-bearer, the divine Son of the Virgin. And even so "it pleased the Father that in Christ should all fulness dwell, and, making peace through the blood of His cross, by Him to reconcile all things."

The old Egyptians pictured departed spirits as birds with human heads, indicating the laying off of the earthly form and the putting on of immortality. But all such figures are represented *holding the cross*, emblematic not only of eternal life, but of that life as in, with, or through the Cross, just as the Gospel teaches.

The old Mexicans, at certain of their holy feasts, made a cross composed of the flour of maize and the blood of a victim offered in sacrifice, which they first worshipped, and finally broke in pieces, distributed the fragments among themselves, and ate them in token of union and brotherhood. The Egyptians and others also had the sacred cake with the form of a cross upon it, which they ate in holy worship. It was but another form of the same idea—life and salvation through the Cross.

And in every aspect in which the figure of this Decan, in its deeper inward significance, appears in the records and remains of antiquity, it connects with deliverance, life, and salvation by means of it. Accordingly, it stands among the starry symbols of the ancient astronomy precisely as it stands in our blessed Christianity. It was placed there as the sign of what holy prophecy had declared should come, just as we reverence it as the sign of what has come in Jesus of Nazareth, the Virgin-born Redeemer of the world. It is the Cross of Calvary prefigured on the sky in token of the price at which our redemption was to be bought.

THE VICTIM SLAIN.

The next in the series of these heavenly signs gives us a still fuller and clearer indication of the nature and payment of that price. Christ was not only "crucified," but He was also "dead and buried." Hence we have in the second Decan of Libra a slain victim, pierced and slain with a dart barbed in the form of the cross—pierced and slain by Centaur himself. "The soul that sinneth, it shall die;" "Without shedding of blood there is no remission." Hence the doctrine of the Scriptures, that Christ's life was made an offering for sin—He who knew no sin consenting to be made a curse for us, that we might be made righteous through Him. He not only felt the cross, enduring its agony and shame, but He died upon it—died for us, that we might have eternal redemption through His blood.

But an important element in the mysterious transaction was, that He sacrificed himself. Men in their wickedness killed Him, but it was He who gave himself into their hands to do it. Without this voluntariness and self-command in the matter the great redeeming virtue of His sacrifice would be wanting. Hence He was particular to say as He went to the cross, "I lay down my life for the sheep. . . . No man taketh it from me, but I lay it down of myself. I have power to lay it down, and I have power to take it again" (John 10 : 15–18). Hence He is preached as

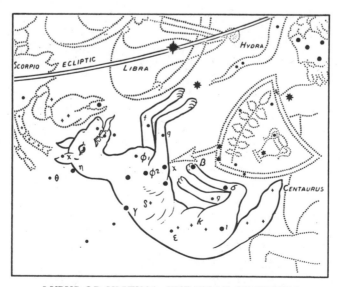

LUPUS OR VICTIMA, THE WOLF OR VICTIM

the great High Priest passed into the heavens, "who through the eternal Spirit offered himself without spot to God," having "appeared once in the end of the world to put away sin by the sacrifice of himself" (Heb. 9 : 11, 26). This was partially prefigured by the Cross in Centaur's path, but more particularly in this Decan, which shows the death infliction by the barbed dart from His own hand.

What this victim of Centaur is, is not very definitely determined. Many of our modern atlases give it as a wolf, but with no ancient authority for it. The Greeks and Latins sometimes called it the wolf; but they were so much in doubt that they more commonly called it *the animal*, the victim, without describing it. Ulugh Beigh says it was anciently called *Sura*, a sheep or lamb. The Arabs use a word in connection with it which means to be slain, destroyed; hence the slain one, the victim. It plainly expresses slaying, sacrifice by death; and so would fall in with that saying of the Apocalypse, that Christ is "the Lamb slain from the foundation of the world."

In some of the Coptic and Egyptian representations this victim is a naked youth, a stripped and unresisting young man, with his finger on his mouth. This youth is *Horus*, the beloved son of Osiris and the virgin, the One to come, who appears in various relations under different names, all more or less connected with the bringing of life and blessedness through humiliation and death. In Phœnician this youth is called *Harpocrates*, under which name he became known to the Greeks and Romans. Harpocrates means justice, or the victim of justice, the vindication of the majesty of law. Among the Romans, Harpocrates was the god of silence, quiet submission, and acquiescence. All of this connects with this Decan as a sign of the promised One, and prefigured Him as quietly and meekly submitting as a victim and sacrifice to justice and the law, even as Christ did actually lay down His life and submit himself as our propitiation. "As a sheep before her shearers is dumb, *so He* opened not His mouth."

In some of the pictures of this youth he is represented with the horn of a goat on one side of his head, as well as with his finger on his lips. This again connects him with sacrifice—willing, silent sacrifice. In some other pictures this horn is detached and held in his hand, filled with fruits and flowers—the original of the *cornucopia*, or horn of plenty; thus signifying that all good to man comes through that meek submission to stripping and sacrifice to satisfy the requirements of eternal righteousness.

So, then, from every side we get the idea of silent submission to death as a slain victim, and the bringing in thereby of a plentiful and everlasting provision for all the wants of man; prefiguring exactly what the Gospel sets forth as fulfilled in Jesus Christ, who, "being found in fashion as a man, humbled himself, and became obedient unto death, even the death of the cross" (Phil. 2 : 5–8).

THE TURN IN THE HISTORY

But the Cross, and Christ's death by the Cross, mark the limit and farthest boundaries of the humiliation for human redemption There was nothing lower than that in the history; and the first two Decans of Libra are the southernmost constellations but one in the ancient astronomy. From the moment that Jesus gave up the ghost the price was paid, the whole debt was discharged, and everything gave token of change. The tide there reached its lowest ebb, and turned, thenceforward to flow in ever-augmenting volume from glory to glory.

The bones of the two thieves were broken, but the death of Jesus, already accomplished, spared His body that indignity. A man high in office and estate moved to take charge of His remains for honorable sepulture in an honorable tomb. Imperial Rome lent its soldiers and its seal to guard and protect them in the place of their rest. The earth and sky gave signs of sympathy, and yielded attestations which drew even from heathen lips the confession of His divinity. A few days, and hell stood confounded before His majesty, and the doors of the grave gave way, and angels in white array stood round the spot to welcome His forthcoming in the powers of

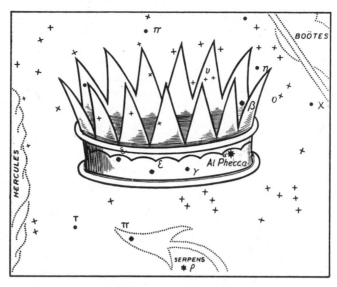

CORONA, THE CROWN

an endless life. Far above all principalities and powers, and every name that is named, He ascended, and for ever sat down at the right hand of the Father, the great Procurer and sovereign Giver of all good and grace. He acepted death, consented to quit his earthly life, agreed to take his place with departed spirits, "died for our sins according to the Scriptures" (1 Cor. 15:3); but thence ascended where the heavens resound with the new song, "*Thou art worthy, for Thou wast slain, and hast redeemed us to God by Thy blood.*" Now, then, "we see Jesus, who was made a little lower than the angels for the suffering of death, crowned with glory and honor" (Heb. 2:9). His shameful Cross issued in a glorious Throne.

The Northern Crown.

And so we find it foreshown in these starry pictures. That Southern Cross connects with the Northern Crown. The one is *a Cross* formed of stars, and the other is equally *a Crown* formed of stars. The third Decan of Libra is the *Corona Borealis*, vertical over Jerusalem once in every revolution of the earth.

> " The golden circlet mounts, and, as it flies,
>   Its diamonds twinkle in the distant skies."

The Greeks say that this was the bridal-gift of Bacchus to Ariadne, the woman who through her love for Theseus came to her death by the hand of Artemis, or, according to another story, was so ill treated in her affection that she put an end to her own life, but was saved by the god, who became so pleased with her beauty that he raised her to a place among immortals, and gave her this crown of stars. It was but a clumsy and carnalized version of the story recorded in the primeval astronomy. Not a woman, but a man, even the Seed of the woman, is the subject. It was through His great love to mortals that He came to grief, neglect, persecution, and death. That death was the divinely-exacted price which had to be paid in bringing the object of His love out of the dark labyrinth of sin and condemnation; but it was at the same time by His own free will and choice. He was brought up again out of death in immortal beauty and glory, and through the good pleasure and delight of the Father was awarded an imperishable crown in heaven. And that heavenly crown had its sign in this beautiful constellation. In its true original this story of Ariadne and her crown is the same as that of the great Redeemer, giving up, and himself sacrificing, His life for the objects of His love, raised from the dead in immortal glory, that at the name of Jesus every knee should bow, and every tongue confess that He is Lord, to the glory of God the Father.

Thus, then, the prophetic sign in the stars is fulfilled in the facts of the history.

A Sneer.

I have heard intimated that this is all speculation. It may suit some to dismiss it in that way. But will those who think it nothing but speculation tell us, then, what is not speculation? The French *savants*, whom many reverence as the high priests of reason over against all credulity and superstition, take it as solid enough to build on it an argument *against* Christianity; why, then, is it not solid enough to build on it an argument *for* Christianity? Some think it speculation to hold for truth that there is a personal God; that the Bible contains a revelation from Him; that man has a soul to live beyond death; that there is to be a future judgment; that the earth is a globe in motion ever rolling around the sun; or that Jesus Christ is the appointed and only Saviour of fallen man;— are we therefore to put all these things from us as empty dreams? Believing the Bible, we believe that God from the beginning promised a divine Seed of the woman to bruise Satan's head, and through suffering and death to bring in everlasting redemption for man; that He has come as the Son of the virgin, born at Bethlehem, crucified on Calvary, buried in Joseph's tomb, resurrected the third day, opening the kingdom of heaven to all believers. Dare we for an instant allow that this is mere speculation? And if what we read in the book of God is not speculation, can it be mere speculation when we find it written with the same clearness on the stars? It is not above a child's capacity to judge whether the story thus told by the constellations answers to the story of the Gospel or not; and, seeing the correspondence, are we not to conclude that the one is the prophetic foretelling and anticipation of the other? If not, I am at a loss to know what, in all the rounds of human belief or unbelief, is not mere speculation. No, no; the story of the Cross of Christ *is true*, and the word on the heavens unites with the word in the Book to assure us of the certainty of our faith.

" My trust is in the Cross; there lies my rest,
 My fast, my sole delight.
Let cold-mouthed Boreas, or the hot-mouthed East,
 Blow till they burst with spite;
Let earth and hell conspire their worst, their best,
 And join their twisted might;
Let showers of thunderbolts dart round and round me,
 And troops of fiends surround me:
All this may well confront; all this shall ne'er confound me."

5

THE TOILING DELIVERER

Thou shalt treat upon the lion and adder: the young lion and the dragon shalt Thou trample under foot. —Psalm 91:13

IT is generally accepted by the old interpreters that the word "lion" in this text should be taken as denoting some venomous thing, either reptile or insect, of a class with serpents. Bochart thinks it means "the black serpent." Patrick takes the description as meaning "serpents, asps, and dragons, with all the rest of those venomous sorts of creatures." The Saviour recurs to this passage where He says, "I give you power to tread on serpents and scorpions, and over all the power of the enemy" (Luke 10:19). Accordingly, we find both the Psalmist and the Saviour using the precise imagery of the sign of the Zodiac and its Decans which we are now to consider. A gigantic scorpion, serpent, and dragon, with a mighty man in conflict with them, mastering them and treading them under foot, is the figure before us.

Some have attempted to explain the origin and meaning of these signs of the Zodiac as gradual formations for season-marks, of sowing, reaping, fishing, hunting, cattle-culture, and the like. Abbé Pluche, in his *History of the Heavens*, thinks to exhaust the whole matter after this manner, though it is hard to see the need for such high and elaborate memorials of what was otherwise far more obvious to the senses. And although some of these signs apply, and have been used, in this way, the abbé is obliged to admit that the scheme does not fit to Egypt, where many say these signs originated; neither does it fit anywhere else; whilst it leaves all the Decans of these signs wholly unexplained. And, however well the theory may here or there fall in with some of the signs, it is much perplexed and disabled when it comes to such as *Scorpio*, since the scorpion is nowhere a thing of game or cultivation, and has no particular season. The best the abbé can do with it on this theory is, to expound it as a sign of autumnal diseases, to tell the people when they were most likely to be sick! Had the abbé taken the very significant hints given in some of his quotations, telling how these signs were explained to those initiated into the more famous ancient mysteries, he would have saved himself such puerilities, and found what he so trifled with to be the records of truths relating to the highest spiritual and eternal interests of man.

THE ANCIENT MYSTERIES.

Pluche quotes from Isocrates, Epictetus, and Tully on the subject, who unequivocally testify that there these signs were explained throughout in a manner indicating most important truths of a sort to give peace in life and hope in death. "Those who are acquainted with the mysteries," says the first, "insure to themselves very pleasing hopes against the hour of their death, as well as for the whole course of their lives." "All these mysteries," adds Epictetus, "have been established by the ancients to regulate the life of men and to banish disorders therefrom." Tully says: "When these mysteries are explained and brought again to *their true meaning*, we prove not to have learned so much the nature of the gods [heathen deities] as that of the things themselves or of the truths we stand in need of. . . . The instructions given there have taught men not only how to live in peace and gentleness, but *how to die in the hopes of a better state to come.*" But what had the raising of good crops, the production of calves, lambs, and goats, and the timing of the fishing and hunting seasons to do with the hopes and prospects of the soul sinking away from earth into the mysterious eternity? And if these signs and asterisms, in "their true meaning," had reference to the soul and its immortal hopes, and were so explained in the noblest of the mysteries, it only shows that among the pagans, notwithstanding all their idolatry and darkness, the true prophetic light still feebly lingered by means of these primeval writings on the stars. And, with the rest of these comforting and hopeful records on the sky, this sign of the Scorpion has equal place and significance.

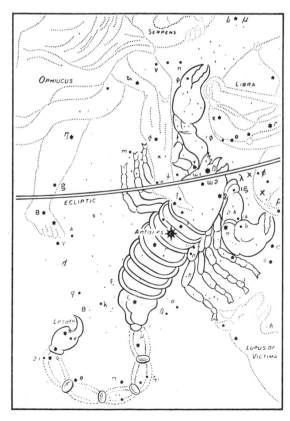

SCORPIO, THE SCORPION

THE SIGN OF SCORPIO

The name of this sign in Arabic and Syriac is *Al Akrab*, which, as a name, means the scorpion, but also *wounding, conflict, war*. David uses the root of this word (Ps. 144 : 1) where he blesses God for teaching his hands to *war*. In Coptic the name is *Isidis*, attack of the enemy—a word from the same root which occurs in Hebrew (Ps. 17 : 9) in the sense of *oppression* from deadly foes. The word *scorpion* itself is formed from a root which means *to cleave* in conflict or battle, and this sign in the Zodiac is the house of Mars, the god of war and justice. The principal star in this sign is called *Antares*, wounding, cutting, *tearing*.

The scorpion, as a living thing, is a spider-like insect, formed something like a small lobster, with an extended chain-like tail ending in a crooked horny sting loaded with irritant poison. To be struck by a scorpion is often fatal, though not necessarily so; but the pain from it is the intensest that can be inflicted on the human body. It is the most irascible and malignant insect that lives, and its poison is like itself. And in this sign we have the figure of a mammoth scorpion, with its tail uplifted in anger as in the act of striking. The figure, the names, and all the indications agree in telling us that we here have the story of a most malignant conflict, and of a deadly wounding in that conflict.

THE SUFFERING SAVIOUR.

How clearly and fully all this corresponds to the great conflict of Christ, and His dear-bought victory in achieving our redemption, any one can easily trace. The text exhibits Him as victor in just such a conflict. Though it refers to the success of God's people in general, and their security under the shadow of the Almighty, the New Testament applies the passage to Christ, who is always the kernel of everything pertaining to the powers and triumphs of His people. What they get, they get in and through His going before them in the matter. He is to His Church what the head is to the body—the chief of the whole thing, without which all the rest is powerless and nothing. Therefore we must understand the declaration as including Him and as referring pre-eminently to Him. It accordingly represents Him as in conflict with serpents, scorpions, asps, dragons, and all deadly and venomous things, just as in this sign and its Decans.

In the Egyptian Zodiac this sign is represented by a monster serpent, Typhon, or Python, the hundred-headed son of a malignant, envious, and intractable shrew, the father of the many-headed dog of hell, of the Lernæan Hydra, and of the three-headed, fire-breathing Chimæra. In the Hebrew Zodiac this sign was counted to Dan; and Dan is described as "a serpent by the way, and an adder in the path." *Scorpio* certainly ranks with the Serpent, and stands in close affinity with the Dragon.

The Serpent's seed is everywhere and always the enemy of the woman's Seed; and the conflict is above all between Christ and the Devil, until all evil is finally subdued and crushed. The great office of the divine Son of the woman, and his experience in it, were sketched from the beginning, as the bruising of the Serpent's head and the bruising of His heel. No sooner did Christ come into the world than the Dragon sought to devour Him through Herod's executioners. No sooner had He come up from the waters of baptism, attested from the open heavens as the Messiah, the Son of God, than the Devil made attack upon Him. And as He came to the final act of discharging the debt of a condemned world, the most terrible of all the assaults of the powers of darkness had to be encountered.

We know something of the wrestling and agony which our Saviour suffered in the Garden of Gethsemane. We know how sorrowful was His soul, as though His immortal being were about to be broken up. We know how He was inwardly wrung with anguish until every pore issued sweat of blood, clotting on His body and falling in great drops to the ground. It was "the hour of the powers of darkness," as He himself explained. It was an experience of agony the like of which never had been, and never could be again. It was the sting and poison of the great

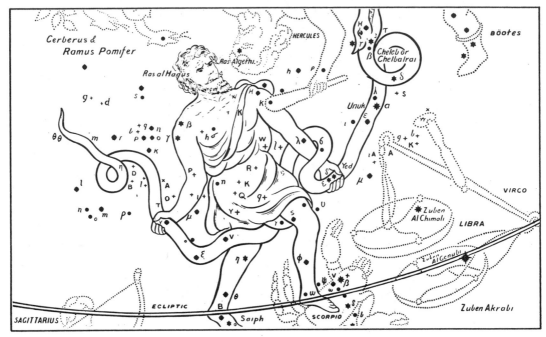

SERPENS, THE SERPENT
OPHIUCHUS, THE SERPENT HOLDER

Scorpion struck into the Son of God, making all His glorious nature vibrate as if in dissolution. It was the prophetic sign of the Zodiac fulfilled in the Seed of the virgin.

THE SERPENT

A further confirmation that we are on the right track in thus interpreting this sign is the fact that the first Decan, or illustrative side-piece, presents us with a picture of the Serpent itself in all its giant proportions.

It was the particular admonition to the Church in Philadelphia: " Hold fast that thou hast, that no one take thy crown." We have likewise seen in the preceding sign that there was held forth a celestial crown for Him who was to suffer on the cross. It was for the joy thus set before Him that the Apostle says He "endured the cross, despising the shame." On the other hand, mythology represents Python as aiming to acquire the sovereignty of gods and men, and only prevented from gaining it by the struggle which ensued between him and the greatest of the Olympian gods. That myth was simply the story of

this constellation, for here the Serpent is stretching after the celestial Crown, has almost reached it, and is only kept from taking it by being held fast by a manly figure grasping him firmly with both hands.

This serpent in the Decan is, of course, to be construed with the Scorpion in the sign, as the one is expository of the other; just as *Spica* in Virgo is to be construed with the Infant in *Coma*. The conflict in both cases is the same, only the images are changed to give a somewhat further impression of it. In the first instance it is the Evil One attacking and inflicting the intensest of anguish; in the other, it is a fierce contest for the Crown.

I will not here discuss the question whether it was a literal serpent that tempted Eve. I suppose some earthly serpentine form in the case, but whether it had wings or organs of speech matters not to the integrity of the record or of the ideas meant to be conveyed. The simple narrative, as it strikes the common mind, is as clear and satisfactory as any learned expositions can make it. The physical creature was not the real enactor of the temptation but was the image associated with a dark and subtle intelligence operating in that form to deceive and ruin our first parents. And from that, for ever afterward, the figure of a serpent became the universal symbol and representative of that Evil Spirit, hence called the Dragon, that old Serpent, the Devil, and Satan, who is the arch-enemy of all good, the opponent of God and the deceiver of men. And it is as the symbol of this evil power that these serpentine figures appear in the constellations.

The Bible everywhere assures us of the existence of a personal Devil and Destroyer, just as it everywhere describes a personal God and Redeemer. It tells us plainly whence he came, what he is, what power he wields, and what is to be his fate, just as it tells whence Christ is, who He is, for what purpose He came into the world, and what is to be the result of His marvellous and complex administrations.

The doctrine of a Saviour necessarily implies the doctrine of a destroyer. The one is the counterpart of the other, and belief in both is fundamental to the right explanation of things, as well as to our proper safety. Men may doubt and question, and treat the idea of a personal Devil as a foolish myth, but their language nevertheless bewrayeth the unfittingness of their skepticism. The doctrine is in the oldest, worthiest, and divinest records ever made for human enlightenment, and in the common belief of all nations and peoples from the beginning of the world. And here we have it pictured and repeated at every turn of the starry configurations, precisely as we find it presented in the sacred Scriptures. Nor can we be on the safe side without honestly receiving and believing it. People may make a jest of it if they will, but they will find out some day that this story of the Serpent is a terrible reality.

OPHIUCHUS.

Any attentive reader of the Scriptures will observe how constantly the Redeemer of the world is represented in the attitude and character of a Physician, a Healer, a Mollifier of wounds, a Deliverer from the power of disease and death. Before He was born the prophets fore-announced Him as "the Sun of Righteousness" who should "arise with healing in His wings"—as He "with whose stripes we are healed"—as He who "healeth the broken in heart, and bindeth up their wounds"—as He who saith, "O death, I will be thy plagues; O grave, I will be thy destruction." So the record of Him in the New Testament is that He "went about all Galilee, preaching the Gospel of the kingdom, and healing all manner of sickness and all manner of disease among the people," and giving every demonstration of power to make good His word, that if any one would receive His teachings and believe on Him that sent Him, the same should never see death, and be raised to life eternal at the last day. His great complaint against men ever was, and is, that they come not unto Him that they might have life. And this again is accurately and most strikingly presented in the second Decan of Scorpio and the myths connected with it.

We have here the figure of a mighty man wrestling until he is bald with a gigantic serpent, grasping the same with both hands, disabling the monster by his superior power, and effectually holding him fast so that he cannot get the crown. With one foot lifted from the scorpion's tail as stung and hurt, he is in the act of crushing that scorpion's head with the other. He thus appears as the one who hath power over the Serpent and over death, holding, disabling, and destroying them, though himself wounded in His conflict with them. Such is also the representation of Krishna in two sculptured figures in one of the oldest existing pagodas of Hindostan.

In one of the old Egyptian spheres the picture is that of a man enthroned, wearing the head of an eagle or a hawk, the enemy and slayer of the serpent, and assigned a Coptic name which means *the chief who cometh*. But the more common figure is that which appears on our modern atlases, whom the Greeks in their own language called *Ophiuchus*, the Serpent-holder, otherwise, from two Arabic words signifying the same thing, *Cheleb Afei* or *Æsculapius*, who figures so illustriously in the mythologies and worships of Greece and Rome.

THE GREAT PHYSICIAN

This Æsculapius was held to be one of the worthiest of the gods. It was to him that the great Socrates in his last hours sacrificed a cock. His temples were everywhere, and everywhere frequented and honored. But, though regarded as a god, the son of Apollo, or the Sun, Homer applies epithets to him never applied to a god, and the greatest of his achievements are mostly ascribed to him in the sphere and activities of a man. He therefore comes to view as both god and man, after the same style as the Seed of the woman in the Scriptures. He is assigned seven children, who were simply personifications of his own qualities and powers, their names further describing him as the Healer, the Physician, the Desired One, the Health-giver, the Beautifier with good health, the One who brings cure, the Universal Remedy. The story is, that he not only cured all the sick, but called the dead to life again by means of blood from the side of the goddess of justice and from the slain Gorgon, and finally himself suffered death from the lightnings of heaven because of the complaints against him by the god of hell, but was nevertheless raised to glory through the influence of Apollo. In all the representations he is invariably accompanied with the symbol of the serpent.

Many hypotheses have been broached to account for the origin of the story and illustrious worship of Æsculapius; and I cannot but wonder that no one has ever thought of tracing it to the primeval astronomy and to this conspicuous constellation of *Serpentarius*, to which it most certainly belongs. Taking these signs, as I hold them to be, the pictorial records of the primitive revelation concerning the Seed of the woman, we at once strike the heart of a complete explanation of every feature of the myth, which at the same time very wonderfully confirms the correctness of so accepting these signs. Here is the man with the serpent, as was Æsculapius. Here is the Seed of the woman, the Son of God. Here is the Serpent-holder and the Death-vanquisher, hence the matchless Physician and Healer.

It may seem strange to identify Æsculapius with Christ, nor do we say that Æsculapius was Christ; but we do say that the constellation out of which came the heathen legend concerning Æsculapius was the picture and sign of the promised Sun of Righteousness, the Healer and Saviour of mankind. As truly as *Spica* denotes the Seed of the virgin, *Serpentarius* denotes that same Seed; and the whole story of Æsculapius thus found its hero, its features, and its names from the primitive prophecies and promises concerning the Virgin's Son, as pictured in this constellation. Everything characteristic in the myth was in some sense prophetic of what should be, and was, fulfilled in Jesus of Nazareth. Christ is the true Sun of Righteousness, the great Healer, the heavenly Physician, the Desired One, the sublime Restorer of soul and body, the Beautifier with health and salvation, the Bringer of cure for suffering and perishing humanity, the Universal Remedy for all the ills which sin has wrought. He is the potent Holder of the Serpent, the Vanquisher of death. He is the Resurrection and the Life, who raiseth up the dead by virtue of the blood taken from the virgin in taking her nature, and the blood of the Gorgon vanquished by His power. And He it was who died from the divine thunderbolts as a Sin-bearer to silence the clamors of perdition, and yet, on the plea of His merit and divinity, was raised up and enthroned in highest heaven as the very God of salvation.

His identity with what the myth represented appears also very strikingly in a certain ancient prophetic hymn to Æsculapius, fabled as inspired and sung at the time of his birth—a hymn with these remarkable lines, which the angels might be supposed to sing over the manger of Bethlehem:

" Hail, great Physician of the world! all hail!
Hail, mighty Infant, who, in years to come,
Shall heal the nations and defraud the tomb!
Swift be Thy growth! Thy triumphs unconfined!
Make kingdoms thicker and increase mankind:
Thy daring art shall animate the dead,
And draw the thunder on Thy guilty head;
For Thou shalt die, but from the dark abode
Rise up victorious, and be twice a God!"

The whole showing of the constellation, and of the mythic story connected with it, thus wonderfully accords with what the prophets anticipated and the New Testament teaches concerning the divine Son of the virgin.

HERCULES

And still more fully is the Messianic work of the bruising of the Serpent's head set forth in the third constellation belonging to this sign. Here is the figure of a mighty man, down on one knee, with his heel uplifted as if wounded, having a great club in one hand and a fierce three-headed monster held fast in the other, whilst his left foot is set directly on the head of the great Dragon. Take this figure according to the name given it in the Egyptian hieroglyphics, and you have a picture of *Him who cometh* to bruise the Serpent and "destroy the works of the Devil." In the head of this figure is a bright star, the brightest in this constellation, which bears the name of *Ras al Gethi*, which means *the Head of him who bruises;* whilst the name of the second star means *The Branch kneeling*. The

Phœnicians worshipped this man five generations before the times of the Greeks, and honored him as representing *a saviour*. Smith and Sayce trace the legend of him in Chaldea four thousand years ago. On the atlases he is called *Hercules*. So the Romans called him, but the Greeks called him *Herakles*, whom they worshipped and honored as the greatest of all their hero-gods, principally on account of his twelve great labors.

According to the mythic accounts, Herakles or Hercules was the god-begotten man, to whose tasks there was scarce an end. From his cradle to his death he was employed accomplishing the most difficult and wonderful of feats laid upon him to perform, and all in the line of vanquishing great evil powers, such as the lion begotten from Typhon, the many-headed Hydra sprung from the same parentage, the brazen-footed and golden-horned stag, the Erymanthean boar, the vast filth of the Augean stables, the swarms of life-destroying Stymphalian birds, the mad bull of Crete which no mortal dared look upon, the flesh-eating mares of Diomedes,

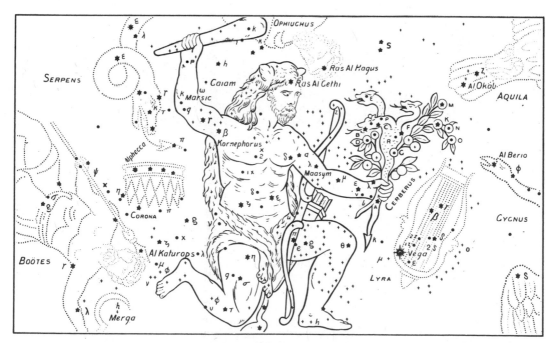

HERCULES, THE MIGHTY ONE

the queen of the devastating Amazons, the triple-bodied Geryones and his dog, the Dragon which guarded the apples of the Hesperides, and the three-headed snaky monster which kept the gates of hell.

Some have argued that the story of Herakles is a purely Greek invention, but it certainly dates back in all its essential features, in Egypt, Phœnicia, and India, to a time long anterior to the Greeks. By their own confession the Greeks did not even understand who or what Herakles was, or what was meant by all his great labors. They took him for the sublimest of the hero-gods, as the accounts came to them, and here and there, as in so many other things, appropriated all to their own country and people; but Aratus, who sung the song of the ancient constellations, and from whose song the Apostle Paul makes a quotation, speaks of Herakles as

> " An image none knows certainly to name,
> Nor what he labors for,"

and, again, as

> " The inexplicable image."

Ptolemy and Manilius refer to him in corresponding terms. They could not make out their greatest hero, or any meaning to his works! Not with them, therefore, did the mythic story of the powerful laborer originate. Its true original is in the ancient constellations of the primeval astronomy, which, like the Scriptures, pointed to the coming Seed of the woman to bruise, vanquish, and destroy the Serpent, and everything of the Serpent born or belonging to the Serpent's kingdom.

A Picture of Christ

Stripped of its foul heathenisms and admixtures, we can easily trace throughout the myth all the outlines of the astronomic picture, and that picture anticipating the sublime work of the Virgin's Son, as depicted by the prophets and recorded in the Gospel, even the battering and vanquishing of Satan and all the powers of darkness. Christ is the God-begotten man. He it is that comes against the roaring satanic " lion " who " go-

eth about seeking whom he may devour." He it is that came into the world to strike off the heads of the great Serpent, lurking in the bogs to ravage and destroy. He it is who comes forth to free the world of all its monsters and hellish pests, and purge it of its vast uncleanness. He it is who had it laid upon Him to fight and slay the Dragon, and thus recover access to the fruits of the Tree of Life, though having to bear the whole weight of a guilty world in making the grand achievement. And He it is who " descended into hell," before whom the spirits of the under-world cowered; to whose power the king of perdition yielded; and who grasped the struggling triple-headed dragon-dog in charge of the infernal gates, and bore him off, " leading captivity captive." Wounded He was in the dreadful encounter—wounded in His heel, wounded unto death, yet living still; suffering also from the poisoned garment of others' sins, mounting the funeral-pyre to die of His own accord amid fires undue to Him, and thence ascending amid the clouds to immortal honor in heaven, with his foot for ever on the head of the foe.

The heathen in their blindness could not understand the story, and knew not what to make of the foreshowing; but in the light of God's fuller revelation, and of the facts attested by the Gospel, we read the origin and meaning of it all, and see how God has been all these ages proclaiming from the starry sky the glories, labors, sufferings, and triumphs of His only-begotten Son, our Saviour.

There is no character in mythology around which great and wondrous incidents crowd so thickly as around Herakles, and there is no character in the history of the world upon whom so much of interest and sublime achievement centres as upon Jesus Christ, the true Deliverer. With Him was the wielding of power unknown to any other man. To kill Him and to be rid of Him has ever been the intensest wish of all the Dragon brood, from the time Herod sought the young child's life even unto this present. With all sorts of ill and wrong was He smitten while He lived, and plotted against in all the ages by the jealous, obstinate, and quarrelsome goddess of false wisdom and serpentine intrigue against the will and word of Heaven. Even the sensual and disgusting loves of Herakles were but heathen and carnal perversions of the devotion to the interest and redemption of man which ever glows in the Saviour's breast and shines in all His varied works. And as Herakles and all his tremendous labors were totally inexplicable on any motives perceptible to ordinary reason, so is Christ the everlasting mystery, incomprehensible and unconstruable, in His life, deeds, or institutes, to all who fail to accept and believe in Him as verily the God-man, come, and still coming, to work the works given Him to do, through suffering, toil, and sacrifice to deliver an afflicted world —come, and still coming, to beat down Satan and spoil all the principalities and powers of evil.

Thus, then, in this sign and its constellations, and in the myths founded on and associated with them, we have the precise picture presented in the text—the picture of the promised Seed of the woman treading on serpents, asps, dragons, and the whole brood of venomous powers—suffering and dying in the conflict, but in the end trampling all enemies in glorious triumph beneath His feet.

We wonder betimes what is to come of this unceasing conflict between right and wrong, good and bad, which we see raging around us in all things—this creeping in everywhere of scorpions and adders to sting and hurt—this twining and hissing of serpents and all horrid things—this everlasting toil, expenditure, and suffering for the better, which never seems to come. A glance at these constellations may serve to tell us, the same as promised in the Holy Book. There can be no deliverance without it, and long and oppressive must the struggle be. Many a serpent must first be strangled, many a hydra attacked, many a wild passion caught and slain, many a pang endured, many a sore reverse experienced. But the cause is secure. The victory must come at last. God and truth and right and good must triumph in the end. The Ophiuchus who holds fast will not lose his crown. The scorpion may sting the heel, but the foot will crush its head. The faithful wielder of the club of righteousness may be brought to his knee, but he shall yet lift up the instrument of his power in glorious success, strangle Cerberus, and bear off in triumph the apples of gold, whilst the great Dragon writhes through all his length with his head under the heel of the Conqueror. For from of old it stands written, "Thou shalt tread upon the serpent and adder; the young lion and the dragon shalt Thou trample under foot."

6

THE TRIUMPHANT WARRIOR

And in Thy majesty ride prosperously, because of truth and meekness and righteousness; and Thy right hand shall teach Thee terrible things. Thine arrows are sharp in the heart of the King's enemies.

— Psalm 45:4, 5

THESE words are from one of the most glowing of the Psalms, in the writing of which David's heart boiled with goodly words. It is marked: "To the chief Musician upon Shoshannim, for the sons of Korah —Maschil. A song of loves." The lily-instrument, the master-performer, and the whole body of singers were called into requisition for its rendering. As a sublime ode it was to be given with the sublimest skill, for it relates to the loveliest of heroes· in the loveliest of His aspects, offices, and relations to His people. This hero is none other than the promised Messiah, the Lord Jesus Christ, in His royal majesty and glory subsequent to His resurrection, and as to be hereafter revealed. When on earth He was despised and rejected of men, but here He is celebrated as " beautiful, beautiful, above the sons of man," endowed with every grace and invested with all authority and power. When on earth He was meek and non-resistant, not breaking so much as a bruised reed; but here

He is contemplated and addressed as a mounted warrior, riding as a king, armed with bow and arrows, shooting down His enemies. His character here is that of the Mighty One, girding himself with honor and majesty, and going forth to victory. John, in his visions of the future, beheld "a white horse; and He that sat on him had a bow; and He went forth conquering and to conquer." It is the same divine Hero, in the same character, offices, and work, in both instances. He has a crown, a throne, and a cause—the cause of righteousness over against injustice, usurpation, and tyranny; which cause He enforces with invincible majesty. His former sufferings are now turned to aromatic perfumes upon Him. Out of the ivory palaces He is gladdened with the sound of the harp. And in glory and triumph He rides forth unto victory, hailed by the daughters of kings and worshipped by the queen at his right hand arrayed in the gold of Ophir.

The picture is particularly magnificent.

We cannot contemplate it without sharing the enthusiasm with which the inspired Psalmist sketched it. But the surprising thing is, that it is also in the Zodiac, and appears at full length in

The Sign of Sagittarius

In this sign we have again the double-natured Seed of the virgin, the Son of God as the Son of man. The figure is that of a mighty warrior with bow and arrows, riding prosperously. In all tongues he is named, as in our charts, *the Archer*, the Bowman, He who sends forth the arrow. In form he is the *Centaur*, the Piercer—not now, however, in connection with the Cross, far down toward the hidden regions, offering himself as a victim and sacrifice to satisfy the demands of justice, but lifted up on high, stationed on the path of the Sun, himself the Sun of Righteousness rising in His majesty.

The Greeks called him *Cheiron*, the Executer, the chief centaur, whom they described as "the righteous-dealing centaur," precisely as this Psalm represents the Horseman and Hero of whom it speaks. Other centaurs were considered mean and beneath humanity, as Christ was accounted in His humiliation; but with Cheiron everything noble, just, refined, and good was connected, even superhuman intelligence, dignity, and power. The artists in picturing him labored to blend the greatest beneficence and goodness with the greatest strength and majesty. And such is the description of the divine Hero of this Psalm.

According to the myths, Cheiron was the great teacher of mankind in heavenly wisdom, medicine, music, and all noble and polite arts, and from whom the most exalted heroes and the most honored of men received their tuition. And so it is said of this sublime King that every grace was poured upon His lips, and that He is the One specially blessed of God, whose name every generation shall remember, and whom the people shall praise for ever and ever. The barbed arrows of this Archer are aimed at the heart of the Scorpion. It was sung of Cheiron,

SAGITTARIUS, THE ARCHER

" 'Midst golden stars he stands refulgent now,
And thrusts the scorpion with his bended bow."

And thus the "arrows" of the divine Hero of the text "are sharp in the heart of the King's enemies." His war is with the whole Serpent-brood, and His going forth is for their destruction. Whether we understand it of the moral and renovating power of the Gospel, or of the judicial administrations of the Son of man at the end of the present Gospel dispensation, or more naturally of both, it is the office and purpose in all the doings of the glorified Christ to pierce and wound the Serpent, to destroy all his works and power, and to disable him for ever. And this is shown in the sign, just as it is declared in the Gospel.

Some of the names in the sign express the further idea of *graciousness* and *delight* in connection with the action signified; which again accords with that saying ascribed to Christ in both Testaments: "Lo, I come: in the volume of the book it is written of me. I delight to do thy will, O my God: yea, thy law is within my heart. I have preached righteousness in the great congregation: lo, I have not refrained my lips."

Swiftness is another idea included in these names; and hence of quick and resistless power, of which horses and horsemen are the biblical images, particularly in connection with the scenes of the great judgment which Christ is appointed to enact. And the coming again of Christ is everywhere described as being with great power and glory, quickly, suddenly, like the lightning's flash. His own word is, "Behold, I come quickly; and my reward is with me;" "The great day of the Lord hasteth greatly;" "For when they shall say, Peace, peace; then sudden destruction cometh upon them."

Cheiron is sometimes represented as occupying Apollo's throne; and so the word to this royal Judge and invincible Warrior is, "Thy throne, O God, is for ever and ever; the sceptre of Thy kingdom is a right sceptre." In the Indian sacred books there is a tenth avatar predicted, when Vishnu, the second in the divine Triad, is to come as a man on a white horse, overthrowing his enemies and rooting out all evil from the earth. And so, according to the last book of the New Testament, when the King of kings and Lord of lords comes forth to the battle of that great day to overwhelm the Beast and the false Prophet and all their armies, He comes in the form of a man sitting upon a white horse, in righteousness judging and making war, the same as in Sagittarius.

Thus everything in and illustrative of this sign serves to identify it as a pictorial prophecy of our blessed Lord, answering in all respects to the representations given in the Scriptures. Grotesque and unevangelic as it may seem, it is a showing upon the stars of the same things, under the same images, that we find written concerning the glorified Redeemer in whom all our hopes are centred. He is the sublime Lord and King of salvation, with the two natures in one person, once humbled to death on the cross, but now exalted to glory in heaven. He is the wise, the true, the good, the righteous, who standeth for the defence and administration of righteousness against the Devil and all the powers of the Adversary. He is the mighty Warrior who rideth prosperously, with the bow and arrows of truth and judgment, ever aiming and speeding them at the heart of the foe, and never more giving over until He has carried everything through to everlasting victory, when Death and Hades, and all the powers and children of evil, shall have sunk for ever to their deserved perdition. And the Decans in this sign confirm and further illustrate what we thus read from it.

THE HARP

In connection with this shooting of the Almighty's arrows against His enemies, when His right hand shall find them out and His wrath swallow them up, so that their fruit shall be destroyed from the earth and their seed from among the children of men, the twenty-first Psalm introduces a special celebration of God's exalted strength in the matter, and represents all His holy ones as singing and praising His power. So also in the Apocalyptic visions of the destruction of the

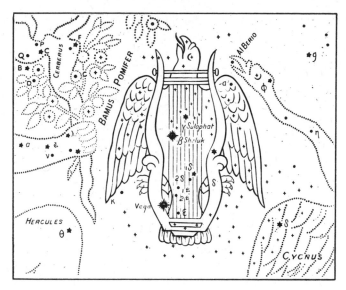

LYRA, THE HARP

destroyers of the earth, the four-and-twenty elders in heaven fell upon their faces and worshipped God, saying, "We give Thee thanks, O Lord God, the Almighty, who art and who wast, because Thou hast taken to Thee Thy great power, and hast reigned"— *i. e.* entered on Thy dominion. Accordingly, also, the first Decan of Sagittarius is the constellation of *Lyra*, the Lyre, the Harp, marked by one of the brightest stars in the northern heavens.

THE LYRE OF ORPHEUS

The harp is the oldest of stringed instruments of music. The ancients ascribed its invention to the gods. We find it named along with the organ, or shepherd's pipe, three hundred years before Adam died (Gen. 4 : 21), and find a specimen of song to be sung to it dating back to the same period (Gen. 4 : 23, 24). The most renowned performer on the harp or lyre in the classic myths is Orpheus, often identified with Apollo. He is called the father of songs and the particular helper of the Argonauts, the noble ones seeking for the Golden Fleece. He is not mentioned by this name by Hesiod or Homer, and subsequent writers place him far anterior

to Hesiod and Homer, and mention all poets and singers as his children or the children of Apollo, to whom he stands in close relation. His art is everywhere associated with religion, prayer, prophecy, and all sacred services, teachings, and anticipations, especially with the joyous element in holy things. At the instance of Apollo and the Muses, it is said, God himself placed the Harp of Orpheus among the stars, where it has ever since been gladdening the celestial sphere with brightness and with song.

The placing of that harp as the first Decan of Sagittarius connects pre-eminent gladness, joy, delight, and praise with the action of this great Archer with his bow and arrows. There is but one such sign in all the ancient constellations, and that is associated with the going forth of this double-natured Bowman aiming his arrows at the Scorpion's heart. It marks him in this particular attitude and act as the achiever of what is the sublimest glory of God and the sublimest joy of heaven.

People often smile and jest at the fabled power of the lyre of Orpheus, at which the rivers for the time forgot to flow, the wild beasts lost their savageness, the trees and rocks on Olympus moved from their places to listen, the ship of the Argonauts glided smoothly into the sea, the mountains became entranced, the dragon that guarded the Golden Fleece sank into sleep, the sufferers in the under-world for the moment lost their pains, and all the potencies of hell yielded homage. But when we connect that lyre with the action of this glorious Archer, and take that action in its true prophetic significance, as the inventors of these signs intended them, these smiles and jests subside, and a scene of glorious achievement opens to our view, which has been the burden of all the songs and prayers and hopes and joyful anticipations of an enthralled and suffering world from the time that Adam was driven out of Eden up till then. That glorious Archer, as he appears in this sign, answers to *the Lamb* as John beheld Him, standing, having seven horns and seven eyes—all the fulness of regal, intellectual, and spiritual power and almightiness—and in the act of lifting the title-deed of the alienated inheritance to take possession again of all that sin has disponed away. Heaven contemplated that act with awe, and grew breathless as it gazed, and a thrill went through the universal heart of living things. A new song broke forth from the living ones and elders around the throne of Deity, and rolled sublime through all the heavenly spheres, till afar in the depths of space the voices of angelic myriads took it up, and every creature in heaven, and on earth, and under the earth, and upon the sea, and all things in these realms, were heard singing, and saying, "To Him that sitteth upon the throne, and to the Lamb, be the blessing, and the honor, and the glory, and the dominion for the ages of the ages!" And this is the true lyre of Orpheus—the joy and gladness and jubilation of the universe at the fulfilment of the burden of all sacred hope and prayer embodied in the words, "*Thy kingdom come—Thy will be done on earth as it is in heaven!*" We thus observe a depth, a splendor, a volume, a pathos, a universality of sacred ardor and poetic outpouring, as just as it is tremendous, and to which all the extravagances of the mythic records do not reach halfway.

With a wonderful appropriateness, then,

which could hardly have come from the unaided powers of man, did the framers of these constellations select the brightest star in the northern heavens to represent this harp, and give to it the name of *Vega*, which signifies *He shall be exalted, The warrior triumphant—* the very name from which our own word *victory* has come—a name which the Apostle uses in its primeval and true connection where he challenges Death and Hades, triumphs over them, and cries his glad thanks "to God who giveth us *the victory* through our Lord Jesus Christ."

In some of the old uranographies this constellation is marked by the figure of an eagle or hawk, the enemy of the serpent, who darts forth upon his prey from the heavenly heights with great suddenness and power; and this eagle is in the attitude of triumph, much as the Mexican eagle is presented victoriously grasping the serpent in its claws. It is the same idea, the triumphant overwhelming of the enemy. From this many of the modern atlases represent the figure of this constellation by an eagle holding the harp, or a harp placed over an eagle, expressing triumphant song springing from the eagle—that is, from the vanquisher and destroyer of the serpent. Whatever the variations of the figure, the same idea is retained, showing the true intention in the marking of this constellation, and the tenacity with which the original thought has clung to it in all ages and in all nations. It is the sign of the Serpent ruled, the Enemy destroyed, the triumphant fulfilment of the sublimest of hopes and sacred promises.

ARA, THE BURNING PYRE

Still further is this signified in the second Decan, which the Arabs call *Al Mugamra*, the completing, the finishing, the making of an end of what was undertaken. The Hebrew uses the elements of the same word where it is said, "The Lord will *perfect* that which concerneth me" (Ps. 138 : 8). The Greeks called it *Ara*, a word which the Latins used to denote a small elevation of wood, stone, or earth made for sacred purposes, particularly for sacrifices; hence *an altar*, and also a *fu-*

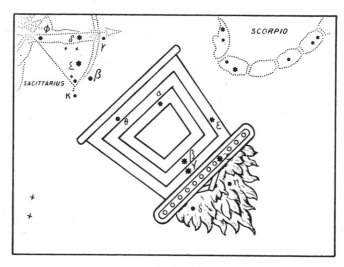

ARA, THE ALTAR, OR BURNING PYRE

neral-pile, whence we have in our charts the figure of an altar covered with burning fire to denote this constellation. The Greeks used the word *ara* sometimes in the sense of prayer, but more frequently in the sense of an imprecation, a curse, or the effect of a curse—bane, ruin, destruction. Personified, it was the name of the goddess of revenge and destruction. In Æschylus it is the name of the actual curse of Œdipus personified. It connects directly with the Hebrew *mara* and *aram*, which mean *a curse, utter destruction.*

THE UNDER-WORLD

In the latitudes in which these constellations were originally formed *Ara* was on the lowest horizon of the south. The regions beyond this were contemplated as the lower regions, the under-world, the regions of darkness, "outer darkness;" just as the regions toward the north pole are contemplated as the upper regions, the regions of light and heaven. And, singularly enough, these ara-fires burn downward, toward the dark and hidden abyss, toward the covered and invisible south pole. The whole significance of the name and figure thus connects with ultimate perdition, the completed curse, the sending into "the lake of fire."

In the Zodiac of Dendera the figure is dif- ferent, but the idea is the same. There we have a throned human figure wielding the flail, the implement of threshing and bruising, and that figure at the same time set over a jackal, often identified with the dragon. Here is the unclean and cunning animal of darkness brought under dominion and judgment, threshed, bruised, punished. This throned and threshing figure has a name which signifies *the Coming One*, the same as in Scorpio. The meaning of the sign is therefore plain. The idea is, victory over the enemy, the thrusting of him into the regions of darkness, the threshing and bruising of him beneath the feet of the conqueror, the beating of him down into final punishment.

According to the Scriptures, the spoiling of Satan and his kingdom by the Virgin-born Son of God is to go on, step after step, to complete overthrow and final perdition. A curse was pronounced upon him at the beginning, fore-announcing that his head should be bruised under the heel of the promised Seed of the woman. Though a strong man armed, a stronger than he was to come upon him, take from him his armor, and subdue all things unto himself, spoiling principalities and powers, triumphing over them. Christ tells us of "everlasting fire, prepared for the Devil and his angels." John, in his vision of what must shortly come to pass, heard the heavens resounding with the song, " Now is come salvation, and strength, and the kingdom of our God, and the power of His Christ: for the accuser of our brethren "—" the great Dragon, that old Serpent "—" is cast down." He also saw a messenger from heaven laying hold on the same, binding him and casting him into the abyss, whence he was finally " cast into the lake of fire and brimstone," where he " shall be tormented day and night for ever and ever." Such is the curse upon the great Enemy, and the finishing of him as set forth in the Holy Scriptures. And what we find thus written in the book is identical with what is pictured on the heavens in connection with *Sagittarius*. To some the idea may seem far-fetched, and so different from ordinary thinking as to be almost absurd; but let them look at the facts as they are, and tell us what other conclusion is possible. What could be more complete than the correspondence of the two records?

The third constellation belonging to the sign of the Bowman is also very significant, and further determines the meaning to be as just expressed.

THE DRAGON

One of the most famous mythological creations in the history of human thought is the horrid serpentine monster called the dragon. Together with the serpent, and other things of the same repulsive and dangerous class, this is the universal symbol of evil—of some living power inimical to God and all good, and the just terror of all men. The Serpent stands for that form of the Evil One in which cunning, artifice, deceit, and malignant subtlety are the characteristics. The Dragon represents the same power armed, defiant, and putting forth in imperial forms, and devastating by force. The Serpent is the sly and creeping deceiver, smoothly gliding in to betray, insinuating his poison and destroying by stealth. The Dragon is the terrific oppressor, assailing with teeth and claws, armed all over with spikes, lifting speary wings and tail, spouting fire and fury, and rushing upon its prey with every vehemence

of malignant energy. The Serpent and the Dragon are one and the same, only in different modes of manifestation. Hence the Devil is called " the Dragon, that old Serpent." Whenever the power of evil is clothed in political sovereignty, persecuting, tyrannizing, and oppressing, it is always the Dragon, or some rampant figure of destruction answering to it.

Among all nations we find this terrible image. Chinese and Japanese legend and art superabound with it. The pages of the classic poets of Greece and Rome teem with it. We find it in the religious books, traditions, and ideas of men of all classes, in all sections of the world, in all the ages. It is in the Old Testament, in the Apocrypha, and in the New Testament. Jews and Gentiles, Christians and heathen, civilized and savage, the Teutons, Scandinavians, and Celts of Europe, as well as the myriads of Asia and the remotest isles of the sea, alike have it, and connect with it the same family of ideas. And everywhere the vanquishing of this monster is the work of gods, heroes, and saints.

Many have wondered and speculated as to how such an imagination obtained this universal hold of the human mind. There is nothing in earthly zoology to serve as the original for the picture, or to account for conceptions and ideas so uniform all the world over. No man ever saw a dragon, living or dead, yet all men talk of the dragon, and adopt it into all their religion, heraldry, and art as the symbol of some well-known reality. Where did it come from? Admit the doctrine which I am endeavoring to elucidate respecting these primeval constellations, and the whole thing is at once and completely explained as nothing else can explain it. Here is the Serpent in all forms of manifestation, and particularly the Dragon, wound about at least one-half of the northern sky, his tail alone extending over the territory of " the third part of the stars." Here is the divine Hero, armed with bow and arrows, riding like St. George, and aiming his weapons at the heart of that Dragon's representative. Here is this precise symbol of the evil power in all his various shapes and attributes, and the great Son of the virgin revealed for his destruction, and going forth in His benevolent majesty to make an utter end of the terrible beast. In all the ages has this image been before the eyes of men in the primeval astronomy, pictorially portraying in the stars the very ideas that figure so conspicuously in their myths and traditions. And this, and this only, is the true original of all these ethnic conceptions—the true original by inspiration given.

And as Sagittarius goes forth in war against the enemy to complete upon him the curse, to make all clear and unmistakable the great constellation of the Dragon is added as a third explanatory side-piece, denoting exactly who it is that this mighty administration strikes, thus waking all the triumphant songs of heaven. It is the final fall of the Dragon-power before the arrows of the invincible warrior-Seed of the woman. It is the ultimate victory fore-announced.

In the Apocalyptic visions of the consummation John beheld a great red Dragon, having seven heads and ten horns, upon his head seven diadems, whose tail was drawing along the third of the stars of the heaven. He stood before the woman eager to devour her child as soon as born; but in spite of him that child was caught away to God and to His throne. And then came war in heaven: Michael and his angels warring with the Dragon,

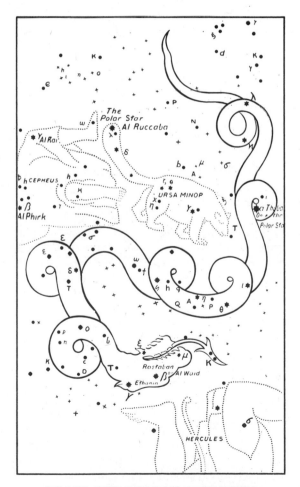

DRACO, THE DRAGON CAST DOWN

who was cast down, and all his angels with him. And then it was that the great voice of song was heard in heaven, because the Accuser, the great Adversary, was conquered and cast down. For a while his persecutions continued upon the earth, till the crowned Warrior on the white horse came, destroying his armies, chaining him in the abyss for a thousand years, and then consigning him and all his to the lake of fire, whence the smoke of their torment ascendeth up for ever and ever (Rev. 12 : 19, 20).

Thus also the Psalmist sings : "God is my King of old, working salvation in the midst of the earth, breaking the heads of the dragons in the waters, breaking the heads of Leviathan in pieces" (Ps. 74).

Isaiah refers exultingly to the time when the Lord cometh forth out of His place to punish the workers of iniquity, and says : "In that day the Lord with His sore and great and strong sword shall punish Leviathan the crossing serpent, even Leviathan that crooked serpent ; and He shall slay the Dragon ;" and calls upon all the people of God to sing when that day arrives (Isa. 26 : 27).

And when we lay these foreshowings of the holy prophets alongside of these pictures in the stars, who can question that we have one and the same story in both ? In both we behold the same Dragon, the same worming of himself into the domain of God, the same spoliation of peace and good by his malignant power, and the same vastness and stretch of his evil influences and dominion. In both we have the same divine Hero, arrayed as an invincible warrior, going forth in conquering majesty against the Dragon, wounding him with His arrows, cleaving him with His sword, bruising and crushing him for his wickedness, annihilating his power, and consigning him to his deserved and everlasting perdition. The names, the actions, the implements, the results, and the common joy of the holy universe over the achievement, are one and the same in the constellations, in the Scriptures, and in the myths. Nor could all this possibly have been except from one original source, even the sacred promise and foreshowing of God, variously certified, and ever again repeated through His prophets, even from the foundations of the world.

The name of this great constellation is *Draco*, the Dragon, the trodden-on. The chief star has several ancient names, such as *Al Waid*, who is to be destroyed ; *Thuban*, the subtle ; *Al Dib*, the reptile. This was the pole-star from four to six thousand years ago, singularly answering to the scriptural designation of Satan as the god and prince of this world. To this day this star is still observed as a very important star to nautical men and the direction of commerce upon the seas, just as the Dragon power still largely prevails. The second star in this constellation is *Rastaban*, head of the subtle ; the third, *Etanin*, the long serpent, the Dragon ; another, *Grumian*, the deceiver ; another, *El Athik*, the fraudful ; another, *El Asieh*, the humbled, brought down ; another, *Gianser*, the punished enemy. Roots corresponding to all these words are contained in the Hebrew Scriptures, where they are used in the senses here given.

What shall we say, then, to these things ? Mythology says the Dragon is the power that guarded the golden apples in the famous Garden of the Hesperides, hindering men from getting them. Is not this the Devil, the old Serpent, the Dragon, who has thrust himself in to keep mortal men from the fruits of the Tree of Life ? Mythology says this Dragon was slain by Hercules. And is not Hercules the astronomic sign of the promised Seed of the woman, the One to come as the Serpent-bruiser, and who stands pictured in his constellation with His foot on the head of the Dragon ? Other myths represent the Dragon as guarding the sacred well, and slaying those who came to draw from it, but was slain by the arrows of Cadmus, who had to suffer for it, indeed, but by Minerva's aid freed the way to the well, and built there a noble city. But is not Cadmus the hero sent to seek his sister who was lost, and the same who was offered as the giver of victory to the people who should accept him as their commander ; just as Christ is come to seek and to save that which was lost, through suffering and divinity vanquishing Satan, opening access to the sacred well of the waters of life, building about it the Zion of His Church, and conducting those who take Him as their Lord and King to the blessedness of triumph and everlasting peace? Ay, verily, these signs in the constellations are but another version of what was written by the prophets and set forth in the Scriptures as the true and only hope of man.

"Most wondrous Book! The Author God himself;
The subject, God and man, salvation, life
And death—eternal life, eternal death.
      . . . On every line
Marked with the seal of high divinity,
On every leaf bedewed with drops of love
Divine, and with the eternal heraldry
And signature of God Almighty stamped
From first to last."

7

DEATH AND NEW LIFE

Verily, verily, I say unto you, Except a corn of wheat fall into the ground and die, it abideth alone: but if it die, it bringeth forth much fruit.
—John 12:24

IN connection with these words I continue the study of that evangelic record which we find written on the stars in the ancient astronomy.

As far as we have gone in these investigations, four signs of the Zodiac, with their accompanying Decans, have been discussed— Virgo, Libra, Scorpio, and Sagittarius. Eight more of these signs accordingly remain to be considered; and to these, in their order, I propose that we now direct our attention.

ORDER OF THE SIGNS

Perhaps this is as good a place as any that may offer to remark the fact that these twelve signs of the Solar Zodiac divide themselves into three distinct groups, each group having its own distinct subject. The first group, consisting of the four signs which have already been before us, relates to the Person, Work, and Triumph of the illustrious Re-

deemer, with special reference to himself. The next succeeding group, consisting of Capricornus, Aquarius, Pisces, and Aries, with their several Decans, relates to the Fruits of His Work and Mediatorship—the formation, condition, and destiny of the Church, or that body of people spiritually born to Him through faith, and made partakers of the benefits of His redemptive administrations; whilst the third and last group relates to the final Consummation of the whole in the united glory of the Redeemer and the redeemed, and the exalted condition of things which the Consummation is to realize. All this will be more clearly brought out as we proceed. At present we make our entrance upon the second or middle group.

THE SIGN OF CAPRICORNUS

Here we have the picture of a fallen goat with the vigorous tail of a fish—half goat and half fish.

It may seem singular and far-fetched to connect the text I have read with such a figure. A little consideration, however, will show that the subject-matter in both is in fact identical, though the particular imagery is entirely different. That of the text is the image which we had in *Virgo*, where the illustrious Son of the virgin is likened to a grain of corn or seed, denoted by *Spica*, the ear of wheat. It was necessary for this seed or grain of wheat to fall into the ground and die in order to reach its intended fruitfulness, which fruitfulness arises directly out of such falling and dying. The meaning of the passage is, that Christ was to die as a sacrifice, and that by virtue of His sacrificial death salvation was to come to man and the congregation of saved ones formed. As Wordsworth expresses it, "He compares himself to a grain of corn, which would be buried by the unbelief of the Jews, but would fructify in the faith of the Gentiles. As much as to say, I will die, that they may live. *My death will be their birth*." As the phœnix was said to arise out of the ashes of its consumed predecessor, so the Church, or congregation of saints, rises out of the death of Christ, sacrificed for the sins of the world. This is everywhere the teaching of the Scriptures, and nowhere more pointedly and graphically than in this text. And when we translate this idea into the imagery of the fifth sign of the Zodiac, we find another very graphic and much older picture of precisely the same thing.

TYPE AND ANTITYPE

First of all, we have here the figure of *a goat*. This is a sacrificial animal. God commanded the children of Israel, saying, "Take ye a kid of the goats for a sin-offering" (Lev. 9 : 31). So Aaron "took the goat, which was the sin-offering for the people, and slew it, and offered it for sin" (Lev. 9 : 15). And of the goat of the sin-offering Moses said, "It is most holy, and God hath given it you to bear the iniquity of the congregation, to make atonement for them before the Lord" (Lev. 10 : 16, 17).

In the next place, this goat is fallen down in the attitude of dying. His one leg is doubled under his body, and the other is powerless to lift him up. His head is drooping and sinking in death. This is the identical falling and dying of Christ as the sin-offering to which He refers in the text. It is the same Seed of the woman, in the attitude and condition of a sacrifice for sin. Christ surely was "wounded for our transgressions" and "bruised for our iniquities." "He was cut off out of the land of the living: for the transgression of my people was He stricken."

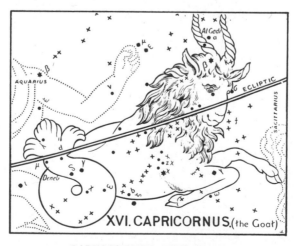

CAPRICORNUS, THE GOAT

As the Head of the flock He suffered in their stead, and laid down His life in sacrifice that they might live. And here it is written on the stars from the earliest ages, and with a vividness of pictorial representation which no one can contemplate without realizing that the picture is intensely striking.

The names in this sign also point to the same thought and significance. *Gedi* and *Dabih* are the most prominent stars in this constellation; and in Hebrew, Arabic, and Syriac these names mean, *the cut-off, the hewn-down, the sacrifice slain.* Other stars in the same constellation have names of similar import, signifying *the slaying, the record of the cutting off.* Even the elements of the name of the sign as we still have it from the Latins, *Capricornus,* mean not only the goat, but *atonement,* sinking or bowed in death. And if there is any significance whatever in these celestial pictures, we have in this sign the symbol of sacrificial death, which is the exact idea of the text.

The Church

But it is at the same time a picture of another kind of life, developed out of this sacrificial death, and vitally conjoined with it. The body of the fallen and dying goat terminates in the body and tail of a vigorous fish. The living fish thus takes its being out of the dying goat, and has all its life and vigor from thence. Accordingly, the Coptic name of this sign signifies *the station* or *mansion of bearing.* In addition to the falling and dying, it is the sign of a mystic procreation and bringing forth. That which is brought forth is *a fish,* which is again a familiar and well-understood sacred symbol.

When Jesus called and appointed His first ministers He said, "I will make you *fishers* of men" (Matt. 4:19). So when God said He will bring the children of Israel again into their own land, His word was, "I will send for many *fishers,* and they shall *fish them*" (Jer. 16:15, 16). So in Ezekiel's vision of the holy waters the word was, "And there shall be *a very great multitude of fish,* because these waters shall come thither" (Ez. 47:1–9).

Christ speaks of His saved ones as "*born of water*" (John 3:5). In the parable of the drag-net and in the miraculous draughts of fishes God's people are contemplated as *fishes.* Hence, in both Testaments fishes stand as the symbol of believers. "Fishes signify regenerate persons," says Dr. Gill. "Fish are those that are wrought upon and brought in by the Gospel, and are so called for six reasons," says Greenhill. "Fish are the men who have attained to life by the Messianic salvation," says Dr. Hengstenberg. The early Christians were accustomed to call believers *Ichthues* and *Pisces*—that is, *fishes.* In the name and titles of our Lord—"*Jesus Christ, the Son of God, our Saviour*"—the initials in Greek form a word or name which signifies *a fish,* and hence the Fathers technically designated Christ as the mystic divine Fish, who in the waters of baptism begets the multitude of fishes—the congregation of His people. Christ is therefore at once the sacrificial goat of the sin-offering and the begetter of a body of reborn men, the Church, the congregation of the quickened and saved. The diction of the Scriptures thus answers exactly to the figure in this sign, which is the dying goat developed into a fish body.

The Mystical Union

Even the great New-Testament doctrine of the Mystical Union of believers with their Saviour is here most strikingly signified. As men naturally are but reproductions and perpetuations of Adam, and live his life, so Christ's people are the reproduction and perpetuation of Christ, living His life. They are *in Him* as the branch is in the vine. They are repeatedly called His body, one with Him, "members of His body and of His flesh and of His bones." And so close and real is their life-connection and incorporation with Him that they are in a sense sometimes called "Christ." What, then, could better symbolize this than the sign before us? This goat and fish are one—one being, the life of the dying reproduced and continued in a spiritual product which is part of one and the same body. The goat of sacrifice sinks into a new creation, which is yet an organic part of itself. The image is grotesque, and has no prototype in Nature, but it is true, exact and graphic. The forgiveness and regeneration of men, and their incorporation with Christ, is something wholly above Nature—something altogether miraculous—which could not be adequately signified by any natural symbols ; and so, as the double nature of the Redeemer himself was denoted by an arbitrary figure, half horse and half man, so the relation between Him as the Sin-bearer and His saved people, who live by virtue of His death, is denoted by another arbitrary figure, made up of a dying goat and a living fish. Nor is it in the power of human genius or imagination to devise another figure capable of setting forth more simply and truly the great and glorious mystery.

The Myths

The pagan myths concerning this sign correspond with these interpretations. This goat is everywhere regarded as Pan, Bacchus, or some divine personage. How he came to have the form of a goat is explained after this fashion : The gods were feasting near a great river, when suddenly the terrible Typhon came upon them, compelling them to assume other shapes in order to escape his fury. Bacchus took the form of a goat and plunged into the river, and that part of his body which was under the water took the form of a fish. To commemorate the occurrence Jupiter placed him in the heavens in his metamorphosed shape. The story is absurd, but through it shines something of the great original idea. It was to secure deliverance from the fury of God's wrath upon sin, and from the ruinous power of the Devil, that the Son of God took upon Him the form of a Sin-bearer and Sacrifice, and in this character was plunged into the deep waters of death. It was by His taking of this form, and His sinking in death as our substitute and propitiation, that life came to those who were under the power of death, whereby they became a living part of Him, never more to be separated from Him. The myth is only a paganized

and corrupted paraphrase of the original reference which the Spirit of sacred prophecy had written in the primeval astronomy, whence the whole conception originated.

Dagon, the half-fish god of the Philistines, and Oannes, the half-fish god of the Babylonians, also connect with this Zodiacal Capricornus, and have embodied in them the same original thought as well as figure. Philo tells us that Dagon means *fruitfulness, the seed-producing ;* and so Christ is the Seed, the Corn of wheat, fallen and dying in the goat, but producing the living fish, the Church, which is the travail of His soul, the true fruit of His atonement. Eusebius says that Dagon was the god of husbandry, the god of seeds and harvests. Pluche says that Dagon among the Philistines was the same as Horus among the Egyptians ; and Horus takes the character of the meek and silent Sufferer from whom comes the horn of blessing and plenty. Dagon had the human form in place of the goat, but that was only a further interpretation of the meaning ; for the goat part of Capricornus stands for the Seed of the woman, and so is in reality the man Christ Jesus.

Berosus speaks of Oannes as likewise half man and half fish. Some of the ancient pictures of him still remain, in which he is figured as a great fish outside, but under and within the fish, and joined with it as its more vital interior, was a tall and vigorous man, standing upright in great dignity, with one hand lifted up as if calling for attention, and in the other carrying a basket or satchel as if filled with treasure. He is fabled as having risen out of the sea to teach the primitive Babylonians the secrets of wisdom, particularly the elements of culture, civilization, and law, organizing them into a prosperous commonwealth. An ancient fragment says of him : "He grew not old in wisdom, and the wise people with his wisdom he filled." The representation is throughout in full accord with what I have been saying of Capricornus. There is a coming up out of the deep in glorious life, and a blessed fruitfulness brought forth thereby, and that fruitfulness in the form of instructed, wise, and disciplined people. It is the fallen Seed of the woman risen up from death after having gone down into the invisible and unknown world, begetting and creating a new order among men—the dying Seed issuing in the believing body, the Church, in which He still lives and walks and teaches and blesses. The myth embodies the exact story of the sign.

SPIRITUAL CONCEPTIONS.

Moreover, the very complexity of the figure of Capricornus, at first so confusing and hard to construe, conducts us into still further particularities of evangelic truth. As far as we have been looking at it, we see the literal death of one being issuing in the spiritual life of other beings, of whose new life He is the life. It is Christ in the one case corporeally sacrificed, and His people mystically resurrected to newness of life in the other. But along with this goes a reflex which it is important for us to observe, as it brings out some of the deep practical spiritualities of true religion. Of course, the rising of the fishes out of the dying goat implies the literal and potent resurrection of Christ himself as the Begetter and Giver of this spiritual resurrection to His people; for if He did not rise, then no preaching or believing would avail to bring us to life or salvation. But as we rise to spiritual life through the power of His resurrection, so there is also implied a dying with Him in order to rise with Him; for there is no resurrection where there has been no dying. We look for a resurrection of the body, because there is first a death of the body. And as God's people are partakers of a mystic or spiritual resurrection, there goes before it a corresponding death. That death out of which their new life comes through and in Christ is twofold. It is first a deadness in sin—existence indeed, but morally and spiritually a mere carcass, with no life-standing to the law or any practical spiritual life toward God and heaven—a life that is nothing but spiritual death and corruption under sentence of eternal death. In the next place, it is death to sin, both as to its penalty and power, a cessation of the mere carnal life and of further existence under condemnation. Now, the great office of religion,

through the Seed of the woman and His sacrificial offering of himself to expiate our sins, is to bring death to this old life in sin and death, and by this wounding, slaying and putting off of the old man of corruption, to generate, evolve, sustain, teach and train the new man, which is renewed after the image of Christ's own resurrection, and which beams with better knowledge and true holiness. Christ corporeally dies for us, and we mystically die to the old death-life with, in, and by virtue of Him. We die to the death-penalty which holds us whilst in the mere carnal life, and put it clean off from us for ever, in the atoning sacrifice of Christ, by accepting Him and believing in Him as our Surety and Propitiation; and in really taking Him as our Redeemer and Hope there is such a force in our faith, and it is in itself such a living and active power, that in the very exercise of it we necessarily die to the pursuit and service of sin. In other words, beginning to live in Christ, we begin to die to the old carnal life. The one is the correlative of the other. Hence the apostolic word: "How shall we that are dead to sin live any longer therein? Know ye not that so many of us as were baptized into Jesus Christ were baptized into His death? Therefore we are buried with Him by baptism *into death;* that like as Christ was raised up from the dead by the glory of the Father, even so we also should walk in newness of life, . . . knowing this, that our old man is crucified with Him, that the body of sin might be destroyed, that henceforth we should not serve sin. For he that is dead is freed from sin" (Rom. 6: 2–7).

This, then, is the meaning of the picture: The Seed of the woman takes our death-penalty on himself, and dies a sacrifice for our sins, so that believers die with Him to all the old life of condemnation and sin; out of this death He springs up in resurrection-power, in which believers rise with Him by being brought to know and accept the truth and to follow His teachings in lively hope of a still further rising in immortal glory at the last; in all of which we behold the much fruit yielded by the seed of wheat falling to the ground and dying.

And with these presentations agree the accompanying side-pieces or Decans.

THE ARROW

The first is Sagitta, the shot and killing *arrow*. It appears naked and alone. It has left the bow, and is speeding to its aim. It is a heavenly arrow, and He who shoots it is invisible. There is a majesty and a mystery about it which startles and awes. It is the death-arrow of almighty justice, which goes forth from the throne against all unrighteousness and sin. It is that death-inflicting instrument which comes with resistless force and sharpness against a world that lieth in sin, and which pierces the spotless Son of God as found in the place of guilty and condemned man. The execution it does is shown in the fallen and dying goat. It is the arrow of divine justice and condemnation upon sin piercing through the body and soul of the meek Lamb of God, who agreed to bear our sins and answer for them.

In the thirty-eighth Psalm we have this very arrow of God sticking fast in the body of the mysterious Sufferer, wounding His flesh and His bones, and completely overwhelming Him. He is troubled and bowed down, as under a crushing burden. His heart panteth, his strength faileth, the light of his eyes fades out. Not only is he the persecuted object of man's hatred, but shut up within the strong bars of divine judgment. It was divine grace that prepared and shot that arrow against the person of the blameless One; but, being found in the room and stead of sinners, God's holy vengeance could not hold back for the sparing even of the only-begotten of the Father. so full of grace and truth. Christ came into the world to die for it; and toward this lowest deep His steps daily led Him as He looked onward to the harvest that was being sown amid these tears. It would seem almost as if the song of the Psalmist had been copied direct from what is thus pictured in these signs.

But this Arrow doubtless covers a further idea. There is a spiritual piercing and slaying in the case of those who come to new life in Christ, akin to the piercing and slaying of Christ himself. Sharp and hurtful words are compared to arrows. And of this character are the words of God as pronounced upon the wicked, judging and condemning them for their sins, bringing them down from their lofty self-security, and killing out of them the vain imaginings in which they live. Isaiah speaks of this sort of shaft or arrow in the Lord's quiver—the arrow of the Word—the arrow of conviction of sin, righteousness, and judgment—a wounding and killing arrow which enters into men's souls, and makes humble penitents of them, that they may come to life in Christ. The death of Christ for our sins also takes the form of a word, preaching, testimony, and argument, even the preaching of the Cross, to kill the life of sin and to cause men to die unto it; so that the very arrow of sovereign justice which drank up the life of Christ as our Substitute and Propitiation passes through Him to pierce also those whose life in sin cost Him all this humiliation and pain; also killing them to that

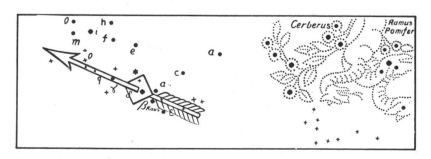

SAGITTA, THE ARROW

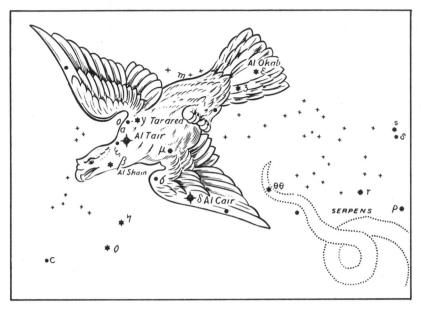

AQUILA, THE EAGLE

ill and condemned life that they may live the Christ-life as His renewed, justified, and redeemed children.

Thus the Arrow fills out precisely the same ideas which we find symbolized in the sign of Capricornus.

The Pierced Eagle

The second Decan adds still further to the clearness and certainty of the meaning. This is the constellation of *Aquila*, the pierced, wounded, and falling eagle. It is but another picture of the grain of wheat falling and dying. The principal star in this constellation is of the first magnitude, and is the star by which the position of the moon—also a symbol of the Church—is noted for the computation of longitude at sea. Its name is *Al Tair*, which in Arabic means *the wounded*. The name of the second star in the same language means *the scarlet-colored—covered with blood*. The name of the third means *the torn*, whilst that of another means *the wounded in the heel*. It is simply impossible to explain how all these names got into this sign and its Decans, except by intention to denote the great fact of the promised Saviour's death.

The myths explain this eagle in different ways. Some say it is Merops, king of Cos, the husband of Ethemea, who lamented for his condemned wife, and was transformed into an eagle and placed among the stars. Some say it is the form assumed by Jupiter in carrying off Ganymedes, whilst others describe it as the eagle which brought nectar to Jupiter while he lay concealed in the Cretan cave by reason of the fury and wrath of Saturn. In short, pagan wisdom did not know what it meant, though holding it in marked regard. And yet, as Christ loved the Church, and gave himself for it, and reigns in glory for its good—as He humbled himself in obedience to death that He might take to himself a glorious Church to serve the eternal Father in immortal blessedness—as He was really brought down into the cave of death, whence He was revived by heavenly virtues after the exhaustion of the fierce wrath of insulted sovereignty,—we can still see some dim reflections of the original truth and meaning even in these confused and contradictory fables.

The eagle is one of the biblical symbols of Christ. "Ye have seen what I did unto the

Egyptians, and how *I bare you on eagles' wings* and brought you unto myself" (Ex. 19: 4), "As an eagle stirreth up her nest, fluttereth over her young, spreadeth abroad her wings, taketh them, beareth them on her wings; *so the Lord alone* did lead him" (Deut. 32: 11, 12). The eagle is a royal bird, and the natural enemy of the serpent. It is elevated in its habits, strong, and swift. It is very careful and tender toward its young, and is said to tear itself to nourish them with its own blood when all other means fail. And here is the noble Eagle, the promised Seed of the woman, pierced, torn, and bleeding, that those begotten in His image may be saved from death, sheltered, protected, and made to live for ever.

But, as in the case of the Arrow, so also in this case, the figure will admit the further idea which takes in the proud sinner, pierced by the arrow of the Word and brought down into the humiliation of penitence, even to death and despair as to all his former hopes in himself. And until the high-soaring children of pride are thus brought down by the arrow of God's Word, and fall completely out of the heaven of their dreams, conformably to Christ's death for them, there can come to them no right life. Paul was alive without the law once, and a very high-soaring and bloodthirsty eagle; but when the commandment came, sin revived, and he *died*—died the death that could alone bring him to right life.

THE DOLPHIN

The third Decan of this sign is the beautiful cluster of little stars named *Delphinus*. It is the figure of a vigorous fish leaping upward. Taken in connection with the dying goat, it conveys the idea of springing up again out of death. Our great Sin-bearer not only died for our sins, but He also rose again, thereby becoming "the first-fruits of them that slept." As the Head and Representative of His Church, He is the principal Fish in the congregation of the fishes. Their quickening, life, and spiritual resurrection rest on His coming forth again after having gone down into the waves of death for their sakes.

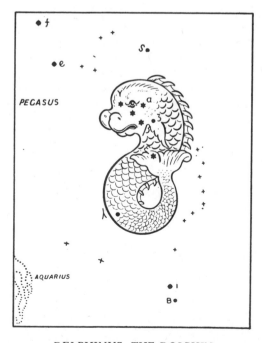

DELPHINUS, THE DOLPHIN

Put to death in the flesh, He was quickened by the Spirit, and in His quickening and resurrection all His people share. Their sins having been buried in His death, their life is by virtue of His resurrection, that "like as He was raised from the dead, so we should walk in newness of life," ever advancing toward a still more complete resurrection to come. The corn of wheat falls into the ground and dies, but from that death there is a springing up again to the intended fruitfulness. Christ dies and rises again, and His people, slain in their old carnal confidence, absolved by His suffering of the penalty due to them, and planting themselves solely upon Him as their Lord and Redeemer, rise with him into the new, spiritual, and eternal life. The picture of the dying goat, with its after-part a living fish, implied this, but the nature of the transition could not be so well expressed in that figure by itself. Hence the additional explanatory figure of an upspringing fish, to show more vividly that the transition is by means of resurrection to a new life of another style. We thus have the vivid symbol of both the resurrection of the slain Saviour as the Head of the Church, and the included new creation of His people, who rise to their new life through His death and resurrection.

In ancient mythology the dolphin was the most sacred and honored of fishes, doubtless because of its place among the ancient constellations, though the myths representing it are very different. It was specially sacred to Apollo, and its name was added to his—some say, because he slew the dragon; others say, because in the form of a dolphin he showed the Cretan colonists the way to Delphi, the most celebrated place in the Grecian world and the seat of the most famous of all the oracles. According to some accounts, it was a dolphin which brought about the marriage of the unwilling Amphitrite with the god of the sea, and for this it received place among the stars. The muddy waters reflect something of the original idea. Christ was the true Son of Deity. It was He who broke the Dragon's power by submitting to become the atoning Mediator. "In all things it behoved Him to be made like unto His brethren, that He might be a merciful and faithful high priest to make reconciliation for the sins of the people." By His death and resurrection He has opened and shown the way by which His people come to the blessed city of which Jehovah is the light. By His mediation He has brought about a marriage between men in flight from their Lord and Him who loved them with a love that passeth knowledge. And in believing foretoken of all this His sign, as the Head of His people, was thus placed in the heavens, where it stands as another form of the parable of the buried corn of wheat rising in new life, of which all who are His are partakers.

SALVATION THROUGH ATONEMENT

Capricornus is thus the illustrious bearer and witness of the most vital evangelical truths. There is no more central or important doctrine of our holy faith than this, that the pure and sinless Son of God, having assumed our nature for the purpose, did really and truly take the sins of the world upon Him, and bore the agonies of an accursed death as the sacrifice and propitiation for our guilt. Whatever difficulty human reason may have in receiving it, it is the very heart and substance of the Gospel tidings, on which all the hopes of fallen man repose. "Thus it is written, and thus it behoved Christ to suffer, and to rise from the dead the third day, that repentance and remission of sins might be preached in His name" (Luke 24 : 46, 47) This "first of all" Paul preached, and Christians received and held, "how that Christ died for our sins according to the Scriptures, and that He was buried, and that He rose again the third day according to the Scriptures" (1 Cor. 15 : 3, 4). "Forasmuch as the children are partakers of flesh and blood, He also himself likewise took part of the same, that through death He might destroy him that had the power of death, that is, the Devil, and deliver them who through fear of death were all their lifetime subject to bondage" (Heb. 2 : 14, 15). Hence the highest apostolic song on earth is that led off by the holy seer of Patmos: "Unto Him that loved us, and washed us from our sins in His own blood, and hath made us kings and priests unto God and His Father; to Him be glory and dominion for ever and ever;" whilst the saints in heaven, in devoutest adoration, fall down before the Lamb, and cry, "Thou art worthy to take the book, and to open the seals thereof; for Thou wast slain, *and hast redeemed us to God by Thy blood*" (Rev. 1 : 5, 6 ; 5 : 9).

And how cheering and confirmatory to our faith to see and know that what Prophets and Apostles have been testifying on earth the heavens themselves have been proclaiming for all these ages! How assuring to know that what we build our hope on now is the same that the holy patriarchs from Adam's time built on as their hope and joy! They believed and expected, and hung their faith and testimony on the stars, that in the fulness of time the Seed of the woman should come, and bow himself in death as the Sin-offering for a guilty world, and rise again in life and fruitfulness of saving virtues, whereby His Church should rise with Him, sharing at once the merit of His atonement and the power of His resurrection, and thus live and reign in inseparable union with himself in life and glory everlasting. Every September midnight of every year for all these centuries has accordingly displayed the sign of it in the middle of the sky, and held it forth to the eyes of mortals as the blessed hope and only refuge of a condemned world, at the same time that it marks the point of change in year and climate, and when the darkness is the greatest opens the southern gateway of the Sun.

Yes, this strange goat-fish, dying in its head, but living in its after-part—falling as an eagle pierced and wounded by the arrow of death, but springing up from the dark waves with the matchless vigor and beauty of the dolphin—sinking under sin's condemnation, but rising again as sin's conqueror—developing new life out of death, and heralding a new spring-time out of December's long drear nights—was framed by no blind chance of man. The story which it tells is the old, old story on which hangs the only availing hope that ever came, or ever can come, to Adam's race. To what it signifies we are for ever shut up as the only saving faith. In that dying Seed of the woman we must see our Sin-bearer and the atonement for our guilt, or die ourselves unpardoned and unsanctified. Through His death and blood-shedding we must find our life, or the true life, which alone is life, we never can have.

> " The wheaten corn which falls and dies,
> In autumn's plenty richly waves;
> So, from the loathsome place of graves,
> With Christ, our Elder, we may rise.

> " From death comes life! The hand of God
> This direst curse to good transforms;
> So purest air is born of storms;
> So bursts the harvest from the clod."

8

THE LIVING WATERS

If any man thirst, let him come unto Me, and drink.
—John 7:37

ONE of the gladdest things in our world is water. In whatever shape it presents itself, it is full of interest and beauty. Whether trickling down in pearly mist from the fragrant distilleries of Nature, or rippling in merry windings through the grassy dell or shady grove; whether jetting from the rocky precipices of the mountain, or gathered into the rolling plains of ocean; whether sparkling in the ice-gem, or pouring in the cataract; whether coming in silver drops from the bow-spanned heavens, or forcing itself out in glassy purity from the dark veins of the earth; whether in the feathery crystals of the snow-flakes, or grandly moving in the volume of the ample river,—it is everywhere and always beautiful. Next to light, it is God's brightest element; and light itself is as much at home in it as in its own native sky. Sometimes, in some connections, it is the symbol of evil, but even there it is the expression of life and energy. Nor is it much to be wondered that in the hot Orient men were moved to deify fountains and erect vo-

tive temples over them, as though they were gracious divinities. The preciousness of bright, fresh waters to parched and needy man is beyond all compare. Where such waters come they bring gladness and rejuvenation, luxuriousness and plenty. Where they pour forth, sinking strength recovers, dying life rekindles, perishing Nature revives, a thousand delights are awakened, and everything rejoices and sings with new-begotten life.

Such an object in Nature could not fail to be seized by the sacred writers to represent the life-giving purity and regenerating power of divine grace and salvation. Accordingly, we find it one of the common and most lively images under which the Scriptures set forth the cleansing, renewing, and saving virtues that come to man in God's redemptive administrations. Thus the Spirit in Baalam's unwilling lips described the goodliness of Israel's tents " as the valleys spread forth, as gardens by the river's side, as the trees of lign-aloes which the Lord hath planted, as cedar trees beside the waters." Thus when the inspired Moses began his song of God's grace to Israel's tribes, he said, "My doctrine shall drop as the rain, my speech shall distil as the dew, as the small rain upon the tender herb, and as the showers upon the grass." The good man is "like a tree planted by the rivers of water, that bringeth forth his fruit in his season, whose leaf also shall not wither." The joy of Messiah's day is the opening of "a fountain to the house of David, and to the inhabitants of Jerusalem, for sin and for uncleanness." Ezekiel beholds the blessed influences of the sanctuary as issuing waters—waters to the ankles, waters to the knees, waters to the loins, waters to swim in —a river of waters. Jesus himself discoursed to the woman of Samaria of the saving benefits of His grace as "living water"—water which slakes all thirst for ever. The people of God are likened to fishes, whose life-element is water. And so in the text the Saviour compares His redeeming virtue and grace to water, and says, "*If any man thirst, let him come unto Me, and drink.*"

In those signs, then, which the primeval patriarchs hung upon the stars as everlasting witnesses of God's gracious purposes to be achieved through the Seed of the woman, we would certainly expect to find some great prominence given to this same significant symbol. And as we would anticipate, so do we really find, especially in the sixth sign of the Zodiac, which we now come to consider.

The Sign of Aquarius

Here is the figure of a man with a great urn upon his arm, from which he is pouring out from the heavens a stream of water which flows with all the volume of a swollen river. Mythology calls him *Ganymedes*, the bright, glorified, and happy One—the Phrygian youth so beautiful on earth that the great King and Father of gods carried him away to heaven on eagles' wings to live in glory with immortals. Some say that he came to an untimely death in this world; and the stories in general combine in representing him as the beloved and favorite of the divine Father, exalted to glory and

AQUARIUS, THE WATER-BEARER

made the chosen cup-bearer of the Deity. Classic art portrays him as a most beautiful young man, sometimes carried by an eagle, sometimes ministering drink to an eagle from a bowl which he bears, and again as the particular companion of the eternal Father. Amid all these earthly varnishes which paganism has daubed over the picture we still may see the sacred image shining through. The true Ganymedes is the beautiful Lord Jesus, "the chief among ten thousand, and altogether lovely." Cut off was He in His early manhood, but divinely lifted up again, borne away to heaven on unfailing wings, seated in brightness and glory beside the everlasting Father, loved and approved as God's only-begotten Son, made the sovereign Lord and Dispenser of grace and salvation, and by His merit procuring and pouring out the very "river of water of life." The urn He holds is the exhaustless reservoir of all the fulness of renewing, comforting, and sanctifying power. And the turning of that holy urn for its contents to flow down into the world below is the precise picture of the fulfilment of those old prophetic promises: "I will pour water upon him that is thirsty, and floods upon the dry ground: I will pour out my Spirit upon thy seed, and my blessing upon thine offspring;" "I will pour out my Spirit upon all flesh; and your sons and your daughters shall prophesy, and your old men shall dream dreams, and your young men shall see visions" (Isa. 44 : 3 ; Joel 2 : 28).

The name of the principal star in this sign —*Sa'ad al Melik*—means *Record of the outpouring*. The Coptic, Greek, and Latin names of the sign itself signify *The Pourerforth of water, The exalted Waterman*, as though specially to designate Him who says, "*If any man thirst, let him come unto Me, and drink.*"

PROMISE OF THE HOLY SPIRIT

When Christ was about to leave the world He said to His followers, "It is expedient for you that I go away; for if I go not away, the Comforter will not come unto you; but if I depart, I will send Him unto you. . . . He will guide you into all truth. . . . He will show you things to come. . . . He shall glorify me: for He shall receive of mine, and shall show it unto you" (John 16). That promise included all the divine life-power issuing from the mediation of Christ for the illumination, regeneration, and salvation of men —all the renewing, cleansing, comforting, and energizing grace for the gathering of the elect and the bringing of believers to eternal life and glory. The Holy Ghost was in the world from the beginning, but here was the promise of a new and enlarged grant and endowment, to lift, nourish, and distinguish Christian believers. The same was gloriously fulfilled on the day of Pentecost, when "suddenly there came a sound from heaven as of a rushing mighty wind, and filled all the house where they were sitting; and they were all filled with the Holy Ghost, and began to speak with other tongues, as the Spirit gave them utterance." And when the Jews mocked and derided, the sacred explanation was that Jesus, being raised up again from the dead and exalted to the right hand of God, and having so received of the Father, was now the Giver and Shedder-forth of this marvellous power. He is thus presented to our contemplation as the glorified Pourer-forth from heaven of the blessed waters of life and salvation; in other words, the true Aquarius, of whom the picture in the sign was the prophecy and foreshowing.

Wherever the Scriptures represent the Spirit and grace of God under the imagery of waters, the idea of unfailing supply and plenteous abundance is also invariably connected with it. Sometimes it is a plentiful rain; sometimes it is a voluminous fountain; sometimes it is a great river flowing with fulness that supplies a thousand life-freighted rivulets. Inspiration tells us that the rock smitten by Moses was the type of the smiting of Christ and the blessings proceeding from Him; but in that case the waters "*gushed;* they ran in dry places like a river." Isaiah sings: "The glorious Lord will be unto us a place of broad rivers and streams." Ezekiel's river was deep and broad, healing even the Dead Sea with the abundance of its flow. Zechariah says these heavenly waters flow out to both seas, and continue without cessation summer and winter alike. God's promise is, "I will open rivers in high places, and fountains in the midst of the valleys: I will make the wilderness a pool of water, and the dry land springs of water;" which, as John Brentius says, "denotes the great plenteousness of the Word and eternal blessedness flowing from Christ the Fountain." And the same is characteristic of the picture in this sign. From the urn of Aquarius flows a vast, constant, and voluminous river. It flows in a bending stream both to eastward and westward, and enlarges as it flows. The imagery of the Scriptures and the imagery of this sign are exactly of a piece, and the true reason of the coincidence is, that both were meant to record and set forth the same glorious evangelic truths.

The Southern Fish

That this sign was really framed to be a picture of the risen and glorified Redeemer

pouring out from heaven the saving influences and gifts of the Holy Ghost, is further evidenced by the first Decan of Aquarius. Those who truly profit by the gifts and powers procured and poured out by our glorious Intercessor are the people who believe in Christ, the regenerate, the saved Church. These, as we saw in our last, are the mystic fishes. And here, as the first Decan of Aquarius, we have the picture of a fish—*Piscis Australis*—drinking in the stream which pours from the urn of the beautiful One in heaven. It is the picture of the believing acceptance of the invitation of the text. Jesus stood and cried, "If any man thirst, let him come unto Me, and drink;" and here is a coming from below—a glad coming to the stream which issues from on high, a drinking in of the heavenly waters, and a vigorous life sustained and expanded by means of that drinking.

The mythic legends do not help us much with regard to the interpretation of this constellation, but they still furnish a few significant hints. Some say this fish represents

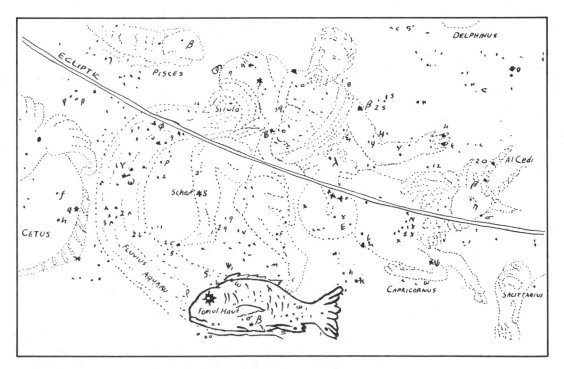

PISCES AUSTRALIS, THE SOUTHERN FISH

Astarte, called Aphrodite by the Greeks and Venus by the Romans, and that she here appears in the form into which she metamorphosed herself to escape the advances and power of the horrible Typhon. Astarte was the moon-goddess, the great mother, the embodiment of the dependent but ever-productive feminine principle. In the symbology of the Scriptures the moon sometimes denotes the mother of the family, as in Joseph's dream (Gen. 37), and both the woman and the moon are representatives of the Church. As the woman was made out of the side of Adam while He slept, so the Church was made out of Christ by means of that deep sleep of death which came upon Him, and to which He submitted for the purpose. The whole mystery of marriage is the symbol of the union between Christ and His Church (Eph. 5 : 23–32). Everywhere the congregation of believers is pictured as the spouse of Christ, the spiritual woman, the mother of us all. And if this fish represents the Astarte of the pagan religion, we have only to strip off the heathen impurities, and understand the reference in the sense and application of the Scripture symbols, in order to find here a picture of the regenerate people of God, the Church, the bride of Christ, the mother of saints.

So understood, the metamorphosis into a fish is also applicable and significant, as in no other interpretation. All true members of the Church are transformed persons, made over again by the power of a new spiritual creation, and living a new life superadded to Nature. It is by this spiritual metamorphosis that we make our escape from the power and dominion of the Devil. And it is by means of this transformation that we have our status and relations in the heavenly economy and kingdom. The light comes feebly through the dark and murky atmosphere of the pagan world; but wherever we get sight of a distinct ray, it easily resolves back into the figures of the primeval constellations, and thence into the sacred story of redemption through the promised Seed of the woman.

PEGASUS

And in perfect consistence with, and as further illustration of, what I have given as the meaning of this sign, is the second Decan. Here is the figure of a great horse pushing forward with full speed, with great wings springing from his shoulders. The elements of his name, as in Isaiah 64 : 5 (4), signify the swift divine messenger bringing joy to those whom he meets, otherwise *the horse of the opening;* or as the Greeks put it, without obliteration of the old Noetic nomenclature, *the horse of the gushing fountain*—a celestial horse, ever associated with glad song, the favorite of the Muses, under whose hoofs the Pierian springs started upon Mount Helicon, and on whose back rode Bellerophon as he went forth to slay the monster Chimæra.

The fables say that this wonderful horse sprang into being from the slaying of Medusa by Perseus; that he was called *Pegasus* (πηγη-συς), *Horse of the Fountain*, because he first appeared near the springs of the ocean; that he lived in the palace of the King and Father of gods, and thundered and lightened for Jupiter; and that Bellerophon obtained possession of him through sacrifice to the goddess of justice, followed by a deep sleep, during which he was divinely given the golden bridle which the wild horse obeyed, and thus he was borne forth to victory, though not without receiving a painful sting in his foot.

In the first chapter of Zechariah the appearance of such horses are the symbols of those whom "God hath sent to walk to and fro through the earth," not simply to see and report the condition of affairs, but to shake and disturb nations, so as to restore liberty, peace, and blessing to God's people. Pegasus is not precisely one of those horses, or all of them combined in one, but still a somewhat corresponding ambassador of God. Pegasus is winged; he moves with heavenly speed. The first part of his or his rider's name, *Pega, Peka,* or *Pacha,* in the Noetic dialects means *the chief;* and the latter part, *sus,* means, not only *a horse,* but *swiftly coming* or *returning,* with the idea of joy-bringing; hence *the chief, coming forth again in*

PEGASUS, THE WINGED HORSE

great victory, and with good tidings and blessing to those to whom he comes. The ancient names of the stars which make up his constellation are—*Markab,* the returning; *Scheat,* he who goeth and returneth; *Enif,* the Branch; *Al Genib,* who carries; *Homan,* the waters; *Matar,* who causeth the plenteous overflow. The names show to what the picture applies.

Gathering up these remarkable items, and combining them, as they all readily combine, in one consistent narrative, we have in astonishing fulness one of the sublimest evangelic presentations; nay, the very going forth of Christ in His living Gospel, as from the scenes of that supper-hall which witnessed the coming of the Paraclete the joyous waters of cleansing and redemption, through His successful mediation, poured their glad flood into our weary world. Then the word was, "Go ye into all the world, and preach the Gospel [Good Tidings] to every creature. He that believeth and is baptized shall be saved." Thenceforward, Parthians and Medes, and Elamites, and the dwellers in Mesopotamia, and in Judæa, and Cappadocia, in Pontus and Asia, Phrygia and Pamphylia, in Egypt, in Lybia, and strangers of Rome, Jews and proselytes, Cretes and Arabians, and people to the farthest ends of the earth, were made to hear, in their tongues, the wonderful works and achievements of God for the renewal and saving of men. Thenceforward the Glad Tidings went, winged with the Spirit of God, waking poetic springs of joy upon the mountains and in the valleys, slaying the powers of darkness and superstition, overwhelming the dominion of the Devil, and bringing song and salvation to every thirsty and perishing soul which hears and obeys the call of the Lord of life to come unto Him and drink. The true Pegasus is the herald and bringer of Christ's mediatorial success and salvation to a famishing world, which the saintly patriarchs looked for from the beginning, and which they thus figured in the constellations in advance as an imperishable witness of what was to come through and by that Coming One in whom all their hopes were centred.

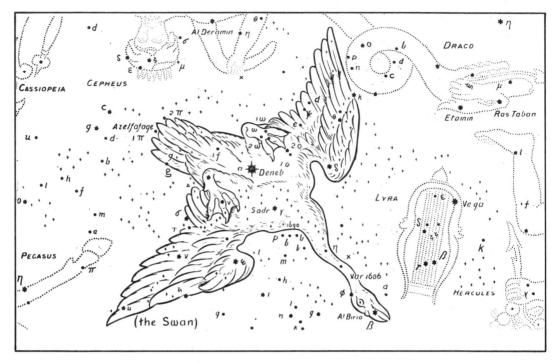

CYGNUS, THE SWAN

THE SWAN

The final side-piece which accompanies the Zodiacal Aquarius accords precisely with this presentation. It is one of the most interesting and beautiful of the constellations, both in its natural peculiarities and in its evangelic references. It consists of eighty-one stars—one of the first or second magnitude, six of the third, and twelve of the fourth; and some of these never set. It embraces at least five double stars and one quadruple. The binary star (61 Cygni) is the most remarkable known in the heavens. It is one of the nearest to our system of the fixed stars. It consists of two connected stars, which, besides their revolution about each other, have a common progressive and uniform motion toward some determinate region, and moving thousands of times faster than the swiftest body known to our system. This constellation has a number of distinct systems in itself, and shows planetary nebulæ which have led astronomers to regard it as the intermediate link between the planetary worlds and the nebulous stars. It has in it specimens of both, and lies in the midst of the great Galactic Stream of nebulous stars. It is therefore remarkably suited to represent that peculiar and complex economy—partly celestial and partly terrestrial, partly acting by itself and partly dependent on the heavenly powers—by which grace and salvation are carried and ministered to the children of men.

The figure in this constellation is the figure of *a swan*, the lordly bird-king of the waters, in all ages and in all refined countries considered the emblem of poetic dignity, purity, and grace. By the Greeks and Romans it was held sacred to the god of beauty and the Muses, and special sweetness was connected with its death. Æschylus sung,

> " The swan,
> Expiring, dies in melody."

As the white dove is the emblem of the Holy Ghost, so the elegant, pure, and graceful swan is a fitting emblem of Him who, dying, sends forth the glad river of living waters, and presides in His majesty over the administration of them to the thirsty children of men. And this is here the underlying idea.

But this swan is *on the wing*, in the act of rapid flight, "circling and returning," as its name in Greek and Latin signifies. It seems to be flying down the Milky Way, in the same general direction with the river which pours from the heavenly urn. The principal stars which mark its wings and length of body form a large and beautiful cross, the most regular of all the crosses formed by the constellations. It is thus the bird of matchless beauty, purity, dignity, and grace, bearing aloft the cross, and circling with it over the blessed waters of life; whilst in the naming of its stars, the brightest is *Deneb*, the Lord or Judge to come; *Azel*, who goes and returns; *Fafage*, glorious, shining forth; *Sadr*, who returns as in a circle; *Adige*, flying swiftly; *Arided*, He shall come down; and other words of like import, we find strong identifications of this lordly bird-king of the waters with Him who, through the preaching of His cross hither and thither over all this nether world, cries and says, "*If any man thirst, let him come unto Me, and drink.*"

Greek and Roman mythology is greatly at a loss to account for the presence of this bird in the sky; but the stories on the subject are not destitute of thought and suggestion corresponding with the evangelic truth. The Greeks enumerated a collection of characters of different parentages and histories, each reputed to have been the original of this swan in the heavens. One was the son of Apollo, a handsome hunter, who in some strange fit leaped into Lake Canope, and was metamorphosed into this swan. Another was the son of Poseidon, an ally of the Trojans, who could not be hurt with arms of iron, but was strangled by Achilles—whose body, when the victor meant to rifle it, suddenly took its departure to heaven in the form of a swan. A third was the son of Ares, killed by Herakles in a duel, who at his death was changed by his father into a swan. A fourth was the son of Sthenelus and a dear friend and relative of Phaeton, who so lamented the fate of him whom Jupiter

destroyed for his bad driving of the chariot of the sun that Apollo metamorphosed him into a swan and placed him among the stars. Some dim embodiments of the true prophetic delineations of this swan, and of that history of the Redeemer through which He came to the position and relations in which this picture received fulfilment, appear in the several myths. Christ was of divine birth and nature. He was in himself invincible. He did submit to death in heroic conflict with the powers of darkness and the just penalties due the sins of the world. It was His great love for those to whom He became a Brother that brought him down to the dark river. His body did take life again after death, and disappear into a new form of brightness and glory to assume position in the heavens. In these several particulars the myths touching this constellation are in remarkable accord with the Gospel history, and help to reflect how minute and clear and vivid were the believing anticipations of the makers of these signs already in the very first ages of our race.

A Beautiful Picture.

Thus, then, in the Zodiacal Aquarius we have the picture in the stars of the heavenly waters of life and salvation; of their source in the beautiful Seed of the woman, slain indeed, but risen again and lifted up in everlasting glory; of the voluminous plenteous ness in which they flow down into all our dry and thirsty world; of the new creation and joyous life they bring to those who drink them; of the swift heralding and bearing of the glad provision to all people; and of the graceful holding forth of the cross to the nations over which, on outspread wings, the Lord of these waters circles, in His meek loveliness ever calling, "*If any man thirst, let him come unto Me, and drink.*"

Beautiful picture of most precious Gospel truths!—a picture which I can interpret no otherwise than as intended by men fully informed beforehand of these glorious facts. And if, perchance, these constellations were not meant in token, testimony, and prophecy of what was foreknown, believed, and expected by the primeval patriarchs who arranged them, the picture is still true to what has since come to pass, and which it is part of our holy religion to accept and rejoice in as the great mercy of God to a fallen world. Christ Jesus is the beautiful Saviour of mankind, Son of God and Son of man. He did come in the flesh and live a human life in which humanity came to its loveliest and highest bloom. He did suffer and die a violent death from offended justice on account of sin which He assumed, but in no degree chargeable to Him. He did rise again from death by the power of the eternal Spirit, changed, transfigured, and glorified, and soar away beyond all reach of enemies, even to the calm heavens, where no revolutions of time can any more obscure His brightness or eclipse the outshining of His glory. He is there as the Lord of life and grace, obtaining by His meritorious intercession an exhaustless fulness of spiritual treasures, like very rivers of renewing and sanctifying mercies, which He has poured, and is ever pouring, down into our world for the comfort, cheer, and salvation of those who believe in Him. He has arranged, and himself conducts and energizes, a great system of means for carrying and proclaiming the same all over the world amid songs of halleluia and rejoicing which can never die. Deep in it all He has embedded the great doctrine of His Cross and Passion as the central thought and brightest substance of the sublime and wonderful economy. And in and amid it all faith beholds Him in His lordly beauty stationed by the true Pierian spring, ever crying and ever calling, "IF ANY MAN THIRST, LET HIM COME UNTO ME, AND DRINK."

"Ho, every one that thirsteth, come ye to the waters; and he that hath no money, come ye, buy, and eat; yea, come, buy wine and milk without money and without price;" "And the Spirit and the Bride say, Come. And let him that heareth say, Come. And let him that is athirst come. And whosoever will, let him take the water of life freely." Blessed tidings! blessed provision! blessed opportunity! O man! awake to the glory and drink; drink deep, drink earnestly, drink with all the capacity of thy soul; for thy Lord and Redeemer saith, "Whosoever drinketh of the water that I shall give him shall never thirst; but the water that I shall give him shall be in him a well of water springing up into everlasting life."

"The Fountain flows! It pours in fullest measure
    Of grace and power—a great and plenteous flood!
Drink—drink, O man! Drink in the crystal treasure,
    Nor thirst, nor die, but live the life of God."

9

THE MYSTIC FISHES

And He said unto them, Cast the net on the right side of the ship, and ye shall find. They cast therefore, and now they were not able to draw it for the multitude of fishes. —John 21:6

OUR blessed Saviour taught by acts, as well as words. He gave out parables in deeds, as well as in stories and descriptions. All His works of wonder were living allegories—pictures and prophecies incarnated in visible and tangible facts. This is particularly true of the miracle to which the text refers. It was a supernatural thing, to prove the divine power of Him by whom it was wrought; but its chief significance lies in its symbolic character as an illustration of that catching of men by the preaching of the Gospel to which the Apostles were called and ordained.

APOSTOLIC FISHING

At the beginning of his ministry, seeing Peter and Andrew casting a net into the sea, He said unto them, " Follow me, and I will make you fishers of men;" that is, ministers of the Word, who by the holding forth of the truth were to cast the great evangelic net into the sea of the world, and enclose people as Christian believers and members of the Church. So He also said, " The kingdom of heaven is like unto a net that was cast into the sea, and gathered of every kind, which, when it was full, they drew to shore, and sat down, and gathered the good into vessels, but cast the bad away." So, likewise, when He commanded Peter to launch out into the deep and let down the nets for a draught, which resulted in taking such a multitude of fishes that the nets brake in the drawing, and two boats were loaded down to the sinking point with the product, He meant to show the disciples not only His divine power, but a picture of that mystic fishing on which he was about to send them, and which was to be the work of His ministers in all the ages. And the miracle before us is a corresponding picture of the same thing—with this difference, that the other instances refer to the Church nominal and visible as it appears to human view, embracing both good and bad, to be assorted in the day of judgment; whilst the reference here is to the inward, true, invisible Church—the Church as it appears to the eye of God—which includes none but the good, the genuine children of grace and salvation, the definite number of real saints.

It is thus abundantly established and clear that in the symbology of the Scriptures and the teachings of Christ the congregation of those who profess to believe in Him—that is, the Church—is likened to *fishes* enclosed in the fisherman's net. The world is likened to a sea, in which natural men range without control, following their own likes and impulses, and belonging to no one. So the Gospel is likened to a net, which the ministering servants of the Lord spread in the waters in order to enclose and gather men—not to destroy them, but to secure them for Christ, that they may be held by His word and grace and be His peculiar possession. And when they are thus secured and brought within the enclosure of the influences and laws of the Gospel as Christ's professed followers, and formed into His congregation, they are His mystic *fishes*, caught by His command and direction and made His peculiar property. The aptness of the figure no one can dispute, and the scripturalness of the imagery is fixed and settled beyond all possibility of mistake. Christ himself makes fishes the symbol of His Church.

But as is the picture in the Scriptures, so we find in the figures of the constellations. The new life that rises out of the death of the sacrificial goat is in the form of a large and vigorous fish. Those who come to the heavenly Waterman to drink in the stream of living influences which he pours down from on high are represented by a great fish. And as the Church is the most important institute, result, and embodiment of the redemptive work and achievements of the Seed of the woman, so we have one of the twelve signs of the Zodiac specially and exclusively devoted to it; and that sign is the sign of *the Fishes*, which we are now to consider.

THE SIGN OF PISCES

This constellation is now the first in the order of the twelve signs of the Zodiac; but in the original order, which I have been following, it is the seventh. The figure by which it is represented consists of two large fishes, one headed toward the north pole, and the other parallel with the path of the Sun. They are some distance apart, but are tied to the two ends of a long, undulating band or ribbon, which is held by the foot of the Ram in the next succeeding sign.

The names of this sign in Hebrew and Arabic, as in the Greek and Latin, mean the same as in English—*the Fishes*. In Syriac it is called *Nuno, the Fish prolonged*, the fish with the idea of posterity or successive generations. In Coptic its name is *Pi-cot Orion, the Fish, congregation, or company of the coming Prince*. Two prominent names in the sign are *Okda, the United*, and *Al Samaca, the Upheld*. And all the indications connected with Pisces tend to the conclusion that in these two great fishes we are to see and read precisely what was symbolized by Christ in the miracle to which the text refers; namely, a pictorial representation of the Church.

THE MYTHS

The origin of this sign, as mythology gives it, is not at variance with this idea. It is said that Venus and Cupid were one day on the banks of the Euphrates, and were there surprised by the apparition of the giant monster Typhon. To save themselves they plunged into the river, and escaped by being changed into fishes—saved by transformation through water. To commemorate the occurrence it is said that Minerva placed these two fishes among the stars.

We have already noted some symbolic connection between the mythic Venus and the Church. The ancient Phœnicians, according to Nigidius, asserted that she was hatched from an egg by a heavenly dove. Cupid, or the ancient Eros, was held to be the first-born of the creation, one of the causes in the formation of the world, the uniting love-power which brought order and harmony to the conflicting elements of Chaos. The later fables of Cupid are remote inventions out of the original cosmic Eros, the ideas concerning whom well agree with the sign, and readily interpret in their application to Christ and the Church. Christ was "the first-born of every creature" (Col. 1 : 15), and is the Head of "the general assembly and Church of the first-born," who, through His uniting love, combines the chaotic elements of humanity into order and union with himself, bringing into being the mystic woman, "born of water and of the Spirit," which is part of His own mystic organism, His body. By that means also those who compose the Church escape the hundred-headed enemy of God and all good. And in so far as this sign of the Fishes was divinely framed and placed in the heavens to commemorate this transformation and deliverance by water, it is nothing more nor less than a divine symbol of the Church—the impersonation of escape from horrible confusion and destruction, as also of that new-creating love of God, the mother of all holy order and salvation.

TWOFOLDNESS OF THE CHURCH

These Fishes are *two in number*. The general idea thus expressed is the idea of *multitude*, which is characteristic of all the sacred promises relating to the success of the Messianic work among men. The Church, in comparison with the great unsanctified world around it, is always a "little flock"—a special elect called out from among the great body of mankind outside of itself—just as the fishes enclosed in a net are but a small portion of the myriads that are in the sea. But, in itself considered, multitudinousness is always one of its characteristics. To Abraham it was figured as the stars of the sky and as the sand on the seashore for multitude. To Ezekiel the sacred waters embraced "a very great multitude of fish." Every symbolic casting of the net at Christ's command took a great multitude of fishes. The very name carries in it the idea of multitude, and the duplication of the symbol gives the still further idea of outspread multiplication—a glorious company of Apostles, a goodly fellowship of Prophets,

a noble army of Martyrs, a holy Church throughout all the world.

But, beyond this, the Church, in historical fact and development, is twofold. There was a Church before Christ, and there is a Church since Christ ; and whilst these two make up the one universal Church, they are still quite distinct in character. The patriarchal Church, which was more definitely organized under the institutes given by Moses, was one. It is a singular fact that the ancient rabbis always considered the people of Israel as denoted by this sign. The Sethites and Shemites, and all adherents to the true God and His promises and worship, were by both themselves and the heathen astronomically associated with these Fishes. They are certainly one set of the great Saviour's fishes. The Christian Church, organized under the institutes of Jesus Christ, was the other of these Fishes. Though in some sense the same old Church reformed, it was still in many respects quite another—so much so that it became apostasy to turn from it to "the beggarly elements" of the former dispensation. Here, then, are the two great branches or departments of the one great universal Church of the promised Seed of the woman. To the one His coming was future, and so it dealt in types, shadows, symbols, and figures of the true. To the other the ancient anticipations have passed into actual fact, and exist as living realities, already far on the way toward the final consummation. The faith of both is the same, and the spiritual life of both is the same. Hence both are mystic Fishes. But the stage of development, the historical place and condition, and the entire external economy, are different, as type and antitype are different, though in interior substance one and the same. The Fish in its multitudinousness symbolizes both. The old Church was the Fish arising out of the slain sacrifice believed in in advance, and signified in the old ordinances ; and the new Church, organized under Christ, is the Fish arising afresh out of the same, which has now become an accomplished and existing reality. Hence the whole thing was fore-signified in the stars under the image of *two Fishes*, which are indeed *two* under one method of conception, and yet *one* and the same in another method of conception. It is the one Fish in both, yet two Fishes in historic presentation and external dispensation.

THE BAND

The Decans of this sign serve to bring out this idea with great clearness. The first Decan is a very long waving Ribbon or Band. The ancient name of it is *Al Risha, the Band or bridle*. It is one, continuous, unbroken piece, and so doubled that one of its ends goes out to the northern Fish, and is tightly bound around its tail; whilst the other end goes out to the other Fish, and is fastened to it in the same way. By this Band these two Fishes are inseparably tied together, so that the one cannot get on without the other. And so the fact is. The patriarchal Church is really tied to the Christian Church. The Epistle to the Hebrews tells us that the ancient saints, from Adam onward, could not be made perfect without us (chap. 11 : 40).

The consummation of all they hoped for was inevitably tied up with what was to be subsequently achieved by Christ, much of which is still a matter of promise and hope. And so the Christian Church is really tied to the patriarchal Church. All the necessary preparations and foundations for Christianity were vouchsafed through the Old Testament. What was then testified, believed, and looked for we must needs also accept, believe, and take in. The Christian does not stand just where the ancient believer stood, but the old was the bridge by which the new was reached. Christ came not to destroy the law and the prophets, but to fulfil them, and to complete what they looked to and anticipated. There could be no Christian Church without the patriarchal going before it, just as there could be no patriarchal Church without the Christian coming after it to complete and fulfil what the old was meant to prepare for. And here is the Band of connection unalterably binding them together in a unity which still is dual.

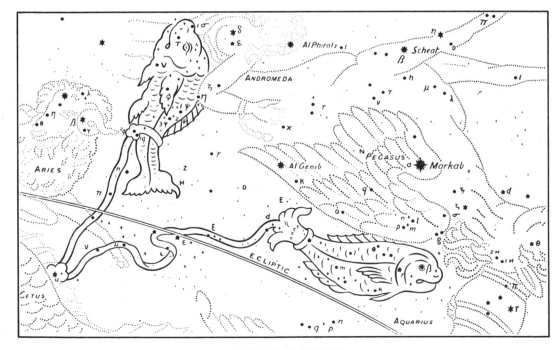

PISCES, THE FISHES
THE BAND

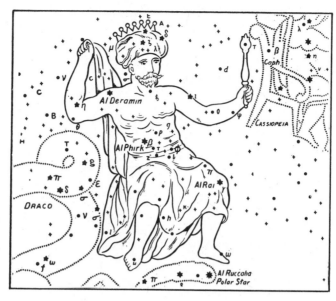

CEPHEUS, THE CROWNED KING

The doubled part of this Band, strange to say, is in the hand or front foot of the symbolic figure in the next succeeding sign; that is, in the hand of *Aries*, the Ram or Lamb. The point of unity between these two Fishes is therefore in Christ and His administrations, by which both are equally affected and upheld. Both belong to Christ in the attitude of the reigning and victorious Lamb. He upholds, guides, and governs them by one and the same Band. These Fishes thus have their places and status by His appointment and authority. They are caught Fishes, no longer roaming at large according to their own will. They are bound together in the hand of the glorious Lamb. They are His, and are upheld, governed, and made to fulfil their offices and mission by His power, will, and grace. And this is precisely the relation and condition of the Church in all dispensations. Like the net of Peter, which held, controlled, and lifted the literal fishes enclosed by it, so this Band holds, controls, and lifts the mystic Fishes which constitute the Church. It is the tie of connection between all saints, and at the same time the tie of connection between them and the glorified Saviour, by whose word they have .been taken and made His precious pos-

session. "Without Me ye can do nothing," was His word when on earth; and ever of old His promise has been: "Thou whom I have taken from the ends of the earth, and called from the chief men thereof, and said unto thee, Thou art my servant; fear not, for I am with thee; be not dismayed, for I am thy God; I will strengthen thee; yea, I will help thee; yea, *I will uphold thee with the right hand of my righteousness.*" And here is the same word pictorially expressed.

CEPHEUS

Who the friend and protector of these Fishes is, the second accompanying side-piece also very sublimely shows. Here is the figure of a glorious king, wearing his royal robe, bearing aloft a branch or sceptre, and having on his head a crown of stars. He is calmly seated in the repose of power, with one foot on the solstitial colure, and the other on the pole-star itself, whilst his right hand grasps the Ribbons. Bearing with us what the Scriptures tell of the present exaltation and glory of Jesus Christ, we here behold every particular so completely and thrillingly embraced that the picture stands self-interpreted.

It so vividly portrays our enthroned Saviour, and fits so sublimely to Him, and to Him only, that no special prompting is necessary to enable us to see Him in it. And if we need further assurance on the subject, we find it in the accompanying star-names.

On the right shoulder of this figure, in glittering brilliancy, shines a star whose name, *Al Deramin*, means *the Quickly-returning*. In the girdle shines another, equally conspicuous, whose name, *Al Phirk*, means *the Redeemer*. In the left knee is still another, whose name means *the Shepherd*. The Egyptians called this royal figure *Pe-ku-hor, the Ruler that cometh*. His more common designation is *Cepheus*, which means *the royal Branch, the King*. Everything thus combines to identify this figure as intended to represent our Saviour as now enthroned in glory, even the Seed of the woman, clothed with celestial royalty and dominion.

In the Zodiac of Dendera the figure in this constellation is a large front leg of an animal connected with a small figure of a sheep, in the same posture as *Aries* in the next sign. It is the strong hand of the Lamb, and so the same which holds the Band of the Fishes. It identifies what is otherwise represented as a glorious king with the upholder of the Fishes, and makes Cepheus one and the same with the victorious Lamb.

Christ has been really invested with all royal rights and dominion. It was predicted of Him from of old, "He shall bear the glory, and shall sit and rule upon His throne" (Zech. 6:13). And so the testimony of the Apostles is that, having been made a little lower than the angels for the suffering of death, and having humbled himself to the cross for our redemption, God hath highly exalted Him, and set Him on His own right hand in the heavens, far above all principality, and power, and might, and dominion, and every name that is named, not only in this world, but also in that which is to come, and hath put all things under His feet, and gave Him to be Head over all things to the Church, which is His body, the fulness of Him that filleth all in all (Eph. 1:19–23). Hence also it is said to all believers, "Ye are complete in Him, which is

the Head of all principality and power" (Col. 2:10). With *a high hand and an outstretched arm* He sitteth in royal majesty to help, uphold, and deliver His Church; "and of the increase of His government and peace there shall be no end."

ANDROMEDA

A still further representation of the Church is supplied in the third Decan of this sign. This is the picture of a beautiful woman, with fetters upon her wrists and ankles, and fastened down so as to be unable to rise. This woman in the Decan is the same as the Fishes in the sign. The change of the image argues no change in the subject. The Church is often a woman, and oftener than it is a net full of fishes; but it is both—sometimes the one, and sometimes the other—in the representations of the Scriptures. Besides, in some of the ancient planispheres these Fishes were pictured with the heads of women, thus identifying them with the woman.

Greek mythology calls this woman *Andromeda (andro-medo)*, *man-ruler*, but with what idea, or for what reason, does not appear in the myths. The name is perhaps derived from some ancient designation of similar significance, which has no meaning in the Greek fables, but which covers a most important and inspiring biblical representation respecting the Church. Here we discover the true *Andromeda*—the mystic woman called and appointed to rule and guardianship over men. When Peter wished to know what he and his fellow-disciples should have by way of compensation for having forsaken everything for Christ, the blessed Master said: "Ye which have followed Me, in the regeneration, when the Son of man shall sit in the throne of His glory, ye also shall sit upon twelve thrones, judging the twelve tribes of Israel" (Matt. 19:28). Hence Paul spoke to the Corinthians as of a well-understood fact, "Do ye not know that the saints shall judge the world?" (1 Cor. 6:2). Hence the enraptured John ascribes everlasting glory and dominion to the divine Christ, not only for washing us from our sins in His own blood, but that He "hath *made us kings*

ANDROMEDA, THE CHAINED WOMAN

and priests unto God" (Rev. 1 : 5, 6). The true people of God, the real Church, are the elect kings of the future ages. Even now already they are embodiments and bearers of the heavenly kingdom and dominion upon earth. Through them the word goes forth for the governing of men, and the regulation of their hearts and lives, and the bringing of them under a new spiritual dominion, so that none ever come to forgiveness and glory except as they come into submission to the truth and the teachings of the Church. The great All-Ruler has so united the Church to himself, and so embodied himself in it, that by its word, testimonies, and ordinances He rules, governs, tutors, and guards men, and brings them under His saving dominion. The Prophets, Apostles, Confessors, Pastors, and Teachers which He has raised up in the Church, with those associated with them in the fellowship of the same faith and work, are the true kings and guardians of men, who have been ruling from their spiritual thrones for all these ages, and will continue to rule more and more for ever as the spiritual and eternal kingdom is more and more revealed and enforced. Most significantly, therefore, may the Church be called *Andromeda;* and the fact that the mystic woman in this constellation is so called, with no other known reason for it, goes far to identify her as verily intended to be a prophetic picture of the Church, which she truly represents beyond anything else that has ever been in fable or in fact.

ANDROMEDA'S CHAINS

But this woman is in chains, bound hand and foot. The names in the sign mean *the Broken-down, the Weak, the Afflicted, the Chained.* The fables say that she was the daughter of Cepheus and Cassiopeia, promised to her uncle Phineus in marriage, when Neptune sent a flood and a sea-monster to ravage the country in answer to the resentful clamors of his favorite nymphs against Cassiopeia, because she boasted herself fairer than Juno and the Nereides. Nor would the incensed god be pacified until, at the instance of Jupiter Ammon, the beautiful Andromeda was exposed to the sea-monster, chained to a rock near Joppa in Palestine, and left to be devoured. But Perseus, on returning from the conquest of the Gorgons, rescued her and made her his bride.

Here, then, was a case of malignant jealousy and persecution resulting in the disability, exposure, and intended destruction of an innocent person. And thus, again, we have a striking picture of the unfavorable side of the Church's condition in this world. Jealous rivals hate her and clamor against her. The world-powers in their selfishness fail to protect her, and lend themselves for her exposure and destruction. Innocently she is made to suffer. Though a lovely and influential princess, she is hindered by personal disabilities and bonds. It will not be so always. The time will come when those bonds shall be broken and that exposure ended. There is One engaged in a war with the powers of darkness and the children of hell who will presently come this way to rescue and deliver the fair maiden and to make her His glorious bride. But for the present affliction and hardship are appointed to her. She cannot move as she would, or enjoy what pertains to her royal character, her innocence, and her beauty. She is bound to the hard, cold, and ponderous rock of this earthly life. Born to reign with her redeeming Lord, Apostles can only wish that she did reign, that

they might reign with her. She is within the sacred territory, but it is as yet a place of captivity and bonds. She never can be truly herself in this mortal life. Nor is she completely free from the oppressive Phineus until the victorious Perseus comes. The whole picture is true to the life, and shows with what profound prophetic foresight and knowledge the makers of these signs were endowed.

ILL-FAVOR OF THE CHURCH

Among the ancients the Zodiacal Pisces was considered the most unfavorable of all the signs. The astrological calendars describe its influences as malignant, and interpret its emblems as indicative of violence and death. The Syrians and the Egyptians largely abstained from the eating of fish, from the dread and abhorrence which they associated with the Fishes in the Zodiac. In the hieroglyphics of Egypt the fish is the symbol of odiousness, dislike, and hatred. And this, too, falls in exactly with our interpretation. The earthly condition and fortunes of the Church are nothing but unfavorable and repulsive to the tastes and likes of carnal and self-seeking man. The restraints and disabilities which go along with it are what the world hates, derides, and rebels against. These Bands that bind the Fishes together, and hold them with bridles of heavenly command and control, and enclose them with meshes beyond which they cannot pass, are what unsanctified humanity disdains as humiliation and reckons as adversity to the proper joy and good of life. Though people can sustain no charges against the Church, and cannot deny her princely beauty, yet to take sides with her is to them nothing but flood, drowning, and devastation to what they most cherish and admire. Let her be chained, disabled, exposed and devoured, if need be, only so that they are exempt from association with her! Let her suffer, and let her be given to death and destruction, the more and the sooner the better if they only can thereby have the greater freedom for their likes, passions, and enjoyments uncurbed and unrestrained! This is the feeling and this the spirit which have obtained toward the Church in all the ages. And the dislike of men to this sign is but the filling out of the picture in the stars as I have been expounding it. It is another link in the chain of evidence that we have here a divine symbol of the Church in its earthly estate and career. The coincidences, to say the least, are very marvellous. To say that the Church has been formed from and to the signs, as French infidelity would have it, is in the highest degree absurd. The Church has not accepted humiliation, disability, contempt, hatred, and oppression from the world just to conform herself to the indications connected with Pisces; and yet her condition to-day, as in all other time, is precisely that which this sign represents, and has been representing on the face of the sky for all these four or five thousand years. The sign has in no sense or degree conditioned the Church, and yet it truly represents the estate of the Church in all generations. To what other conclusion, then, can we come than that the sign in its place, and the whole system of signs of which it forms a conspicuous part, is from that good and infallible prescience which knows the course and end of all things from the beginning? Let those doubt it who will; for my own part, I have no doubt upon the subject.

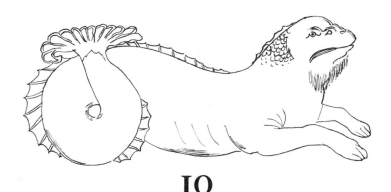

IO

THE BLESSED OUTCOME

Worthy is the Lamb that was slain to receive power, and riches, and wisdom, and strength, and honor, and glory, and blessing.

—Revelation 5:12

THIS is the myriad-voiced response of the heavenly world to the triumphant song of the redeemed after the Church has run its earthly course. It immediately follows that time, now near at hand, when the great voice from the sky, as of a trumpet, shall say, to all the holy dead and to all God's saints, "COME UP HITHER." The whole scene represents that heavenly condition of the elect to be realized at the fulfilment of the apostolic word, which says, "The Lord himself shall descend from heaven with a shout, with the voice of the archangel, and with the trump of God: and the dead in Christ shall rise first: then we which are alive and remain shall be caught up together with them in the clouds, to meet the Lord in the air" (1 Thess. 4 : 16, 17). It is the same scene to which Jesus himself referred when He said: "Wheresoever the body is, thither will the eagles be gathered together" (Luke 17 : 37). And it is precisely this scene that is signified by the eighth sign of the Zodiac—the last of the quaternary relating more especially to the Church.

The text celebrates the worthiness, glory, and dominion of *the Lamb*, who is further described as appearing to have been slain, but here as standing in the midst of the throne, having the perfection of strength and wisdom, and the fulness of spiritual and divine energy operative in the world for the complete salvation of His people; for this is what is meant by the "seven horns and seven eyes—the seven Spirits of God sent forth into all the earth." And in the sign of *Aries* we have this same *Lamb*, or Prince of the flock, the Son of man as the Head, Sacrifice, and High Priest of the Church, lifted up upon the path of the Sun, looking forth in the repose of power, and working that very translation and glorification of His people which the Scriptures everywhere set before us as the blessed hope of all saints.

To this interesting presentation, then, let us now direct our attention.

THE SIGN OF ARIES

The figure here is that of a vigorous *Ram*. It is called *Aries, the Chief, the Head;* as *Aryan* means *the Lordly*. So Christ is the Chief, the Head and Lord of His Church. The English name, *Ram*, means high, great, elevated, lifted up. In Syriac the name is *Amroo, the Lamb*, the same as John 1 : 29, where it is said, "Behold *the Lamb* of God, which taketh away the sin of the world;" also *the Branch, the Palm-branch*, recognized by the Jews as denotive of Christ's royal coming to His Church. The Arabic calls this figure *Al Hamal, the Sheep, the Gentle, the Merciful.* The principal stars included in this figure are called *El Nath* or *El Natik*, and *Al Sharetan*, which mean *the Wounded, the Bruised, the Slain.* Over the head of the figure is a triangle, which the old Greeks said exhibited the name of the Deity, and its principal star bears a name signifying *the Head, the Uplifted*, hence the Lamb exalted to the divine glory, to the throne of the all-holy One.

It is unreasonable to suppose that all this could have happened by mere accident. There was manifestly some intelligent design by which the whole was arranged. And the entire presentation is in thorough accord with what the Scriptures say concerning the Seed of the woman. As the Son of man He is continually represented as the Head and Prince of the flock, *the Lamb*—"the Lamb that was slain"—the Lamb lifted to divine dominion and glory. In His pure, meek, and sacrificial character the Scriptures style Christ "the Lamb of God, which taketh away the sin of the world." In His exaltation He is represented as "the Lamb in the midst of the throne." In the administrations of judgment upon the wicked world He is contemplated as the Lamb, whose wrath is unbearable. As the Bridegroom and Husband of the Church He is also the Lamb, to whose marriage-supper the Gospel calls us. As the Keeper of the Book of life in which the names of the saints are written, the Lifter of the title-deed of our inheritance, and the Breaker of the seals by which the earth is purged of usurpers and the mystery of God completed, He is presented as "the Lamb." As the consociate of the eternal Father in the joy and sovereignty of the world to come, in which the saints glory for ever and ever, He is still referred to as "the Lamb," by whose blood they overcome and in whose light they live world without end. And in whatever attitude He appears, back of all He is still the Lamb.

THE MYTHIC STORIES

The mythic stories concerning Aries still further identify him with the Lamb of the text. This noble and mysterious animal was given by Nephele to her two children, Phrixus and Helle, when Ino, their mortal stepmother, was about to have them sacrificed to Jupiter. It was by seating themselves on its back and clinging to its fleece that they were to make their escape. *Nephele* means *the Cloud*. She is reputed the queen of Thebes; and *Thebes* was *the house, city*, or *congregation of God*. We thus have the cloud over God's house, or congregation, precisely as the Scriptures tell of the cloud of God's gracious manifestations to His ancient people—in their deliverance from Egypt, in their journeyings in the wilderness, and in their worship in the tabernacle and the temple. God visibly dealt with them as their merciful Guide, Instructor, Protector, and Ruler; and His gracious presence was almost uniformly manifested in the form of *the cloud*. Also in Job's time "thick clouds" were His covering. It was by these cloud-manifestations that He called and formed the congregation of His people, assembled them around Him, and kept them in communion with himself as His Church or city.

The two children of the cloud are therefore the same with the two Fishes in the preceding sign; that is, the multitudinous twofold Church, which is born of these merciful divine manifestations. These children were all under sentence of death. So the Church, consisting of men who had fallen under the power of incoming sin, was in danger of being sacrificed. From such a fate believers are delivered by means of the blest "Lamb of God, which taketh away the sin of the world."

This Lamb was furnished to these children

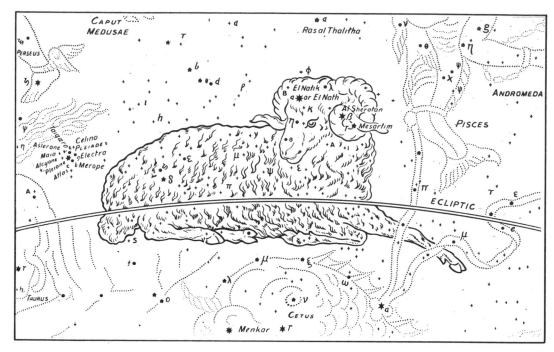

ARIES, THE RAM

from the same cloud of which they themselves are born; and so Christ was begotten by the power of the Highest coming upon and overshadowing the Virgin of Nazareth, and upon himself at His baptism and transfiguration.

The safety of these children of the cloud rested exclusively in this Lamb, and so the name of Jesus is the only name given under heaven among men whereby we can be saved. Both of them in fact were safe, and carried far aloft from Ino's reach and power, so long as they both continued firmly seated on this Lamb; and so the Church is lifted far above all condemnation by virtue of its being planted on Jesus Christ as its Help and Redeemer. Helle, one of these cloud-children, became giddy in the heavenly elevation to which she was lifted by this Lamb, lost her hold upon his back, and fell off into the sea, thereafter called *Hellespont*, or Helle's Sea; and so the antediluvian Church apostatized and was drowned in the flood; as likewise the Israelitish Church, becoming giddy in its sublime elevation, let go its hold on the Lamb by rejecting Christ, and dropped from its heavenly

position into the sea of the common world Phrixus, the more manly part of this mystic cloud-seed, held on to the mystic Lamb, and was brought in safety to *Colchis, the citadel of reconciliation*, the city of refuge. So likewise there has ever been a true people of God remaining faithful amid the apostasies around them, who never let go their hold on the Lamb of God, and are securely borne to the citadel of peace and salvation.

Nephele's Lamb was sacrificed to Jupiter as those who were saved by him would have been without him; and so Christ, the true Aries, was sacrificed for us, and died in our stead. He is "the Lamb slain from the foundation of the world." And it was this Lamb of Nephele that yielded the Golden Fleece, which made him who possessed it the envy of kings, and which constituted the highest treasure to be found by the children of men. And this, again, is a most striking image of the heavenly robe of Christ's meritorious righteousness, the sublimest and most enriching treasure and ornament of the Church, which ever sings—

> " Jesus, Thy blood and righteousness
>   My beauty are, my glorious dress;
>   'Midst flaming worlds, in these arrayed,
>   With joy shall I lift up my head."

It is wonderful to see how these traditional legends of the constellations interpret on the theory that they have come from prophecies and sacred beliefs touching the promised Seed of the woman and the Church which He has purchased with His blood.

It is also worthy of remark that the Egyptians celebrated a sacred feast to the Ram upon the entrance of the Sun into the sign of Aries. They prepared for it before the full moon next to the spring equinox, and on the fourteenth day of that moon all Egypt was in joy over the dominion of the Ram. Everybody put foliage or boughs, or some mark of the feast, over his door. The people crowned the ram with flowers, carried him with extraordinary pomp in grand processions, and rejoiced in him to the utmost. It was then that the horn was full. The ancient Persians had a similar festival of Aries. For all this it is hard to account except in connection with what was prophetically signified by Aries. But taken in relation to what the Scriptures foretell of the Lamb, in the period when He shall take to Him His great power for the deliverance and glorification of His Church, we can easily see how this would come to be one of the very gladdest and most exultant of the sacred feasts. It is when the Lamb thus comes upon the throne, and appears for the taking up of the deeds of the inheritance, the gladdest period in all the history of the Church and people of God is come. Then it is that the songs break forth in heaven in tremendous volume of Worthiness, and Blesssing, and Honor, and Glory to the Lamb for redeeming men by His blood, and making them kings and priests unto God, and certifying unto them that now they " shall reign on the earth."

And when we turn to the accompanying Decans of this sign, the very work and doings ascribed to the Lamb in this entrance upon His great power are still more specifically set before us, in which the joy in Him on the part of His Church and people comes to its culmination. The first of these is

CASSIOPEIA

This is nothing less than a picture of the true Church of God lifted up out of all evils,

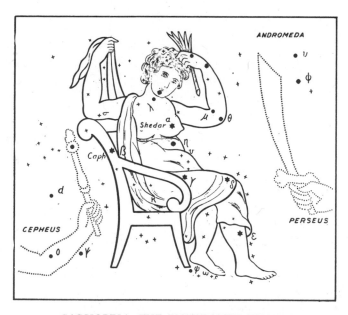

CASSIOPEIA, THE ENTHRONED WOMAN

bonds, and disabilities, and seated with her glorious Redeemer in heaven. The figure is that of a queenly woman, matchless in beauty, seated in exalted dignity, with her foot on the Arctic Circle, on which her chair likewise is set. In one hand she holds aloft the branch of victory and triumph, and with the other she is spreading and arranging her hair, as if preparing herself for some great public manifestation. Albumazer says this woman was anciently called "the daughter of splendor," hence "the glorified woman." Her common name is *Cassiopeia*, the beautiful, the enthroned; or, as Pluche derives the name, *the Boundary of Typhon's power, the Delivered from all evil.* The constellation itself is one of the most beautiful in the heavens.

> " Wide her stars
> Dispersed, nor shine with mutual aid improved;
> Nor dazzle, brilliant with contiguous flame:
> Their number fifty-five."

Four stars of the third magnitude, which never set, form the seat upon which this woman sits. The star on her right side is on the equinoctial colure, and on a straight line with Al Pherats in Andromeda's cheek to the north pole. The constellation embraces a binary star, a triple star, a double star, a quadruple star, and an extraordinary number of star-clusters of similar constituents to the general field of greater stars.

About three hundred years ago there occurred in this constellation what was a great mystery to astronomers. A star, surpassing in brilliancy and splendor all the fixed stars, suddenly appeared on the tenth of November, 1572, and, after shining in continuous glory for sixteen months, disappeared, and has never since been seen, just as the Church disappears in the shadow of death, or is presently to be caught away to the invisible world.

And if there is any one constellation of the sky, or any figure among these celestial frescoes, specially fitted to be the symbol and representative of the Church, particularly in its enfranchised and glorified condition, it is this. The names are equally significant. The first star marking the figure of this woman is called *Shedar*, which means *the Freed*, and

Ruchbah and *Dat al Cursa*, signifying *the Enthroned, the Seated.* On her right hand is also the glorious star-crowned King, holding out his sceptre toward her, whilst all the accounts pronounce her his wife, just as the Scriptures everywhere describe the Church as affianced to Christ, hereafter to be married to Him as " the bride, the Lamb's wife."

Cassiopeia is universally represented as the mother of Andromeda; and so the Apostle refers to the heavenly Church as the mother of the earthly Church. The Jerusalem that is above "is the mother of us all." The whole presentation is that of deliverance and heavenly triumph, precisely as we speak of the Church triumphant; and the ready-making is for the great marriage ceremonial. (Compare Rev. 19:7, 8.)

The perfection of this woman's beauty, fairer than Juno and the envy of all the nymphs of the sea, likewise answers exactly to the Scripture descriptions of the Church: " Thy renown went forth among the heathen for thy beauty; for it was perfect through my comeliness, which I put upon thee, saith the Lord" (Ezek. 16:14). Christ is to present it to himself, " a glorious Church, not having spot, or wrinkle, or any such thing, but holy and without blemish" (Eph. 5:27). Cassiopeia is an enthroned queen; and this is also uniformly the biblical picture of the Church when once it comes to enter upon its promised glory. John saw thrones, and they sat upon them, and they reigned with Christ. And it was further said that so "they shall reign for ever and ever." The Church is " *the queen* in gold of Ophir" of which the Psalmist (45:9) so enthusiastically sung.

CETUS

But when the time comes for the Church to enter upon her royal exaltation and authority, another very important and marked event is to occur. John beheld it in apocalyptic vision, and writes: " I saw an angel come down from heaven, having the key of the bottomless pit and a great chain in his hand. And he laid hold on the Dragon, that old Serpent, which is the Devil, and Satan, and bound him a

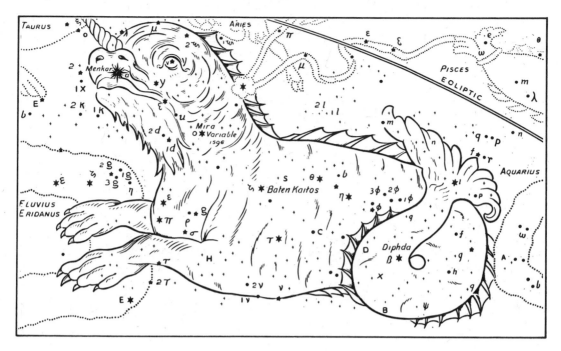

CETUS, THE SEA MONSTER

thousand years, and cast him into the bottom-less pit, and shut him up, and set a seal upon him, that he should deceive the nations no more, till the thousand years are fulfilled; and after that he must be loosed a little season" (Rev. 20 : 1–3). And this is pictorially given in the second Decan of Aries.

The picture is that of a great sea-monster (*Cetus*), the true Leviathan of Job and Isaiah, which covers the largest space of any one figure in the sky. It is a vast scaly beast, with enormous head, mouth, and front paws, and having the body and tail of a whale. It is generally called "the Whale" on our plani-spheres. It is an animal of the waters and marshes, and the natural enemy and devourer of the fishes. It is the same which the sea-god sent to devour Andromeda, and hence the particular foe and persecutor of the Church. It is a downward constellation, bor-dering on the lower regions. One of its cha-racteristic stars, *Mira*, situated in the neck of the scaly monster, is the most wonderfully variable and unsteady in the heavens. From a star of the second magnitude it dwindles away so as to become invisible once in about

every three hundred days, and Hevelius af firms that it once disappeared for the space of four years. It is a striking symbol of the arch-Deceiver, and, singularly enough, its name means *the Rebel*. And what is specially re-markable in the case is, that the doubled end of the Band which upholds the Fishes, after passing the front foot or hand of the Lamb, is fastened on the neck of this monster, and holds him firmly bound. The name of the first of the Cetus stars, *Menkar*, refers to this; for Menkar means *the chained Enemy*. And so the name of the second star, *Diphda*, means *the Overthrown, the Thrust-down*.

Satan is loose now. Peter writes: "Your adversary, the Devil, as a roaring lion, walk-eth about, seeking whom he may devour" (Pet. 5 : 8). God speaks of him, and puts the confounding questions: "Canst thou draw out Leviathan with an hook? or his tongue with the cord which thou lettest down? Canst thou put a hook into his nose? or bore his jaw through with a thorn? Will he make many supplications unto thee? will he speak soft words unto thee? Will he make a cov-enant with thee? wilt thou take him for a servant for ever? Wilt thou play with him as with a bird? or wilt thou bind him for thy maidens? Shall thy companions make a banquet of him? shall they part him among the merchants? Canst thou fill his skin with barbed irons? or his head with fish-spears? Behold, the hope of him is in vain: shall not one be cast down even at the sight of him? None is so fierce that dare stir him up" (Job 41 : 1–10). But he whom no man can take or bind, the Lamb has in His power, and will yet lay hold upon, and fasten with a great chain, from which he cannot break away. By the same power with which He upholds the Fishes He restrains the devouring Enemy; and with that same power He will yet fasten up the monster for final destruction. Of old, Isaiah prophesied of a day when "the Lord with His sore and great and strong sword shall punish Leviathan the piercing Serpent even Leviathan that crooked Serpent, and He shall slay the Dragon that is in the sea" (Isa. 27 : 1). And here we have the same forepictured in the stars, showing how the enthroned Lamb will bind and punish Leviathan, even as the written word of prophecy describes. The sign in the heavens answers precisely to the descriptions in the Book, proving that one is of the same piece with the other, and that both are from the same eternal Spirit which has moved to show us things to come.

PERSEUS

But in still greater vigor and animation is this whole scene set out in the third accompanying side-piece to this sign of the enthroned Lamb. Micah (2 : 12, 13) prophesies of a time when the flock of God shall be gathered, their King pass before them, and the Lord on the head of them; and says that this shall be when "*the Breaker is come up before them.*" Whatever may have been in the foreground of this prediction, it is agreed that "the Breaker" here must needs be Christ, the very Lamb of our text, breaking the way of His people through all the doors and gates of their present imprisonment and disability, and dashing to pieces all the antagonizing powers which

stand in the way of their full deliverance and redemption. So the Lamb in the Apocalypse is the Breaker of the seals and of apostate nations, the same as the Son in the second Psalm. And this Breaker, in these very acts, is the precise picture in this constellation.

Here is the figure of a mighty man, stepping with one foot on the brightest part of the Milky Way, wearing a helmet on his head and wings on his feet, holding aloft a great sword in his right hand, and carrying away the blood-dripping head of the Gorgon in his left. His name in the constellation is *Perets*, Græcised *Perses* or *Perseus*, the same as in Micah's prophecy—*the Breaker*. The name of the star by his left foot is *Atik, He who breaks.* The name of the brightest middle star in the figure is *Al Genib, the One who carries away*, and *Mirfak, Who helps.* And when Perseus comes to the meridian the most brilliant portion of the starry heavens opens out its sublimest magnificence in the eastern hemisphere.

THE MYTHS

Now, one of the most beloved and admired of all the hero-gods of mythology was this *Perseus.* He was the son of the divine Father, who came upon Danæ in the form of a shower of gold. No sooner was he born than he and his mother were put into a chest and cast into the sea: but Jupiter so directed that they were rescued by the fishermen on the coast of one of the Cyclades, and carried to the king, who treated them with great kindness, and entrusted to them the care of the temple of the goddess of wisdom. His rising genius and great courage made him a favorite of the gods. At a great feast of the king, at which the nobles were expected to make some splendid present to their sovereign, Perseus, who was so specially indebted to the king's favors, not wishing to be behind the rest or feebler in his expressions than were his obligations, engaged to bring the head of Medusa, the only one of the three horrible Gorgons subject to mortality.

These Gorgons were fabled beings, with

bodies grown indissolubly together and covered with impenetrable scales. They had tusks like boars, yellow wings, and brazen hands, and were very dangerous. Their heads were full of serpents in place of hair, and their very looks had power to turn to stone any one on whom they fixed their gaze. To equip Perseus for his expedition Pluto lent him his helmet, which had the power of rendering the wearer invisible; and Minerva furnished him with her buckler, resplendent as a polished mirror; and Mercury gave him wings for his feet and a diamond sword for his hand. Thus furnished, he mounted into the air, led by the goddess of wisdom, and came upon the tangled monsters. He,

> " In the mirror of his polished shield
> Reflected, saw Medusa slumbers take,
> And not one serpent by good chance awake;
> Then backward an unerring blow he sped,
> And from her body lopped at once her head."

Grasping the same in his left hand, he again mounted into the air, and

> " O'er Lybia's sands his airy journey sped;
> The gory drops distilled as swift he flew,
> And from each drop envenomed serpents grew."

By this victory he was rendered immortal, and took his place among the stars, ever holding fast the reeking head of the Gorgon. It was on his return from this brave deed that he saw the beautiful Andromeda chained to the rock, and the terrible monster of the sea advancing to devour her. On condition that she should become his wife, he broke her chains, plunged his sword into the monster that sought her life, fought off and turned to stone the tyrant Phineus who sought to prevent the wedding, and made Andromeda his bride, begetting many worthy sons and daughters, and by varied administrations of miraculous power changing portions of the earth and its governments and rulers, returning betimes to bless the countries that honored him.

PERSEUS AND CHRIST

No natural events in the seasons or in the history of man could ever serve as a foundation for such a story as this. Here is a divine-human son, begotten of a golden shower from the Deity, a child of affliction and perse-

cution from his very birth, but predestined by the heavenly powers to live and triumph. By his high qualities he is made the keeper and conservator of the temple of wisdom and sacred worship. Out of devotion to his king he undertakes to destroy the Gorgons as far as they are destructible. For this he descends into hell, and brings forth armor from thence. He is in communion with the divine wisdom, and thereby is girded in splendor and led unerringly. He is winged, and given a diamond sword, as Heaven's messenger and herald to undo the powers of evil and administer deliverance and prosperity. He wounds the dire Gorgons in the head, and carries off their power. He punishes Leviathan with his " sore and great and strong sword." He breaks the bonds of Andromeda, and makes her his bride amid high festival, at which he puts down all opposition. And thereupon he goes forth to countries far and near, punishing and expelling tyrants and usurpers, rooting out untruth and corrupt worship, and blessing and rejoicing the city and kingdom of heroes. All this interprets with wonderful literalness and brilliancy when understood of the promised Seed of the woman, the Lamb that was slain, going forward at the head of His people as *the Breaker*, bringing death and destruction to the monsters of evil, setting wronged captives free, and joining them to himself in glory everlasting. Nor is there anything else of which it will interpret or that can adequately account for the existence of the story.

MEDUSA'S HEAD

And that we are so to understand this figure is still further manifest in the facts and names in the reeking, snake-covered head grasped by the hero. *Medusa* means *the Trodden under foot*. The name of the principal star in this head, *Al Ghoul*, contracted into *Algol*, means *the Evil Spirit*. The same is also a variable star, like *Mira*. It changes about every three days from a star of the second magnitude to one of the fourth, and makes its changes from one to the other in three and a half hours. *Rosh Satan* and *Al Oneh* are other names of the stars in this

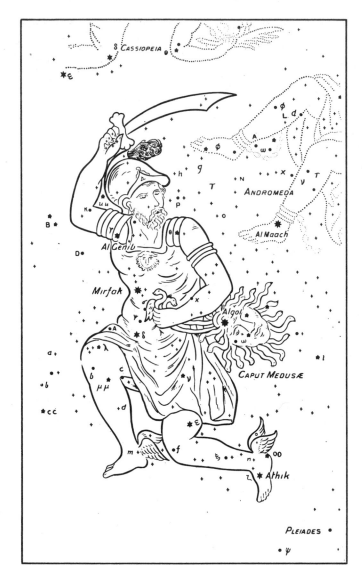

PERSEUS, THE BREAKER

head, which mean *Satan's head, the Weakened, the Subdued.* And the invincible Subduer and Breaker is none other than "the Lamb," the biblical *Peretz*, the Persian *Bershuash*, taking to himself His great power, and enforcing His saving dominion and authority for the full redemption of His people.

The Church's Hope

With great vividness, beauty, and fulness does this sign of Aries thus symbolize the blessed outcome of the Church, whose earthly estate and career were signified in the three preceding. Out of the sacrificial death and mediation of the Seed of the woman, the slain Lamb, the Church obtains its being. By the unfailing stream of the spiritual waters, which pour down from heaven as the fruit of His mediatorial intercession, it is quickened into life and celestial fellowship. By the bands of royal power with which He has been crowned at the right hand of eternal

Majesty it is upheld, directed, and governed amid this sea of earthly existence, turmoil, danger, and temptation. Helpless in its own strength, despised, hated, threatened by the serpents of Medusa's head, and exposed to the attacks of the monster lord of this world, it is still sustained and preserved by the right hand of Him whose is the dominion. And the time is coming when He who walks amid the golden candlesticks and holds in His hand the seven stars shall lift the title-deed of its inheritance, and call its members up from this doomed world to meet Him in the air, whilst He proceeds to punish and dash in pieces all enemies, cutting off Medusa's head, putting Leviathan in bonds, and lifting the chained Andromeda to Cassiopeia's starry throne. And then it is that all heaven rings with the song, "Worthy is the Lamb that was slain, to receive power, and riches, and wisdom, and strength, and honor, and glory, and blessing;" whilst all creation thrills with "Blessing, and honor, and glory, and power, unto Him that sitteth upon the throne, and unto the Lamb for ever and ever."

Dear friends, may I not here turn to ask, Have you been brought into fellowship and communion with this Church and congregation of the Lord? If so, then thank God for it, and be glad before Him that He has bestowed upon you so great a favor. Bless His name for the grace that has led you into those holy gates, and for the treasures and dignities of which He has thus made you heirs. Trials, dangers, and disabilities may be upon you now, but the Lamb is in the midst of the throne to uphold, protect, and comfort you, and by His blood and intercession you are safe. Cling to Him and His golden fleece, and no malignity of the Destroyer shall ever be able to touch a hair of your head. Wait and pray on in patience and in hope; the victorious Perseus comes for your deliverance and to share with you His own triumphant immortality.

Or does the present moment find you still lingering without the gates, and far aside from the assembly and congregation of God's flock? These starry lights that look down so lovingly upon you are hung with admonitions of your danger, and in diamond utterance point you to the better way. "There is no speech nor language, their voice is not heard; but their line is gone out through all the earth, and their words to the end of the world," marking out the tabernacle of the Sun of Righteousness, in which alone there is covenanted safety and salvation for exposed and helpless man. In full harmony with the written Book night by night they hold forth their pictorial showings to corroborate the testimony of Prophets and Apostles, that the erring seed of Adam may learn wisdom, enter the chambers of security, and shut themselves in to life and glory against the time when the Breaker shall come. The light-bearers in the sky join with the light-bearers in the Church in giving out the one great testimony of God: "He that believeth on the Son hath everlasting life; and he that believeth not the Son shall not see life; but the wrath of God abideth on him" (John 3 : 36).

II

THE DAY OF THE LORD

My horn shalt Thou exalt like the horn of an unicorn.
—Psalm 92:10

MANY of the Jewish writers and the Jewish Targum ascribe the authorship of this psalm to Adam, the first man. The Jewish ritual appointed it as the special psalm for the Sabbath day. It celebrates, first of all, the glories and blessings of creation. It then anticipates a period of great apostasy, wickedness, and prosperity to the enemies of Jehovah. But beyond that it contemplates the speedy and invincible overthrow and destruction of the workers of iniquity, followed by a glorious Sabbath of everlasting righteousness and peace. And in connection with the violent scattering and perishing of the enemies of the Lord it particularly emphasizes a special and peculiar exaltation of the power and dominion of the Messiah, who speaks in the Psalmist, and says that His "*horn*"—His power, His active dominion—shall be "*like the horn of an unicorn.*"

THE UNICORN, OR REEM

It has long been a question what animal is meant by the *Reem*, which is so often referred to in the ancient Scriptures, and which translators have generally called the *unicorn*. But modern research and discovery have served to clear up the subject in a manner entirely satisfactory. The *reem* is not a one-horned creature, like the rhinoceros, as has generally been supposed, but a pure animal of the ox kind, though wild, untamable, fierce, and terrible. Two passages prove that it was a great two-horned and mighty creature, now, so far as known, entirely extinct, but once common in North-western Asia, Assyria, and Middle Europe. Remains of it have of late years been discovered in the north of Palestine, and Cæsar, in the account of his wars, describes it as being hunted in the Hercynian forest in his day. It was known as the primeval ox, or wild bull, different altogether from the bison or the great antelope, sometimes taken for it. It was a formidable animal, "scarcely less than the elephant in size, but in nature, color, and form a true ox." Its strength and speed were very great, and it was so fierce that it did not spare man or beast when it caught sight of them. It was wholly intractable, and could not be habituated to man, no matter how young it was taken. This fact is set out in the book of Job (39 : 9–12), where it is said: "Will the *reem* be willing to serve thee, or abide by thy crib? Canst thou bind the *reem* with his band in the furrow? or will he harrow the valleys after thee? Wilt thou trust him because his strength is great? or wilt thou leave thy labor to him? Wilt thou believe him that he will bring home thy seed, and gather it into thy barn?"

This animal was particularly distinguished for its great, outspread, sharp, and irresistible horns, to which the horns of ordinary oxen were not to be compared. Hence Cæsar says, when a hunter succeeded in killing one, pitfalls being the chief means of capture, he made a public exhibition of the horns as the trophies of his success, and was the wonder and praise of all who beheld. Joseph (Deut. 33 : 17), in his superiority of power, is likened to the *reem*, of which his two sons, Ephraim and Manasseh, were the two great horns which were to push the people to the ends of the

earth. And to this mighty, untamable, and invincible primeval ox the Messiah compares himself in connection with the great judgment upon the wicked world; for then His horn shall be exalted like the horn of a *reem*. Toward His Church He is the Lamb, but toward the unsanctified world He finally becomes the terrible *reem*.

But, what is very marvellous, the picture which the Messiah appropriates to himself so exultingly in the text is precisely the picture which is presented in the sign of the Zodiac which now comes before us—the sign of *Taurus*, the first of the final quaternary in the celestial circle.

I have already explained that the twelve Zodiacal signs are arranged in three sets of four each, each set having a particular subject of its own in the grand evangelic history. In the first set we were shown the Seed of the woman in His own personal character and offices. In the second set we were shown the formation, career, and destiny of the Church. And in the third set, upon which we now enter, we are shown the great judg-

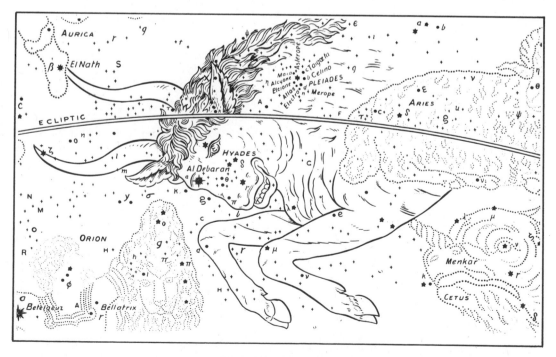

TAURUS, THE BULL

ment-period and the completion of the whole mystery of God respecting our world and race.

THE JUDGMENT

I may also remark here that it is a great mistake to conceive of the judgment-time as limited to a period of twenty-four hours. It is called "the *day* of judgment" only after the manner in which "the *day* that the Lord made the earth and the heavens" is spoken of as *a day*. The *day* of judgment is simply the period or *time* of the judgment. The common notion on the subject, which crowds up everything in one grand assize, is wholly at variance with the Scriptures, and a source of endless troubles to expositors in attempting to construe the very numerous and very diverse prophecies which refer to it. It can be clearly demonstrated, from the teachings of Christ and His Apostles, as well as from the ancient prophets, that everything does not end with the termination of the present Church period, and that the end or consummation itself includes a variety of administrations, in most of which the glorified saints are to take active part.

And what is thus set forth in the Scriptures is correspondingly represented in the signs as given in the primeval astronomy. Four of the Zodiacal signs set forth the career of the Church up to the time of its transfer to glory, when, under the great power of the Lamb, the chained and exposed Andromeda is transformed into the enthroned Cassiopeia. But beyond that we still have four additional signs before all is finally complete. These begin and end with scenes of judgment, and so relate to a great judgment-period, which begins at the house of God by the ereption of God's ready and waiting saints to himself in the heavenly regions, and then breaks in fury upon the ungodly population still left upon the earth. And then it is that Jehovah's enemies shall perish, and all the workers of iniquity be scattered, and the horn of the Seed of the woman be exalted like the horn of the *reem*, to fulfil all His desire upon His foes; which is the precise scene pictorially represented in

THE SIGN OF TAURUS

The names of this sign, in Hebrew, Arabic, Syriac, Latin, and Greek, mean the same as the English name, *the Bull*. But the figure is not that of the common bull of any known class. The horns are greater and differently set from those of domestic cattle, whilst the toes also have horns. The attitude and energy displayed are likewise far fiercer and more nimble than the common ox ever shows. It is the *reem* of the text, the aurochs, the bull of yore, the fierce, mighty, and untamable wild bull of the primeval ages, and a most expressive symbol of Christ as the irresistible and angry Judge.

This terrific animal appears here in the intensest rage, dashing forward with swift and impetuous energy, and with his great sharp horns set as if to run through everything that comes in its way. The Egyptians called it by names signifying *the Head, the Captain, the mighty Chieftain who cometh*. The chief star in this sign is situated in the Bull's eye; and its name, *Al Debaran*, means *the Captain, Leader*, or *Governor*. The middle and hinder part of the enraged animal includes the body of the enthroned Lamb, out of which it seems to rise. It is also the direct opposite of the Scorpion, so that when it rises the Scorpion sets and disappears.

THE MYTHS

In mythology this Bull was always accounted snow-white, the color of righteousness and royal judgment. According to some of the accounts, this form was assumed by Jupiter out of his passion for the beautiful Europa, whom he won by his gentleness and bore on his back across the seas to Crete. The god of the sea demanded that he should be offered in sacrifice, but because of his beauty the king preserved him. Afterward he became mad, and wrought great havoc and destruction among the Cretans, and could neither be caught nor tamed except by Herakles.

This story remarkably interprets with reference to Christ and His Church, and the anger with which He is to visit the wicked world after the Church of the first-born has been safely landed in heaven. The same becomes the more striking when we take in some other markings of the case.

Among the early nations there was a wide-spread idea connecting this Bull with the Deluge, and the *Pleiades*—the seven stars, the Doves, the peculiar star-cluster of "sweet influences"—with the ark of Noah and those saved by it in that great judgment. "The seven stars," which the Scriptures also connect with the Church (Rev. 1:16; 2:1), are on the back of this Bull, high up on his great shoulder. The *Pleiades*, according to the myths, were the seven daughters of Atlas, the upholder of heaven and earth, who, with their sisters, the *Hyades*, in this Bull's head, were placed in heaven because of their virtues and mutual sympathy and affection. They beautifully symbolize the saints securely supported by the terrible Judge, and who, together with the holy angels whom they are like, thus move with Him and His inflictions upon the guilty world.

THE SACRED PROPHECIES

And when we take this fierce and enraged aurochs as the symbol of the glorious Head of His redeemed people, particularly in those scenes of judgment upon the apostate and unbelieving nations after the saints have been taken away, we have before our eyes in the stars the very picture which Isaiah describes where he prophesies of "the world, and all the things that come forth of it," and says: "The indignation of the Lord is upon all nations, and His fury upon all their armies. He hath delivered them to the slaughter. Their slain also shall be cast out, and the mountains shall be melted with their blood. *The unicorns* [*the reems*, the precise animal which constitutes the figure in *Taurus*] shall come down, and the bullocks with the bulls, and their land shall be soaked with blood. For it is the day of the Lord's vengeance, and the year of recompenses for the controversy of Zion" (34:2–8).

The Scriptures everywhere tell us of a pe-

riod of indignation, when the Lord shall come forth out of His place to punish the inhabitants of the earth for their iniquity; when He will no longer keep silence; when the earth shall disclose her blood, and shall no more cover her slain (Isa. 26:20, 21). He is very long-suffering now. Men sin, but His judgment does not quickly follow upon transgression. Sin is added upon sin, and wickedness upon wickedness, and yet the Lord keeps silence, not willing that any should perish, but that all should come to repentance. But there is a limit to His forbearance. There is a time coming when He will tear in pieces, and there shall be none to deliver. His own word is: "Behold, the day of the Lord cometh, cruel both with wrath and fierce anger, to lay the land desolate, and to destroy the sinners thereof out of it. And I will punish the world for their evil, and the wicked for their iniquity; and I will cause the arrogancy of the proud to cease, and will lay low the haughtiness of the terrible. The earth shall remove out of her place, in the wrath of the Lord of hosts, and in the day of His fierce anger. Every one that is found shall be *thrust through*" (Isa. 13).

These are fearful comminations. And lest we should think that they refer only to the past, the New Testament repeats them, and tells us how "the Lord Jesus shall be revealed from heaven with His mighty angels, in flaming fire taking vengeance on them that know not God, and that obey not the Gospel" (2 Thess. 1:7–9); and how the kings of the earth, and the great men, and the rich men, and the chief captains, and the mighty men, and every bondman, and every freeman, will hide themselves in the dens and in the rocks of the mountains, calling to the mountains and rocks, "Fall on us, and hide us from the face of Him that sitteth upon the throne, and from the wrath of the Lamb: for the great day of His wrath is come; and who shall be able to stand?" (Rev. 6:12–17). Alas, alas, for the wicked, the unbelieving, and the impenitent when that day comes! For the horn of Messiah shall then be like the horn of the enraged aurochs, and there will be no escape from His fury.

ORION

Very impressively also do we find the same still further signified in the constellation of the first Decan of this animated sign. This is one of the grandest of the constellations, and so beautifully splendid that when it is once learned it is never forgotten. When it comes to the meridian a very magnificent view of the celestial bodies presents itself above the horizon. It is specially celebrated in the book of Job, and is mentioned in Amos and in Homer. And because of its great magnificence the flatterers of conquerors like Nimrod and Napoleon selected it for association with the names of these men.

The figure is a giant hunter, with a mighty club in his right hand in the act of striking, and in his left the skin of a slain lion.

> " First in rank
> The martial star upon his shoulder flames ;
> A rival star illuminates his foot ;
> And on his girdle beams a luminary
> Which in vicinity of other stars
> Might claim the proudest honors."

His left foot is in the act of crushing the head of the enemy. He wears a brilliant starry girdle to which hangs a mighty sword, the hilt or handle of which is the head and body of the Lamb. Concerning the idolatrous and the wicked, God hath said: "Behold, I will send for many fishers, and they shall fish

ORION, THE GLORIOUS ONE

them; and after will I send for many *hunters*, and they shall hunt them from every mountain, and from every hill, and out of the holes of the rocks; for mine eyes are upon all their ways: they are not hid from my face, neither is their iniquity hid from mine eyes. I will recompense their iniquity and their sin double" (Jer. 16:16–18). And here is the great Captain and Prince of these hunters in full and mighty action. His name is *Orion, He who cometh forth as light, the Brilliant, the Swift.* The book of Job speaks of Him as invincibly girded, whose bands no one can unloose. *Betelguese*, a star of the first magnitude, flames on His right shoulder; and Betelguese means *The Branch coming. Rigel*, another star of the first magnitude, flames in His lifted foot; and Rigel means *the Foot that crusheth*. In His great belt are three shining brilliants, called *the Three Kings*, also *Jacob's Rod* (Isa. 11:1), also the *Ell and Yard*, giving the rule of celestial and righteous measurement, just as it is said of the Rod and Branch from Jesse's roots, "Righteousness shall be the girdle of His loins, and faithfulness the girdle of His reins" (Isa. 11:5). In His left breast shines a bright star, *Bellatrix*, which means *Swiftly coming* or *Suddenly destroying*. The Arabs call Him *Al Giauza*, the Branch; *Al Mirzam*, the Ruler; *Al Nagjed*, the Prince. He is but another figure of the same invincible Avenger represented by the enraged aurochs—the horn of the Messiah exalted into the horn of the terrible aurochs.

MYTHS ON ORION

According to the myths, though full of confusion and contradictions, Orion was the united gift of the gods, Jupiter, Neptune, and Mercury, and had power to walk the sea without wetting his feet, and surpassed in strength, stature, and handsomeness all other men. He is described as the greatest hunter in the world, who claimed to be able to cope with and conquer every animal on earth. Because of this claim, a scorpion sprang up out of the earth and gave him a mortal wound in his foot; but at Diana's request he was raised to

immortality, and placed in the heavens over against the Scorpion. He is spoken of as skilled in the working and handling of iron, as having fabricated a subterranean abode for the god of fires, and as having walled in Sicily against the inundations of the sea, building thereon a temple to its gods. It is said of him that because he loved Merope her father put out his eyes while he was asleep on the sea-shore, but that, by raising himself on the back of a forgeman and turning his face to the rising sun, he recovered his sight, and went forth with great haste, rage, and energy to avenge the perfidious cruelty of his foes. He is said to have greatly loved the Pleiadic maiden, and that out of affection for her he performed the great work of clearing the country of all noxious wild beasts, bringing the spoils of his successes as presents to his beloved.

There is much rubbish and heathen uncleanness in some of the accounts, but the filthy waters nevertheless reflect the pure image. Christ was born of a woman, as some accounts allege of Orion; and he was at the same time the peculiar gift of Deity to our world, as alleged by other accounts of this hero of the constellation. He was indeed the greatest and sublimest of all men. He did claim to be able to destroy, and came into the world that He might destroy, all the mighty powers of evil and all the works of the Devil. On this account He was stung by the Scorpion of death. Because of His love for the Church He did sink into a deep sleep upon these shores of time, in which the light of His eyes was extinguished, but was restored to Him again by His lifting up from the grave. He was in the world, and passed through it without being wetted or soiled by its waters. He is indeed stationed in immortal glory as the everlasting plague, enemy, and destroyer of death. He it is who has made ready the lake of fire for the Devil and his angels. He is the Protector of the land of His Church, and the Builder of the temple of its worship and security. And so it is also appointed to Him to come forth in His mighty power and vengeance, to bring swift destruction upon His cruel foes, and to

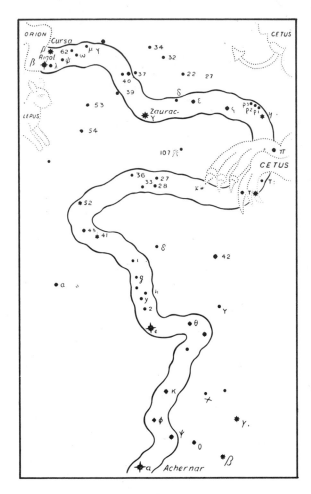

ERIDANUS, THE RIVER

hunt out all the noxious wild beasts that in-fest the earth, that he may clear it for ever of their presence, bestowing all the fruits of His victories upon the Church which He has purchased with His blood.

Eridanus

The second Decan of this illustrious sign carries forward the same idea to still further lengths. From beneath the down-coming foot of Orion, from under the feet of the rampant aurochs, and from before both, there flows out a great tortuous river, eastward and west-ward, and down into the regions of darkness in the under-world. Its name is *Eridanus, the River of the Judge.* It is specially connected in the myths with a confusion in the manage-ment of the chariot of the Sun, by which heaven and earth were threatened with a universal conflagration, during which trouble the vain and obtrusive Phaeton was killed by a thunderbolt and hurled headlong into this river, in which his body burned and consumed with fire, whilst at the same time such burning heat fell upon the world that it dried up the blood of the Ethiops and turned vast sections into sterility and emptiness.

In Daniel's vision of the four beasts, and of God's judgment of them, we find this same *River of the Judge.* Having described the several world-monsters and their ill-doings, the Prophet says: "I beheld till the thrones were set, and the Ancient of days did sit: His throne was like the fiery flame, and His wheels as burning fire. *A fiery stream* [a river of fire] *issued and came forth from before him.*" It is the River of the Judge, for we read, "The judgment was set, and the books were opened." And the Prophet "beheld even till the beast was slain, *and his body destroyed, and given to the burning flame*" (Dan. 7 : 9–11).

So we also read in the Psalms (50: 3) : "Our God shall come, and shall not keep silence: *a fire shall devour before Him*, and it shall be very tempestuous round about Him;" "*A fire goeth before Him, and burneth up His enemies round about Him*" (97 : 3–5).

So again in Isaiah it is written: "Behold, the name of the Lord cometh from far, burning with His anger, and the burden thereof is heavy: His lips are full of indignation, and His tongue as a devouring fire: and His breath as *an overflowing stream* [*of fire*]. Tophet is ordained of old; yea, for the king it is prepared: He hath made it deep and large: the pile thereof is fire and much wood; the breath of the Lord, *like a stream of brimstone, doth kindle it*" (30 : 27–33); "For, behold, the Lord will come with fire, and with His chariots like a whirlwind, to render His anger with fury, and His rebuke with flames of fire. For by fire and by His sword will the Lord plead with all flesh; and the slain of the Lord shall be many" (66 : 15, 16). "Who can stand before His indignation? and who can abide in the fierceness of his anger? *His fury is poured out like fire*" (Nah. 1 : 5, 6).

And so, also, "when the Son of man shall sit upon the throne of His glory" the nations which did not the works of faith and charity shall go away "into *everlasting fire*, prepared for the Devil and his angels" (Matt. 25 : 31–41). Nay, saith the holy Apostle, "The day of the Lord cometh as a thief in the night; in the which the heavens shall pass with a great noise, and *the elements shall melt with fervent heat, the earth also and the works that are therein shall be burned*" (2 Pet. 3 : 10).

Here, then, is the true *Eridanus*, and the fate of the proud and presumptuous Phaeton and all his usurped rule. The River of Fire, issuing from before Taurus and Orion, shall receive them and burn them up in unquenchable flames. The burning breath of the angry Judge shall sweep them headlong to "*the lake which burneth with fire and brimstone*, which is the second death" (Rev. 20 : 14, 15).

These are very dark, painful, and terrifying presentations; but they are true pictures, exactly the same both in the Scriptures and in the constellations. They are given in these alarming terms and figures that wicked, careless, and indifferent people may take warning, turn away from their follies and sins, and flee to the refuge set before us in the blessed Gospel of Christ. And if any man have ears to hear, let him hear.

But the presentations are not all terror and hopelessness.

MERCY IN JUDGMENT

Although the present Church-period will have ended before the promised Seed of the woman takes on the character described in the text and in these signs, probation will not have entirely ended. The possibility of securing salvation will not yet have been completely cut off. Though the dispensation is then changed from that of the present silent forbearance and long-suffering on God's part into one of active and terrific judgment, and though all chance of reaching the first honors of the kingdom will then have passed away for ever, there still will be a chance for being "saved so as by fire;" and many there will be who will also embrace that remaining opportunity.

In the very nature of things the breaking in of the great and terrible fact that the day of judgment is come, and with the startling and convincing proofs of its actual presence spread all around, there cannot but be some awakening and revolutionizing effect on the hearts and thinking of multitudes who up till then have made themselves very easy about these matters of salvation. Hence Isaiah prophesied: "When Thy judgments are in the earth, the inhabitants of the world will learn righteousness" (26 : 29). So also the Psalmist (64 : 7–9) says: When God shall shoot

AURIGA, THE SHEPHERD

His arrows at them that encourage themselves in evil, and shall suddenly wound them, "men shall fear, and shall declare the work of God; for they shall wisely consider His doing." And again: "Thy people shall be willing in the day of Thy power" (110 : 3). So also Daniel prophesies of this very time, and says: "Many shall be purified, and made white, and tried; but the wicked shall do wickedly, and none of the wicked shall understand; but the wise shall understand" (Dan. 12 : 8–10). The wicked shall not understand, seeing, as Paul says, that because they received not the love of the truth, God sendeth them a working of error, that they may believe a lie, and be irremediably condemned (2 Thess. 2 : 10–12). Accordingly, we also read in the Apocalypse, after the ready and waiting saints have been caught up and crowned in heaven, and the great tribulation has already set in upon the earth, of "a great multitude" who were un-

prepared when the first scenes of the judgment broke in, but still succeed in rectifying their errors, wash their soiled robes in the blood of the Lamb, and reach the world of the redeemed, though they never get crowns. And what we find thus set forth in the Scriptures is likewise signified in the constellations.

AURIGA

To the enraged Aurochs, the mighty Hunter, and the fiery River of the Judge there is added another figure in the third Decan, which is thoroughly evangelic and gracious. The Greek myths are totally at a loss with regard to its main features, conclusively showing that these signs were arranged long before the time of the Greeks, and that Greek genius was totally incompetent to produce them. The Greeks could only preserve the traditional figure in this Decan, and let it stand wholly unexplained. The figure itself is that of a mighty man seated on the Milky Way, holding a band or ribbon in his right hand, and with his left arm holding up on his shoulder a she-goat, which clings to his neck and looks out in astonishment upon the terrible Bull; whilst in his lap are two frightened little kids, which he supports with his great hand. The Greeks called him *Hæniochos*, which in their language signified *a Driver* or *Charioteer;* and so our modern atlases call him *the Wagoner*. But as he has neither chariot nor horses, and is thoroughly occupied with the care of his goats, it is very strange that the modern world should have persisted in regarding him as a chariot-driver. But there is one link of connection to show how this absurdity came about. One of the old traditional names of this figure was *Auriga*, or a name framed of the elements preserved in the word *Auriga*, which, in Latin, means *a Conductor of the reins*, a coachman, a charioteer. And as this figure holds a band or ribbon in his right hand, these heathen people could do no better than to take him for a wonderful charioteer. But he is no charioteer at all, and is engaged in performing a wholly different office.

The Noetic elements in the word *Auriga* signify *the Shepherd;* and the Shepherd he really is, even that same Good Shepherd who laid down His life for the sheep and giveth unto them eternal life. This is most clearly shown by His having the mother-goat on His arm, with her feet clasped about His neck, and the little kids on His hand. The band in his right hand is the same Band which we saw in the hand of the Lamb and in the hand of the enthroned Cepheus. It is the Band of power by which the glorious Head of the Church upholds and guides His people on the one side, and binds the enemy on the other. It is therefore a picture of the exalted and almighty Saviour, still exercising His offices of mercy and salvation in the midst of the scenes of judgment, just as the Scriptures tell us that in the midst of wrath He remembers mercy (Hab. 3 : 2). And to this all the indications in this sign agree.

The chief star in this constellation, *Capella*, which is of the first magnitude and of peculiar brilliancy, marks the heart of the mother-goat on Auriga's bosom. The very attitude and expression of this goat are significant. It not only clings to the great Shepherd's neck, as if trembling for its own safety, but is anxiously looking back upon the action of the Bull, as if saying, "I have seen the wicked in great power, and spreading himself like a green bay tree; yet he passed away, and, lo, he is not: yea, I look for him, but he cannot be found" (Ps. 37 : 34–36). The whole picture is in precise accord with Isaiah's prophecy of this very period, where he says : " Behold, the Lord will come with strong hand, and His arm shall rule for Him : behold, His reward is with Him and His work before Him. He shall feed His flock like a shepherd : *He shall gather the lambs with His arm, and carry them in His bosom, and shall gently lead those that give suck*" (40 : 10, 11). Hence the name of the star in the right arm of Auriga, *Menkalinon*, in Chaldaic means *the Band of the Goats* or *Ewes*.

In the Zodiac of Dendera, Auriga holds a sceptre, the upper part of which shows the head of the Lamb, and the lower part the figure of the Cross; which vividly expresses salvation even under the severe administrations of sovereign judgment. And here are the two little kids, just born, having come into place amid these ongoings of the terrible judgment, the one bleating upward after its mother, and the other looking in startled wonder at the dashing career of the enraged Bull, but both safe in the great Shepherd's hand. How touching the picture of the tender mercies of our Saviour, even after the Church of the firstborn has been taken, and He has already risen up as the terrible Aurochs !

A Solemn Outlook

And now what shall we say to these showings of the Holy Ghost ? There is a day of judgment coming, and it hastens on apace. It will be a day of trouble and an hour of trial such as have never yet been seen in our world. It will be a day that shall burn as an oven ; and all the proud, yea, all that do wickedly, shall be as stubble to the fire; and the day that cometh shall burn them up, saith the Lord of hosts, that it shall leave them neither root nor branch (Mal. 4 : 1). Only they that take refuge in Jesus shall find shelter and security. And on the throne of His majesty in the heavens He sits with wide-open arms, saying, "Come unto Me, all ye that labor and are heavy-laden, and I will give you rest. Take my yoke upon you, and learn of Me; and ye shall find rest unto your souls" (Matt. 11 : 28, 29). From the eternal Father the word is: "Unto you that fear my name shall the Sun of Righteousness arise with healing in His wings; and ye shall go forth and grow up as calves of the stall; and ye shall tread down the wicked; for they shall be ashes under the soles of your feet in the day that I do this, saith the Lord" (Mal. 4 : 2, 3).

How, then, should these presentations serve to quicken us to spirituality of living and to all earnestness of watchfulness and prayer, that we may be found of Him in peace, without spot, and blameless! And how should the same animate our hopes as believers, and reconcile us to whatever sacrifices, pains, or losses to which our profession may subject us in this present evil world! What saith the Spirit? Hear it, dear friends, and ponder it:

"Fret not thyself because of evil-doers, neither be thou envious against the workers of iniquity; for they shall soon be cut down like the grass, and wither as the green herb. Trust in the Lord, and do good; so shalt thou dwell in the land, and verily thou shalt be fed. For evil-doers shall be cut off: but those that wait upon the Lord, they shall inherit the earth. For yet a little while, and the wicked shall not be: yea, thou shalt diligently consider his place, and it shall not be. For the Lord loveth judgment, and forsaketh not His saints; they are preserved for ever. Wait on the Lord, and keep His way, and He shall exalt thee to inherit the land: when the wicked are cut off, thou shalt see it. The salvation of the righteous is of the Lord: He is their strength in the time of trouble. And the Lord shall help them, and deliver them: He shall deliver them from the wicked, and save them, because they trust in Him" (Ps. 37).

12

THE HEAVENLY UNION

And so shall we ever be with the Lord.
—1 Thessalonians 4:17

THESE sweet and comforting words relate to a scene of things beyond the resurrection of the dead, and hence to something which is to be brought about during the progress of the judgment-period. After the Lord himself has come forth with the voice of a great trumpet, and the holy dead have been raised, and the living saints have been translated, and both classes have been caught up together to meet the Saviour in the air, then the word is, "*So shall we ever be with the Lord.*" And the particular blessedness which we thus find set forth in the Scriptures we also find in the constellations, and more especially in that sign of the Zodiac which we now come to consider—*Gemini*, usually called *The Twins*.

THE SIGN OF GEMINI

We have here two youthful-looking and most beautiful figures peacefully sitting together, with their feet resting on the Milky Way. Their heads lean against each other in a loving attitude. The one holds a great club in his right hand, whilst his left is clasped around the body of his companion. The other holds a harp in one hand and a bow and arrow in the other. Both the club and the bow and arrow are in repose, the same as the figures which hold them. The club, unlifted, lies against the shoulder of the one, and the bow, unstrung, rests in the hand of the other. The picture looks like a readiness for warlike action, but at the same time like a joyful repose after a great victory already gained. We will presently see that it really means all that it seems, and that it significantly portrays what is set forth in the text and in many places in the Scriptures.

MYTHIC ACCOUNTS

The Greeks and Romans considered these two figures the representatives of two youths, twin brothers, both sons of Jupiter, of very peculiar and extraordinary birth. They are said to have been with the Argonauts in the contest for the Golden Fleece, on which oc-

GEMINI, THE TWINS

casion they displayed unparalleled heroism— the one by achievements in arms and personal prowess, and the other in equestrian exercises. In the Grecian temples they were represented as mounted on white horses, armed with spears, riding side by side, crowned with the cap of the hunter tipped with a glittering star. The belief was, that they often appeared at the head of the armies, and led on the troops to battle and victory—the one mounted on a fiery steed, the other on foot, but both as invincible warriors. After their return from Colchis it is said that they cleared the Hellespont and the neighboring seas from pirates and depredators, and hence were honored as the particular friends and protectors of navigation. An intimation of this is given in the history of St. Paul, as the name of the vessel in which he sailed was that of these two figures. It is further said that flames of fire were betimes seen playing around their heads, and that when this occurred the tempest which was tossing the ocean ceased, and calm ensued. They were said to have been initiated into all the mysteries, and were invited guests at a great marriage at which a severe conflict occurred. They were indissolubly attached to each other, and Jupiter rewarded their mutual affection by transferring them together to heavenly immortality. The Greeks and Romans· sacrificed white lambs upon their altars, and held them in very high regard. It was a common thing to take oaths by their names, as indicative of the utmost truth and verity. Vulgarly, the habit still survives of swearing "by Gemini."

Further accounts represent these two youths as kings, and as divine saviors and helpers of men, though mostly in the character of warrior-judges. They were supposed to preside over the public games, particularly where horses were concerned. War-songs and dances were supposed to have originated with them, and they had much to do in favoring and inspiring the bards and poets. When Menestheus was endeavoring to usurp the government of Attica, they interfered, and devastated the country around Athens until its gates opened to them and the Athenians submitted to them and rendered them sacred honors. They were distinguished in the Calydonian Hunt, and fought and slew Amycus, the gigantic son of the god of the sea, who challenged the Argonauts and had shown himself the enemy of Herakles. They made invasive war to recover the portions of which they had been cunningly cheated, and succeeded in it, and gained much more in addition. In this conflict the authors of the murderous assaults upon them were stricken down and slain by the lightnings of Jupiter. They were assigned great power over good fortune, and particularly over the winds and the waves of the sea.

Such are the mythic representations as they come through the Greeks and Romans. In some other showings, however, these two figures are not of one sex. In the Zodiac of Dendera the figure is that of a man walking hand in hand with a woman. The same are sometimes called Adam and Eve. But the male figure is not the literal first Adam, but the mystic second Adam, the same Seed of the woman who everywhere appears in these celestial frescoes. The figure in the Egyptian sphere has an appendage which signifies *the Coming One* — the Messiah-Prince. And having identified the masculine figure, there can be no difficulty in identifying the accompanying female figure. The Lamb has a bride, a wife, bone of His bone and flesh of His flesh, and destined for an everlasting union with Him in glory and dominion. And this Eve, made out of His side in the deep sleep of death to which He submitted for the purpose, is none other than the Church, which here appears in celestial union with her sublime Lord. Even the word *Gemini*, in the original Hebrew, Arabic, and Syriac, whence it has come, does not run so much on the idea of two brought forth at the same birth, as upon the idea of something *completed*, as of a year come to the full or as of a long betrothal brought to its consummation in perfected marriage. The old Coptic name of this sign, *Pi Mahi*, signifies *the United, the Completely joined.*

THE STAR-NAMES

And when we closely examine the names still retained in this constellation, we find ample indication that these figures were meant to set forth Christ and His Church in that great marriage-union which is to be completed in the heavens during that very judgment-period to which these last four signs refer. In the left foot of the southern figure of Gemini shines a conspicuous star, named *Al Henah, the Hurt, the Wounded.* This figure, then, must refer to Him whose heel was to be bruised. So the principal star in his head is called *Pollux, the Ruler, the Judge,* and sometimes *Herakles,* or *Hercules,* the mighty sufferer and toiler, who frees the world of all otherwise unmanageable powers of evil. In the centre of his body is another bright star, called *Wasat,* which means *Set, Seated,* or *Put in place,* as where it is said, " I am *set* on the throne of Israel," " there are *set* thrones of judgment," " the judgment was *set,*" " I am *set* in my ward;" which specially describes what is prophesied of Christ in connection with the completion of His marriage with His Church.

And, in perfect accord with these indications, this figure holds in his right hand the great club of power, as the One who bruises the Serpent's head and breaks in pieces all antagonisms to His rule or to His people's peace. The Egyptians called him *Hor,* or *Horus, the Coming One,* the son of light, the slayer of the serpent, the recoverer of the dominion. Horus is described in an extant Egyptian hymn as " the son of the sun," " the mighty, the great avenger, the observer of justice," " the golden hawk coming for the chastisement of all lands, the divinely beneficent, the Lord omnipotent;" which corresponds again with the descriptions of the *Merodach* of the ancient Babylonians, who is called the Rectifier, the great Restorer. It is the biblical description, almost literally, of the promised Redeemer of the world in connection with the judgment.

The variation as to the sex of the other figure, which is sometimes contemplated as a woman and sometimes as a masculine hero,

LEPUS, THE HARE OR THE ENEMY

corresponds also with the biblical representations of the Church. God calls Israel His *son*, and also His *spouse*, the wife of which He is the Husband, the one chosen out from among the maidens and wedded to himself. The bride of the Lamb in the Apocalypse is at the same time described as "*a man-child*," who was to rule all nations with a rod of iron, and to that end was "caught up unto God and to His throne."

CHRIST'S UNION WITH HIS CHURCH

But the two figures in this sign, though in some sense distinct, are really *one*, as Christ and the Father are one, and as the man and his wife are one flesh. The union is such that one is in the other, and the two are so conjoined that one implies and embraces the other. There is no Christ apart from His Church, and there is no Church except in Christ. They are two, and yet they are one —He in them, and they in Him—so that what is His is theirs, and what is theirs is His. As He is the peculiar Son of God, they are peculiar sons of God in Him, and are joint-heirs with Him to all that He inherits. Again and again the Scriptures comprehend *Him* in the descriptions of the Church, and embrace *them*

in the predictions concerning Him. Hence, in the truer and deeper meaning of the Psalms, He and His people speak the same words, pass through the same experiences, receive the same assurances, and rejoice in the same promises, hopes, and honors. The king often disappears in the body politic, and the body politic still oftener disappears in the king. And so it is in these two figures. They are no more twins than Christ and His Church are twins, yet they are both the peculiar sons of God; whilst the birth of the one was virtually and really the birth of the other.

Hence, also, the names and qualities which appear in the one are at the same time construable with both, because they coexist in one another. They are Bridegroom and bride, but they are at the same time together the one Man-Child appointed to rule all nations with a rod of iron. Accordingly, the one is called *Pollux* and *Herakles*—the Ruler, the Judge, the Toiling Deliverer; and the other is called *Castor* and *Apollo*—the Coming Ruler or Judge, "born of the light," who punishes and destroys the wicked and unrighteous, who brings help and wards off evil, who has the spirit of prophecy and sacred song, who protects and keeps the flocks, and who delights in the founding and establishment of cities, kingdoms, and settled rule and order among men. It is not the one by himself in either case, but the one in and with the other, conjoined and perfected in the same administration—Christ with the Church, and the Church with Christ, as the one all-ruling Man-Child under whom the whole earth shall be delivered from misrule and oppression, the eternal kingdom come, and the entire world enjoy its unending Sabbath.

At present this union of Christ with His Church, though real and the very life of Christianity, is mystic, hidden, and not yet fully revealed. The Church is yet intermixed and held down by earthiness and the power of mortality and death. All this needs to be stripped off and immortality put on, as has been accomplished in the case of Christ the Head, who is now already at the right hand of the Father. What has happened in His deliverance, triumph, and exaltation needs also to be wrought out in the case of His members, the Church. Our *complete* union with Him can only be when this mortal has put on immortality and death is swallowed up of life; which occurs when the sainted dead are raised, and they, together with those of His who are then still alive, are caught up in incorruption to meet Him in the heavenly spaces. But what is as yet mystic and unrevealed is hereafter to be openly, formally, and most gloriously exhibited and shown in living and eternal fact.

The Marriage of the Lamb

Hence, in the Apocalyptic pictures of the ongoing judgment-period, after the Man-Child has been born into immortality, and is caught up to God, and has overcome the opposing Dragon and his angels by the blood of the Lamb and the word of their testimony, and immediately before Christ and His people come forth riding on white horses for the overthrow of the Beast and his armies, we hear the voice of gladness and rejoicing, and the giving of glory to the All-Ruler, in that "*the Marriage of the Lamb is come*," and the word of blessing goes forth upon all who are "called to the marriage-supper of the Lamb" (Rev. 19 : 7–9).

Just what this marriage of the Lamb is, or what celestial formalities and demonstrations it embraces, no man is able definitely to tell. We know, in general terms, that the Bridegroom is Christ, after He has taken to Him His great power and is about to proceed to the utter destruction of His enemies, and that the bride is the Church, the completed assembly of the elect, after they have all been gathered to their Lord in triumphant immortality. We know also that it involves some formal and manifest ceremonial, by which He takes, acknowledges, and fully endows His glorified Church as thenceforward and for ever conjoined with himself in closest and inseparable unity, to move as He moves, to reign as He reigns, to judge and make war as He judges and makes war, and to be one with Him in all the possessions, administrations, joys, honors, and achievements which pertain to Him then and world without end. It is the formal and eternal perfecting of them in Him, and of Him in them, in a union as ineffable as it is unending.

And this is the precise thing alluded to in the text and pictorially given in the sign of *Gemini*. The very name, the attitudes of the figures, and the order of place occupied by this sign, as well as the star-names in it and all the mythic stories connected with it, combine to fix this as its truest and fullest meaning, as intended by the mind that framed it and gave out the original instructions concerning it. It is God's sign in the heavens of the coming marriage and union of the Seed of the woman with His redeemed Church, precisely as the same is set forth in all His word as the hope and joy of His people, to be fulfilled at His revelation and coming.

Thus, then, we find the true Castor and Pollux, the peculiar sons of God, whose bravery secures the prize of the Golden Fleece, who share in the same trials, sufferings, labors, triumphs, and glories, and with whom is the holy wisdom, the prophetic inspiration, the leadership of armies that fight for human rights and liberty, the patronage of holy heroism and sacred song, the upholding of truth and righteousness, the only salvation for oppressed and afflicted man. These are the true kings, ordained to rule all nations with a rod of iron, to chastise and destroy the rebellious and incorrigible, to hunt out and punish wickedness unto the ends of the earth, and to be revealed in flaming fire as warrior-judges on white horses, to put down usurpers, fight the gigantic son of the god of this world, hurl the dread Antichrist and his hordes to sudden perdition, revenge the blood of martyrs on those who shed it, apportion law and destiny to the earthly peoples, and sit and reign in immortal regency over all the after generations. (See my *Lectures on the Apocalypse*, vol. iii.)

And what we thus find in the sign is further signified in the accompanying Decans.

LEPUS

The first of these, as given in our planispheres, is *Lepus*, the figure of a gigantic hare. In the Arabic it is called *Arnebeth*, which means *the Hare*, but also has the signification of *Enemy of the Coming*. In the Persian and Egyptian Zodiacs the figure is a *serpent*, trodden under Orion's foot, with this further addition in the Egyptian, that the serpent is also caught in the claws of a seeming hawk. It is also called *Bashti-Beki, the Offender confounded*. The mythic account of this hare is, that it is one of the animals which Orion most delighted in hunting, and hence was placed near him in the stars. In the picture Orion is in the act of crushing this hare with his great foot. And the names of the stars which it includes—*Nibal, Rakis*, and *Sugia*—mean *the Mad, the Caught, the Deceiver*.

From these indications it is sufficiently manifest that this constellation was meant to show and record the nearing end of the Enemy, and the close proximity of his utter overthrow when once the heavenly marriage is celebrated.

And this is precisely the showing made in the Scriptures, particularly in the Apocalypse. The lifting of the Church into its destined union with Christ in glory is a stunning blow to the whole empire of darkness, and the sure herald of its utter dissolution then speedily to follow. No sooner is it announced that "the marriage of the Lamb is come" than the heaven opens, and He who is called Faithful and True rides forth upon the white horse, in righteousness to judge and make war, and all the armies of heaven follow Him on white horses, and the Beast and the False Prophet are taken, and the kings of the earth and their armies are slain with the sword of this invincible host (Rev. 19 : 6–21).

SIRIUS

The second Decan confirms and sustains the same presentation. This is the great *Dog*, anciently the *Wolf*, the special hunter and devourer of the hare. In the Dendera Zodiac the figure is the *Eagle* or *Hawk*, the particular enemy of the Serpent, having on his head a double mark of crownings with power and majesty, and standing on the top of a great mace as the triumphant royal Breaker and Bruiser of the powers of evil. The principal star in this constellation is the most brilliant and fiery in all the heavens.

> " All others he excels ; no fairer light
> Ascends the skies, none sets so clear and bright."

But it is associated with burning heat, pestilence, and disaster to the earth and the children of men. Homer sung of it as a star

> " Whose burning breath
> Taints the red air with fevers, plagues, and death."

Virgil speaks of blighted fields, a smitten earth, and suffering beasts, because this star

> " With pestilential heat infects the sky."

This star is called *Sirius*, from *Sir* or *Seir*, which means *Prince, Guardian, the Victorious*. Taken in connection with the name of the figure in the Egyptian sphere, as often given, we have *Naz-Seir* or *Nazir ;* and we know who it was that was to be called *Naz-seir-ene*. *Naz-Seir* means *the Sent Prince*. So the Rod promised to come forth from the stem or stump of Jesse is called *Netzer* in the Hebrew Bible, there translated *the Branch*, the princely Scion, who should "smite the earth with the rod of His mouth, and slay the wicked with the breath of His lips." Not, then, only because Christ spent His earlier years at an obscure little village by the name of *Nazareth*, but, above all, because He was *the Sent Prince, the Messiah, the Branch*, at once the *Netzer* of Isaiah and the *Naz-Seir* of these equally prophetic constellations. From the earliest ages of Christianity till now interpreters and defenders of the Scriptures have been at a loss to explain by what prophet or in what sacred prophecy it was said, as claimed by the Apostle, that Christ should be called a *Nazarene;* but here, from a most unexpected quarter, we find the nearest and most literal foreshowing of that very name, given in place as a designation of the Seed of the woman, and describing Him as *the Sent Prince*, the lordly Eagle, the appointed tearer in pieces and extirpator of the whole serpent brood. And in this *Naz-Seir*, or *Naz-Sirius*, we are to see Him of whom Matthew said, " He came and dwelt in a city called *Nazareth*, that it might be fulfilled which was *spoken by the prophets*, He shall be called NAZ-SEIR-ENE" (Matt. 2 ; 23).

In accord with this, the second star of this constellation is called *Mirzam, the Ruler;* the third, *Muliphen, the Leader, the Chieftain;* the fourth, *Wesen, Shining, Illustrious, Scarlet;* the fifth, *Adhara, the Glorious;* and another, *Al Habor, the Mighty*. It would verily seem as if we were selecting a list of scriptural expressions concerning our Redeemer when we thus give the sense of these astronomic names. Their meaning is most truly significant when understood of Christ, but they are worse than absurd if we are to understand them of an Egyptian *dog*. Nor will these showings interpret at all except as applied to the scene, subject, and period of which *Gemini*, as I have explained, is the central sign.

THE SUBLIME PRINCE

A magnificent picture of the Sun is that which the Psalmist gives, where he represents him as a bridegroom, glowing under his wedding-canopy, exulting like a mighty man to run his race, and going forth from one horizon to the other with a power of heat and brightness from which nothing can hide. But what is thus said of the natural Sun is still more thrillingly true of the Sun of Righteousness in the case before us. He is the Bridegroom, for " the marriage of the Lamb is come." He stands under the wedding-canopy, the Illustrious, the Glorious, ready for revelation in the brightness of His appearing, and exulting to go forth in all His invincible energy to search and try the earth from end to end, revealing everything, testing everything, and bringing burning, death, and destruction to whatever is found lifting itself against Him as " the King of kings and Lord of lords."

In this attitude and in these relations He is the Hunter and Destroyer of the Hare, the true *Naz-Seir-ene, the Appointed Prince*, the lordly Eagle, the Destroyer of the Serpent. Here especially He is the mighty, the glorious, the Prince of the right hand, as the Arabic has it, the Chief leading His hosts to effective victory. Here heat and burning and plague and death attend upon His going forth, and men are smitten and scorched; as it is written: "Their flesh shall consume away while they stand upon their feet, and their eyes shall consume away in their sockets, and their tongue shall consume away in their mouth" (Zech. 14: 12) ; " for the day of the Lord of hosts shall be upon every one that is proud and lofty, and upon every one that is lifted up, and the loftiness of man shall be bowed down, and the haughtiness of men shall be made low, and the Lord alone shall be exalted in that day" (Isa. 2 : 12–17) ; "And out of His mouth goeth a sharp sword, that with it He should smite the nations; and He shall rule them with a rod of iron ; and He treadeth the winepress of the fierceness of the wrath of Almighty God" (Rev. 19 : 15).

It is the same picture of the same identical scene described by Isaiah (63), where it is asked, "Who is this that cometh from Edom, with dyed garments from Bozrah? this that is glorious in his apparel, travelling in the greatness of his strength?" To which He answers: "I that speak in righteousness, mighty to save." And where the further inquiry is put: "Wherefore art thou red in thine apparel, and thy garments like him that treadeth the winefat?" And the further an-

CANIS MAJOR, THE DOG

swer is: "I have trodden the winepress alone; and of the people there was none with me: for I will tread them in mine anger, and trample them in my fury; and their blood shall be sprinkled upon my garments, and I will stain all my raiment. For the day of vengeance is in mine heart, and the year of my redeemed is come. . . . And I will tread down the people in mine anger, and make them drunk in my fury, and I will bring down their strength to the earth." Here is the true *Pollux*, the real *Sirius*, the mighty Chief-

tain, the Wolf or Eagle coming upon the enemy, the glorious Hero of salvation, arrayed in brightness and scarlet, and triumphing in the greatness of His strength.

All the features in the sign thus harmoniously weave into one consistent and magnificent showing, which is the same in the stars as in the written prophecies.

THE COMPANION OF SIRIUS

But when the glorious Sun of Righteousness thus comes forth in His majesty from under the wedding-canopy, "clothed with a vesture dipped in blood," riding upon the white horse, and sending out His mighty sword to smite the nations and hurl the Beasts and their followers to perdition, He comes not alone. The armies of the heaven follow Him on white horses, wearing the clean linen of saintly righteousness. He is the Head, the Leader, the Chief, but behind Him are His elect myriads, warrior-judges like himself. He is married now, and His bride is with her Husband. "To execute vengeance upon the nations and punishments upon the people; to bind their kings with chains, and their nobles with fetters of iron; to execute upon them the judgment written: *this honor have all the saints*" (Ps. 149 : 7–9).

And to bring out this feature there is added a third Decan of Gemini—the second Dog or Wolf. It differs from the first only in being smaller and feebler, and following a little behind the first; for the saints by this time are all like unto their Lord, and follow Him whithersoever He goeth. Princeliness is in

them also, though the Arabic astronomy designates them as the Prince of the left hand, as it calls Him the Prince of the right hand. In the Egyptian Zodiac this constellation has a human figure with the Eagle's head; hence a sign of humanity exalted to power and authority against the Serpent-seed. It is called *Sebak*—that is, *Conquering, Victorious.*

The name of the principal star, a very bright star of the first magnitude—and from that star the name of the constellation itself on our planispheres—is *Procyon*, which, in its Noetic elements, is associated in meaning with redemption, and may mean *Redeemed* or *Redeeming*, or both, and well describes the body of the glorified saints. The term *Al Mirzam* occurs here also, as in the second Decan, and ascribes rulership to what is here symbolized, the same as to the Head Prince going before; just as Christ has promised to His faithful people that they shall share His throne and sovereignty and "reign with Him for ever and ever." The second star in this constellation bears the name of *Al Gomeiza*,

CANIS MINOR, THE SECOND DOG

which in signification also refers to redemption, and seems to include particularly the previous history of the saints, as, like their Lord, once *burdened, loaded down, enduring for the sake of others.*

THE MYTHS

The myths touching this Dog are varied. Some say he represents the Egyptian god *Anubis*, which was the god that took charge of the dying and carried them to judgment. Others say it refers to Diana and her hunting and destroying of wild beasts. Some say he is the dog of Icarus, who revealed the place where the murderers of his master had hid the body of their victim, and thus was the occasion of various sad and disturbing calamities. And still other accounts represent this Dog as one of the hounds of Actæon, which in madness devoured their master after Diana had turned him into a stag. Actæon was a trained and cunning hunter who was impertinent toward Artemis, the goddess of purity and justice, and had command over sufferings, plagues, and death. He boasted himself against her, and even appropriated to himself and associates what was sacred to her. Hence these judgments came upon him and made an end of him.

These stories agree in nothing except in the recognition of some good agency or heavenly power at work to bring the erring to account, and to give trouble and death to the proud, the offending, and the intractable. But in this they all accord with the character and office which the Scriptures ascribe to the glorified Church in connection with what follows immediately on the marriage of the Lamb. They help to strengthen the chain of evidence identifying Procyon as the starry symbol of those heavenly armies which come forth along with the King of kings and Lord of lords to the battle of the great day of God Almighty, to make an end of misrule and usurpation on earth, and clear it of all the wild beasts which have been devastating it for these many ages.

SUMMARY ON GEMINI

Thus, then, the records in the stars combine with the records in the Book to picture to us a most sublime destiny for the congregation of believers. They are betrothed to Christ even now, and love Him, and oft have sweet and blessed communion with Him; but it is only through veils and intervening ordinances, by faith and not by sight. The time is coming when these veils shall be removed, and God's people shall meet Him face to face, and see the King in His beauty, and be joined with Him in all the intimacies of love, fellowship, and oneness, being made copartners with Him in all He has and is and does, yea, the loved and loving participants in all His glory, throne, and immortal administrations. They shall not only "stand in the judgment," but they shall be lifted when it comes, "caught up to meet the Lord in the air," to be with Him as no other beings are with Him, even as His bride and wife. And when His power goes forth to plague the wicked world, avenge the blood of the martyrs, overwhelm the great Beast and his armies, rid the world of all the wild beasts of usurpation and unrighteousness which have infested it so long, and reduce the refractory nations and peoples to just and rightful authority by the force of an iron sceptre to which all must bow or be dashed to pieces, they shall be one with Him in the terrific manifestations and be co-administrants of that irresistible almightiness. They in Him, and He in them, shall be the Castor and Pollux of the world to come, supremely blessed in each other, and making blessed, putting glad songs where tears and groans have moaned their *miserere*, and settling everything into the order, peace, and permanence of that divine kingdom when all shall be "on earth as it is in heaven."

O glorious outcome for these toils and fears and trials and misgivings in faith's weary pilgrimage! Death gone! Mortality swallowed up of life! Union with the King complete! Vicissitude, peradventure, doubt, and disability clean swept away for ever! The throne, the dominion, and the glory secure! What a blessedness is this! Who shall sing it as it merits?

"Blest seats! through rude and stormy scenes
I onward press to you."

13

THE BLESSED POSSESSION

I will multiply thy seed as the stars of the heaven, and as the sand which is upon the sea-shore; and thy seed shall possess the gate of his enemies.
—Genesis 22:17

THIS is part of the oath which God swore unto Abraham after the test of his faith in the offering of his son Isaac. It applied in part to the believing patriarch's natural seed, but more especially to Christ and the multitudinous seed of faith, who are also "the seed of Abraham." This is made clear in the writings of St. Paul, who tells us that "to Abraham and his seed were the promises made; not to *seeds*, as of many, but as of one—thy *Seed*—which is Christ" (Gal. 3:16); "and if ye be Christ's, then are ye Abraham's seed, and heirs according to the promise" (Gal. 3:29)

We do not therefore strain or misapply the text when we understand it of Christ and the Church, and say that to these the divine promise is to multiply them as the stars of the sky and the sands on the sea-shore, and to give them victory and success to take the gate of their enemies, and possess the same for ever. And the ultimate fulfilment of this promise is what we find symbolized in the stars by the sign of *Cancer* and the constellations which form its Decans.

THE SIGN OF CANCER

In our planispheres we have here the picture of a gigantic *Crab*. It is the same in the Parsi, Hindoo, and Chinese Zodiacs, and hence is supposed to have been the same in the Chaldean and original representations; but in the Egyptian sphere the figure is the *Scarabæus*, or sacred beetle, which some take as having been the original figure. It is difficult to decide which is the most ancient, but either serves well to express the meaning which clearly attaches to this sign.

THE CRAB

The crab is an animal born of the water, as the Church is "born of water and of the Spirit." Its rows of legs, on opposite sides, give the idea of multitudinous development and numerous members, as the promise here is with regard to the Church, and as is signi-

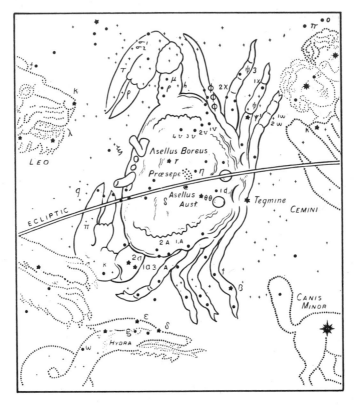

CANCER, THE CRAB

fied in the sign of the Fishes, which is a special symbol of the Church.

In the progress of the crab's development and growth it undergoes important changes. The most marked of these is the periodic throwing off of its old shells and the taking on of new ones. In its earlier life these changes involve alterations in the whole form and shape of the animal. And so the Church, in the process of its earthly development and growth, passes from dispensation to dispensation, and each individual saint first puts off the old man with his deeds, and puts on the new man which is renewed after the image of Him that created him, and then lays off " the body of this death" in order to be "clothed upon with our house which is from heaven, that mortality might be swallowed up of life." And these several changes, both general and personal, are all entirely completed by the time the Church comes to occupy the place indicated by this sign.

The crab is also armed with two powerful hands or claws, by which it grasps hold with wonderful force and securely retains whatever it takes. And so it is with the people of God. Having, like Mary, "chosen the good part," or, like the patriarchs, " embraced the promises," or, like the apostles, "lain hold of the hope set before us," they come into the possession of the incorruptible and heavenly inheritance, and retain it with a grasp so firm and strong that it "shall not be taken away."

The Scarabæus

And so again with the *scarabæus*. This is a creature whose career exhibits very marked and significant transformations. The first period of its existence is passed in a dark, drear, subterranean abode, where its senses are feeble, its powers circumscribed, ungladdened by pleasant sights, oft terrified by unintelligible voices from the sunlit world above, compelled to eat and live amid filth, and with no worthier employment than to grow and wait for future changes. And so it is with the earthly Church and the children of God in this present life. With all that may be said of us here, we are the slaves of toil and suffering, full of darkness, doubt, and uncertainty, loaded with grovelling cares, the sport of ever-recurring accidents which we cannot explain, pushed and cramped and crowded by others no better off than ourselves—mere knots of incapacities and troubles like earthborn and dirt-fed grubs, though bearing in us the germs and beginnings of eventual glory and blessedness.

Having dragged out the time apportioned to its first condition, the scarabæus is next transformed into quite another. Nature's hand now swaths it into a chrysalis. Activity ceases. Food can no longer be taken. The avenues of the senses are closed. The functions of life are put in abeyance, though soon to open out into still another form of existence. And so our earthly life terminates in death and passes into the mummy condition—that peculiar middle stage in which our inner being still lives on, but in quiescence and rest, which the Scriptures call "sleep," which no cares or wants invade, and in which the embalmed body awaits the call of resurrection to reappear with new and augmented powers.

And when this period of peaceful inaction is completed the swathed creature suddenly breaks from its chrysalis, and bursts forth into an exaltation of being which has for ever left behind it every vestige of the low conditions in which its earlier life was spent. What painfully and gloomily crawled in the filthy earth and darkness now spurns the dust takes wings like a bird, soars at large in the bright sunshine whithersoever it will, and becomes a dweller in air, with the liberties of a free heaven. Filled now with loving affections and marvellous sagacity, it builds a house for its treasure, and holds it fast as it rolls it out with unwearied devotion into the vast unknown. And thus from the mummy form of the sleeping saints there is

to come a sudden bursting forth, when bodies terrestrial shall be supplanted by bodies celestial, and what was earthy becomes heavenly, and what was corruptible puts on incorruption, and what was ignoble becomes glorious, and what was natural takes all the attributes and capacities of enfranchised spiritual being, to mount up with wings as eagles, and to enjoy the light and love and liberty of heaven, in no way inferior to the angels. And thus, with the goal of our being reached and the treasure of our hearts in hand, the promise is that we shall hold it secure world without end.

There was scarce a creature on earth which the old Egyptians made so much of as this scarabæus beetle. The stones of their finger-rings and shoe-latchets, the seals of their priests and nobles, the ornaments and amulets worn on their bodies, the tokens of their guilds and orders, the memorials of their marriages, and the last mark put upon the mummies of their dead, were shaped into the form of the scarabæus. Men have wondered why this was, and faulted the taste of people so attached to a filthy *bug*. It was not on account of its beauty surely, nor on account of any great service rendered by it to their country or their crops. But it was the figure in their Zodiac—the star-sign of perfected being, the progress of which from darkness to light, from death to resurrection, from earthly disability to heavenly glory, from the vicissitudes of time to the secure possession of the treasures of eternity, they could see and trace in this beetle at almost every step throughout all their land, and with which the primitive traditions had taught them to connect the most precious hopes of man. This explains the mystery and tells the story, and helps us greatly in identifying the meaning which the primeval patriarchs understood and intended to express in this eleventh sign of the Zodiacal series.

Præsepe

In the centre of this constellation there is one of the brightest nebulous clusters in the starry sky, and sufficiently luminous to be

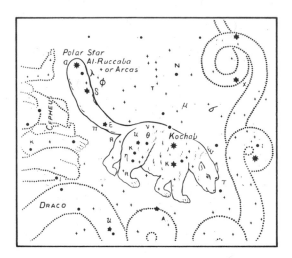

URSA MINOR, THE LITTLE BEAR

be seen betimes with the naked eye. It looks like the nucleus of a great comet, and has often been taken for one. It is made up of a multitude of little stars, and is often designated in modern astronomy as the *Bee-hive*. The ancients called it *Præsepe*, which, in its Arabic and Hebrew elements, means *the Multitude, Offspring, the Young, the Innumerable Seed*—the very idea in the text. The Latins understood by it the manger from which the asses were fed, the stall, the stable, the fold, and hence a house of entertainment, the place into which travellers gathered for refreshment and rest. The same idea is expressed by Moses in connection with Issachar, to whom the Jews referred this sign, where he speaks of Issachar as being gathered into tents, called to the mountain, offering the sacrifices of righteousness, and sucking the abundance of the sea and all the hid treasures of its sands (Deut. 33: 18, 19). In Jacob's blessing of his sons we have corresponding allusions and still further identifications with the particulars in this sign. In many of the classic references to the Zodiac the figures here are two asses, particularly represented by the two stars, the one north and the other south of Præsepe. And so Jacob prophesies of the coming *Shiloh*, that to Him shall the gathering of the people be, and that, having washed His garments in the blood of grapes, as when He treads the winepress of the fierceness of the wrath of Almighty God, and having accomplished the destruction of His enemies, as when He rides forth on the white horse to destroy all hostile powers, "He shall bind His foal to the vine, and His ass's colt to the choice vine." Issachar himself is likened to the great and strong ass which reclines between the two folds or resting-places, seeing that "the rest is good and the land pleasant," even that for which he was willing to bow his shoulder to the burden, and to serve and pay tribute to possess (Gen. 49: 10–15).

The Scriptures thus not only give us the imagery found in this sign, but connect the sign itself—which was assigned to Issachar—with the final results of the achievements of the promised Seed of the woman—with the rest that remains for the people of God—with the ultimate home-gathering of the multitudinous seed of faith—with the peaceful and secure entrance of the Church upon the "inheritance, incorruptible and undefiled, and that fadeth not away, reserved in heaven for those who are kept by the power of God through faith unto salvation ready to be revealed in the last time" (1 Pet. 1: 4–6).

THE MYTHS

The myths concerning this sign are faint

and feeble, but what is given amply conforms to what the Scriptures record in connection with it. The two asses which the Greeks accepted as the figures of Cancer they explained to be the animals by which Jupiter was assisted in his victory over the giants, but in repose now by the side of the celestial crib. They would thus admirably identify with the white horses on which Christ and His heavenly armies rode when they came forth for the destruction of the beasts, kings, and armies that made war with the Lamb. They would seem, indeed, to stand for the same, but now resting in immortal glory after the victory.

Other myths associate this Crab with the famous contest of Hercules with the dreadful Lernæan monster, and affirm that this was the animal from the sea which Juno's envy of the hero caused to bite his foot, but which, being quickly despatched, was rewarded by being placed among the heavenly constellations. Hercules was the symbol of the Seed of the woman as the suffering and toiling Deliverer, the great Overcomer and Slayer of the powers of evil, who, for the sake of His people, endured the sting and bruising of His heel; and yet, for all the pains they caused Him, He brings them at last to the enjoyment of eternal rest and glory, having slain their enmity by His cross.

The Names

The Egyptians called this sign *Klaria, the Folds, the Resting-places.* We call it *Cancer,* which in later vocabularies means *the Crab,* but which, in its Noetic roots, explains what we are to see in this Crab. *Khan* means the traveller's resting-place, and *ker* or *cer* means *embraced, encircled,* held as within encircling arms. And so *Can-cer* means *Rest secured*— the object of desire at length reached, compassed, possessed, and inalienably held. Hence also the chief star in this sign is named *Acubens,* the sheltering, the place of retirement, the good rest. Hence also other names in this sign (*Ma'alaph* and *Al Himarein*) mean *assembled thousands, the kids or lambs ;* whilst the whole is called in Hebrew, Arabic, and Syriac by a name which signifies *holding, possessing, retaining.* It is the sign of the saints' everlasting rest, in which the head of the Serpent is beneath their feet, as under the feet of this Crab.

And what we thus find in the sign itself is further illustrated and fully corroborated in its accompanying Decans.

Ursa Minor

The first of these is what is now called *Ursa Minor, the Lesser Bear.* But this was not its original name ; nor is it a bear at all. Those who figure it as a bear are obliged to give it a long uplifted tail, such as no bear ever had. And what is very astonishing, on the supposition that we here have to do with the form of a bear, is, that the most remarkable star in this constellation, and the most observed and rested on by man in all the heavens, is located far out on this unnatural tail. Where is the sense that would lead any astronomer, ancient or modern, to locate the Pole Star of the heavens in an imaginary tail of a feeble little bear ? The very idea is absurd, and such an absurdity that we may be sure the great old primeval astronomers are in no wise chargeable with it. It is said that the North American Indians connected the North Star with a bear, and that hence the figure here must have been primitively known as " the Bear ;" but it is not proven that these Indians belong to the primitive peoples, whilst they at the same time criticise and ridicule those who name it a bear, as not knowing what a bear is, or they never would have given it a long and lifted tail.

The way in which Ursa Minor and Ursa Major may have come to be called *Bears* is perhaps from the fact that the ancient name of the principal star in the latter is *Dubheh* or *Dubah,* and as *Dob* is the word for bear, the Greeks and others took the name of that star as meaning *the Bear,* and so called these two corresponding constellations *the Bears.*

But *Dubheh* or *Dubah* does not mean *bear,* but a collection of domestic animals, *a fold,* as the Hebrew word *Dober.* The evidence is that, according to the original intent, we are to see in these constellations not two long-tailed bears, but two *sheepfolds* or *flocks*, the collected and folded sheep of God's pasture.

The ancient Danes and Icelanders called *Ursa Minor* the Chair or Chariot of Thor, and the old Britons ascribed the same to Arthur, their great divine hero. This is coming much nearer to the astronomical facts of the case, as also to the original ideas connected with this constellation. It has seven principal stars, often called *Septentriones*—the seven which turn. The Arabs and the rabbins called them *Ogilah, going round*, as wheels; and hence also they are called *Charles's Wain, the King's Wagon*, or the thing which goes round. These noted *seven stars* are in themselves sufficient to suggest some connection with "the seven churches" which John saw as "seven stars" in Christ's right hand. The whole number of stars in this constellation is twenty-four, which suggests connection again between it and the "four-and-twenty elders" whom John beheld "round about the throne, clothed in white raiment,

and having on their heads crowns of gold" (Rev. 4), which denote the seniors of the elect Church in heaven. The ancient names in this constellation are *Kochab, the Star*, allied perhaps with the promise in Rev. 2 : 28, otherwise rendered by Rolleston *waiting the coming ; Al Pherkadain, the Calves, the Young*, Hebraically, *the Redeemed ; Al Gedi, the Kid, the Chosen of the flock ; and Al Kaid, the Assembled*, the gathered together. These are all applicable to the Church of the first-born, and particularly describe it as it finally comes to its inheritance.

Aratus says that Jupiter transferred both these bears to the sky from Crete during his concealment in the Idæan cave; but bears were never known in Crete, though it was plentiful enough in flocks and herds. But the story agrees with the scriptural account in this, that Christ mysteriously transfers the Church of the first-born to heaven whilst yet unmanifested to the rest of the world.

The Greeks called *Ursa Minor*, if not both the Bears, *Arcas*, or *Arktos*, a name which

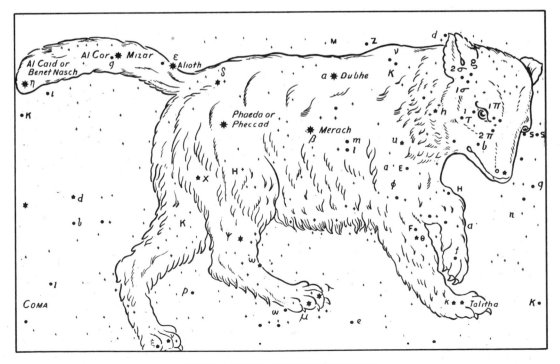

URSA MAJOR, THE GREAT BEAR

Harcourt derives from *Arx, the stronghold of the saved*. The myth concerning Arcas is, that he was the son of Jupiter and the nymph Callisto, that he built a city on the site of the blasted house of him who was served up as a dish to try Jupiter's divinity, and that he was the progenitor, teacher, and ruler of the Arcadians; which readily interprets in good measure of what is written of the Church of the first-born, particularly in its offices in the mysterious future.

THE POLE-STAR

It is part of the promise of the text that the seed of faith is to "possess the gate of his enemies"—that is, to take the house or possession of the foe—and thenceforward to hold what the enemy previously held. Now, at the time these constellations were formed, and for a long time afterward, the Pole-Star was the Dragon Star, *Alpha Draconis*. Thus this central gate, or hinge, or governing-point of the earth's motion, was then in the enemy's possession. But that Dragon Star is now far away from the Pole, and cannot again get back to it for ages on ages, whilst the Lesser and higher Sheepfold has come into its place; so that the main star of Arcas is now the Pole-Star. The seed of faith thus gets the enemy's gate. And understanding *Ursa Minor* of the Church of the first-born in heaven, instated in the government of the earth, we have in it a striking picture of the old prophecy fulfilled, when once Satan is cast down and the saints reign with their Lord in glory everlasting.

It is also an interesting fact that no traces of these Greek Bears are to be found in the Egyptian, the Persian, or the Indian planispheres, but only what is thoroughly agreeable to the idea that we are here to see the assembly of God's flocks in their heavenly glory, authority, and dominion, as over against the Serpent and the whole serpent dominion.

URSA MAJOR

And this is made the more evident in the second Decan of Cancer—*Ursa Major, the Great Bear*, anciently, *the Great Sheepfold*, the resting-place of the flock. The Arabs still call this constellation *Al Naish* or *Annaish*, the ordered or assembled together, as sheep in a fold.

In the centre of the miscalled tail of this so-called Bear we find the name *Mizar*, which means *guarded or enclosed place*. The chief star of all is *Dubheh, herd* or *fold;* the second is *Merach, the flock;* another, *Cab'd al Asad, multitude of the assembled*. Here we also have the names *El Acola, the sheepfold; Al Kaiad, the assembled; Alioth, the ewe* or *mother; El Kaphrah, the protected, the covered, the Redeemed; Dubheh Lachar, the latter herd* or *flock*, as distinguished from a former in Ursa Minor. The book of Job refers to "Arcturus and his sons"—to *Ash*, or *Aish*, and "her" progeny. The old Jewish commentators say that *Aish* here means the seven stars of the Great Bear. The word is often collective, denoting *a community*, hence the flock, the congregation. And in the so-called tail of this Bear we find the name *Benet Naish, the daughters of Aish*, part of the flock going out after Boötes, the Shepherd.

The myths say that this Bear is the nymph *Callisto*, the mother of Arcas, the son of Jupiter, and that she was metamorphosed into a bear by Juno. In the word *Callisto* we find the Shemitic root which we again meet as *Caulæ, a sheepfold, an enclosure*. And with this idea in mind a glance at these "seven stars" shows how well the presentations answer to an enclosure, from which the great flock goes forth from the fold at the corner led by their great Shepherd and Guardian, to whose coming all the ages have been looking from the beginning.

In the Dendera Zodiac this constellation has a great female figure with the head of a swine, the enemy of the Serpent, the tearer of the earth, and holding in her hand a great ploughshare, emblematic of tearing up, bruising, turning under; and the name by which it is called is *Fent-Har, the Serpent-bruiser, the Serpent-horrifier*. This ploughshare appears in both these constellations, and may have given rise to the association of *the plough* with these stars; but the whole significance is that of the seed of faith in power and triumph over the Serpent and its progeny.

All this sufficiently shows that we here have to do with the happy sheepfold, the flock of God, in heavenly glory and dominion, and not in the least with the anomalous wild bears of the Greeks and the later Western peoples. The picture is that of the seed of faith spoken of in the text in its twofoldness—the Church of the first-born round about the throne, signified by the Polar centre, and the Church of the after-born in still ampler numbers, led and guarded by the great Boötes amid the everlasting pastures.

Argo

And to make this the clearer, the third Decan of Cancer was framed. This is *Argo*, the mysterious ship of the mysterious Argonauts returned from their successful expedition to recover the Golden Fleece. Since the time of Homer, and long before Homer lived, the world has been full of noise about this ship and these gods and demigods of the Argonautic Expedition. But that same world till now has been floundering about to find a key to unlock the mystery in which the story is enveloped. Many are the suggestions to explain it, but all as empty of satisfactoriness as they are beneath the importance and significance always and everywhere attached to it. The trouble is, that men have ever persisted in trying to interpret it with reference to the affairs of ordinary human history or of some wild conceits of dreaming poets; whereas it belongs to the mystic, spiritual, and prophetic ideas frescoed on the stars, and to nothing else under heaven. Taken in these relations, and construed with the rest of these signs as we found their true application to be, we can have no difficulty. That Golden Fleece was the lost treasure of human innocence and righteousness, of which the subtlety of the Serpent had bereft mankind in the Garden of Eden, and so held and guarded it that no mere men could ever find or recover it. In the grove of *Mars*, the fierce god of justice, at *Colchis*, the citadel of atonement, it lay, the Serpent watching it

with jealous and ever-wakeful eyes. Nor was there a mortal to be found able to approach it until the true *Jason, the Recoverer, the Atoner, the Healer*, even JESUS, came, organized His *Argo*, His *company of travellers*, made up of heroes under His command and leadership, and went forth through various trials, conflicts, and sufferings, helped by the holy oracles that went along, and sustained by the heavenly ointments and powers to heal the wounds and hurts that had to be encountered, and took the precious prize, and then through varied fortunes brings the heroes back victorious to his own home-shores. And here, in the constellation of *Argo*, we have the picture of that return—the ship and the brave travellers come home, with the lost treasure regained, their toils and hazards and battles over, and blessed rest their lasting inheritance. Here the story fits in every part. It is the old ship of Zion landed in the heavenly port. Understand it so, and every feature takes on an evangelic light and a meaning commensurate with its fame. Nor is it possible to contemplate the vivid correspondence without wonderment at the prophetic knowledge and spiritual understanding and anticipations of those primeval sages who framed these signs and gave out their meaning.

The Names

And what we thus read in the story of the Argonauts is confirmed by the names in the constellation itself. The brightest star in the group is *Canopus* or *Canobus*. And this is the name of the great hero and helmsman, who died from the serpent's bite, but whom the Egyptians worshipped as a divine being. The name itself means *the possession of Him who cometh*, and thus explains why the Egyptians represented Canobus by a great treasure-jar. Other names are also here which tell us what we are to understand. *Sephina* means *multitudinous good, the very abundance* of the seas and of treasures referred to by Moses under the sign of Issachar. *Tureis* means *the firm possession in hand*, the treasure secured. *Asmidiska* means *the travellers released*. And *Soheil* means *what was desired*.

ARGO, THE SHIP

In the Dendera Zodiac we have here the figure of a great ox enclosed, with the cross suspended from his neck, the symbol of the great possession marked with the ancient token of immortality and eternal life. And the name of this figure is *Shes-en-Fent, rejoicing over the Serpent*. All this expresses exactly what I have said is the great subject of Cancer.

In the Persian Zodiac we have here three young women walking at leisure, the same with the daughters of Aish, signifying the Church in its final inheritance.

Thus the whole presentation binds up and links together from all sides to fix upon the sign of *Cancer* and its Decans the intention to make it the recorded symbol, prophecy, and hope of the heavenly rest for the redeemed which shines so conspicuously in all the scriptural promises. It is the star-picture of the multitudinous seed of faith at length possessing the gate of the enemy, rejoicing over him in life eternal, and going forth in abundant peace and blessedness, with the Serpent's head effectually trodden beneath their feet.

A Sweet Consolation

It is a blessed consolation to the oft-weary toilers and travellers in this world to know that there does remain a rest for the people of God. With all the trials and hardships to which they are subjected here, there is to come a blessed recompense. Jesus says: "Let not your heart be troubled; in my Father's house are many mansions. I go to prepare a place for you; and if I go, and prepare a place for you, I will come again, and receive you unto myself, that where I am ye may be also" (John 14 : 1–3). Isaiah sings: "The ransomed of the Lord shall return, and come to Zion with songs and everlasting joy upon their heads: they shall obtain joy and gladness, and sorrow and sighing shall flee away" (35 : 10). John in prophetic vision looked over into that other world, and writes: "I beheld, and lo, a great multitude which no man could number, of all nations, and kindreds, and peoples, and tongues stood before the throne, and before the Lamb, clothed with white robes, and palms in their hands. These are they which came out of great tribulation, and have washed their robes, and made them white in the blood of the Lamb. Therefore are they before the throne of God, and serve Him day and night in His temple: and He that sitteth upon the throne shall dwell among them. They shall hunger no more, neither thirst any more; neither shall the sun light on them, nor any heat. For the Lamb which is in the midst of the throne shall feed them, and lead them unto living fountains of waters: and God shall wipe away all tears from their eyes" (Rev. 7 : 9–17); "And there shall be no more death, neither sorrow, nor crying, neither shall there be any more pain: for the former things are passed away" (21 : 4). And even from His throne in glory the Saviour sends word to His struggling people: "To him that overcometh will I grant to sit with Me in my throne, even as I also overcame, and am set down with my Father in His throne" (Rev. 3 : 21). Such are the great and precious promises given to us, and such the possession to which we aspire. They are promises also that shall surely be fulfilled. God has pledged himself by His oath to make them good. They are the same that glowed in the hearts of the primeval patriarchs, who saw them afar off, and were persuaded of them, and embraced them, and confessed that they were pilgrims and strangers on the earth. On these imperishable stars they hung and pictured their confident belief and anticipations, whereby they, being dead, yet speak—speak across these many thousands of years—speak for our comfort on whom the ends of the world have come. Let us, then, be encouraged to believe as they believed, to hope as they hoped, laboring and looking for entrance into that same holy rest, even the everlasting kingdom of our Lord and Saviour Jesus Christ.

14

THE CONSUMMATED VICTORY

Weep not: behold, the Lion of the tribe of Judah, the Root of David, hath prevailed to open the book, and to loose the seven seals thereof.

—Revelation 5:5

THE scene of these words was in the heavenly spaces, whither the Apostle John had been caught up to witness what is to come to pass after the present Church-period comes to its close. They bring to view a great and oppressive sorrow and a great and glorious consolation.

In the hand of enthroned Almightiness lay a roll or document written within and without and sealed with seven seals. That roll denoted the title-deed of the inheritance which man had forfeited by disobedience, and which had reverted into the hand of God, to whom the race had become hopelessly indebted. Those "seven seals" attested the absoluteness of the bonds of forfeit, and bespoke how completely the inheritance was disponed away and gone. Nor could it ever be recovered to man, except as some one should be found with worth, merit, and ability to satisfy the claim, lift the document, and destroy its seals. But neither in heaven or earth nor under the earth did any one appear worthy to take up the writing, or even so much as to look upon it. This was the grief which made the Apostle weep. It seemed to say to him that man's patrimony was clean gone for ever. It drew a dark and impenetrable veil over all the promises and over all man's prospects, as if everything hoped for was now about to fail. Could it be that all the fond anticipations touching "the redemption of the purchased possession" were now to miscarry, and the whole matter, of which the saints had been prophesying so long, go by default? So the matter looked, which was a grief indeed that well might overwhelm the soul of an Apostle, even in heaven.

But, though John "wept much," he was not left to weep long. A voice from among the throned elders soon broke in to relieve his anxiety and dry his tears. That voice said: "*Weep not: behold, the Lion of the tribe of Judah, the Root of David, hath prevailed to open the book, and to loose the seven seals thereof.*" This was the consolation which com-

LEO, THE LION

forted the holy Seer, and which he was directed to write for the cheer and comfort of the sorrowing Church in all these ages since. And what was thus said to John, both in substance and in figure, we likewise find written upon the stars in the twelfth and last sign of the Zodiac and its Decans.

THE LION

The text speaks of a mystic *Lion*. The lion is a kingly, majestic, noble, but terrible creature, so strong and courageous as to fear nothing, and so fierce and powerful that no other animal can stand before him. The names of the lion in Hebrew, Arabic, Syriac, and Coptic, though different, all signify about the same, and mean *He that rends, that tears asunder, that destroys, that lays waste.* The name in Greek and Latin is formed from words which express sharp and flaming sight, leaping forth as flames, coming with raging vehemence. From this we see how the earlier peoples were impressed by what they saw and knew of this terrible beast. The

common sentiment of mankind has associated it with royalty and dominion, and awarded it the title of "king of beasts." It scarcely has an equal in physical strength, which is further combined with extraordinary quickness and agility. Ordained to feed on flesh, it is fitted for the work of capture and destruction, and is supplied with the most powerful physical machinery conceivable for the purpose. It can easily kill and drag away a buffalo, and it can crush the skull of a horse or break the backbone of an ox with one stroke of its paw. Its claws can cut four inches in depth at a single grasp. It has great ivory teeth capable of crunching a bullock's bones. The fall of its fore paw in striking is estimated to be equal to twenty-five pounds in weight, whilst it is able to handle itself with all the nimbleness of a cat, to whose family the lion belongs. The possession of such powers, with its instincts for blood, renders this animal wonderfully daring, bold, and self-confident, and the great terror of men and beasts in the vicinity of its haunts. When the lion is assailed and thoroughly aroused, and lifts himself up in proud contemplation of his foes, though banded in troops around him, his composed, majestic, and defiant mien is described as noble and magnificent beyond conception ; whilst the terribleness of his growl and the thunder of his roar contribute to make the picture almost superhumanly impressive. And this is the image which we are called to contemplate in the text as describing the character and majesty of Christ in connection with the final scenes of the taking of the roll from the hand of eternal Godhead, the breaking of its seals, and the clearing of the earth from all enemies and usurpers.

CHRIST AS THE LION

When the dying Jacob blessed his sons, he pronounced Judah *a lion*, whom his brethren should praise, whose hand should be in the neck of his enemies, and before whom his father's children would bow down (Gen. 49 : 8, 9). His words on that occasion were all intensely prophetic. What he said of Judah applied to the warlike and victorious energy which was afterward shown in that tribe. The same received remarkable fulfilment in David, in whom the lion-nature was strikingly exhibited, and whose boast in the Lord was, " By Thee I can dash in pieces the warlike people. I pursue after mine enemies, and overtake them, and turn again until I have consumed them " (Ps. 18). But these lion-qualities assigned to Judah looked onward to a still nobler King, who " sprang out of Judah " as David's lineal descendant and heir, who is at once David's Lord and David's son, and pre-eminently *the Lion* of whom Jacob spoke.

Under the New Testament, and during the course of the existing Church-period, our Saviour is more commonly contemplated as the innocent, uncomplaining, and spotless Lamb of sacrifice, meekly yielding up His life that we might live. Even among the stupendous works of battle and judgment set forth in the Apocalypse, He still appears again and again as " the Lamb "—" a Lamb as it had been slain," " the Lamb slain from the foundation of the world "—by whose blood the saints are washed from their sins, their garments made white, and their final victory over all Satan's accusations achieved. And to His people, even as the eternal Bridegroom, He will never cease to be the Lamb of God, by whose sacrificial death and mediation they have their standing and their blessedness. Neither does He cease to be the Lamb even in connection with His being the terrible Lion. The Lamb is capable of wrath, and in the day of His wrath He is the Lion. He is the one to His friends, and He is the other to His enemies. Nay, He does not come to the exercise of His powers and prerogatives as the Lion, except as he first clears away all impediments and overcomes all embarrassments by means of sacrificial atonement and satisfaction for the sins of those for whom He at length takes the character of the Lion, to tear His and their enemies in pieces. This is what the elder means when he says that this Lion of the tribe of Judah " *hath prevailed*," so as to be in position of worthiness and ability, as the almighty Redeemer, to go forward as a Lion to take the inheritance by destroying all who have obtruded themselves upon it and presume to hold it in defiance of His royal rights.

THE LION-WORK

Nor are the Scriptures sparing in their references to this lion-character and lion-work of the glorious Redeemer when things have once come to ripeness for the sharp sickle of judgment. Not only Jacob and Moses, but all the prophets, have alluded to it. Thus the word of the Lord by Hosea (13 : 7, 8) was : " I will be unto them as a lion. I will rend the caul of their heart. I will devour them like a lion." Thus Zephaniah (3 : 8) prophesied : " Wait ye upon me, saith the Lord, until the day that *I rise up to the prey :* for my determination is to gather the nations, that I may assemble the kingdoms, to pour upon them my indignation, even all my fierce anger : for all the earth shall be devoured with the fire of my jealousy." Thus Isaiah (42 : 13), referring to the period of the judgment, says: "The Lord shall go forth as a mighty man, He shall stir up His jealousy like a man of war: He shall cry, yea, *roar;* He shall prevail against His enemies." Thus Amos declares: "The Lord will roar from Zion, and utter His voice from Jerusalem; and the habitations of the shepherds shall mourn, and the top of Carmel shall wither. Will a lion roar in the forest when he hath no prey?" (1 : 2; 3 : 4, 8). "Consider this," saith the Lord (Ps. 50: 22), "ye that forget God, lest I tear you in pieces, and there be none to deliver."

And here, in the sign of Leo, is this very Lion, thoroughly aroused, salient, and full of majesty, the same in all the pictorial Zodiacs of all nations. It is the same "Lion of the tribe of Judah" to which the text refers, for in the Jewish astronomy this twelfth sign was the sign of Judah. He is the Lion of Judah in the text, and He is the Lion of Judah in the Zodiac. The record of the signs and the record of the Word are here precisely identical. The coincidence is positive and absolute, and rests on no mere inferences from mere likeness or concurring circumstances. The picture in the sky is one and the same with the picture in the Revelation as shown to John in his visions in Patmos.

In the Apocalypse the Lion-Lamb takes the roll from the hand of eternal Majesty amid thrills of exultation which shake the whole intelligent universe from centre to circumference. He tears asunder seal after seal, until the very last is reached and broken, and with each there bursts forth a divine almightiness, seizing and convulsing the whole world as it never before was affected. The white horse of conquering power, and the red horse of war and bloodshed, and the black horse of scarcity and famine, and the cadaverous horse of Death with Hades at his heels, dash forth in invincible energy upon the apostate populations of the earth. The heavens are shaken, and seem to collapse like a falling tent, the earth is filled with quaking, the mountains and islands are moved out of their places, and the mightiest and bravest, as well as the weakest, of men are filled with horror and dismay. The great tribulation,

the like of which never was and never again shall be, sets in. The golden censers of the heavenly temple, filled with fire from the celestial altar, are emptied into the earth amid cries and thunders and terrific perturbations. The judgment-angels sound their trumpets and pour out the contents of their bowls of wrath, filling the world with burning and bitterness and tripled woe, unloosing hell itself to overrun and deceive and torment the nations, developing all their antichristianism into one great and all-commanding embodiment of consummated iniquity, and gathering its abettors at the last into the great winepress of the wrath of God, to be trodden by the divine Avenger till the blood flows in depth to the horses' bridles for more than a hundred miles, and who will no more give over until the beasts from the abyss, and the Devil, and all theirs, are cast into the burning lake of the second death.

Such is the Lion-work of the Root and Offspring of David as it was shown to the Apostle John, and directed to be written for our learning. And what is thus pictured in the last book of the Scriptures is the same that was fore-intimated and recorded in this last sign of the Zodiac before any one book of our present Bible was written.

The Sign of Leo

Here is the great Lion in all the majesty of His fierce wrath—*Aryeh*, He who rends; *Al Sad*, He who tears and lays waste; *Pimentekeon*, the Pourer-out of rage, the Tearer asunder; *Leon*, the vehemently coming, the leaping forth as a consuming fire. The chief star embraced in this figure, situated in the Lion's breast, whence its mighty paws proceed, bears the name of *Regel* or *Regulus*, which means *the feet which crush*, as where it is said of the Messiah that He shall tread upon the serpent and asp, and trample the dragon under His feet (Ps. 91 : 13). The second star in Leo is called *Denebola*, the Judge, the Lord who cometh with haste. The third star is *Al Giebha*, the exalted, the exaltation. Other names in the sign are *Zosma*, the shining forth, the epiphany; *Minchir al*

Asad, the punishing or tearing of him who lays waste; *Deneb al Eced*, the Judge coming, who seizes or violently takes; and *Al Defera*, the putting down of the enemy.

As nearly and fully as names can express it, we thus have the same things in the Zodiacal Leo that we find ascribed to the Lion of the tribe of Judah in the Apocalypse. They both tell one and the same story—the story of the wrath of the Lamb, and His great and final judgment-administrations, in which the kingdom of Daniel's mystic stone, cut out of the mountain without hands, falls upon, breaks in pieces, grinds to powder, and scatters in undistinguishable dust all other kingdoms and powers, and sweeps everything inimical to a common and eternal perdition.

And what we find so vividly pictured and expressed in the sign is still further and most unmistakably corroborated in its accompanying side-pieces or Decans.

HYDRA

The great mission of the promised Seed of the woman was effectually to bruise the Serpent's head. This is the all-comprehending burden of the assurance given to fallen Adam, and his children after him. The Serpent was the subtle and snaky creature which deceived and seduced our first parents into transgression. Whether in the form of a literal *snake* is not worth our while to inquire; but it was some visible serpentine shape by which Eve was approached, and in and behind which was a treacherous, intelligent, evil spirit, who reappears again and again in the histories and prophecies of the Scriptures, even up to the end, as "the great Dragon, that old Serpent, called the Devil, and Satan, which deceiveth the whole world" (Rev. 12: 9). He was once a good angel and a chief among the angels, but "kept not his first estate," left his place as one of God's loyal subjects, abused his free will to sin and rebellion, and fell under bonds of condemnation, in which he is held over unto the judgment of the great day. Meanwhile, he is exerting his great powers to the utmost in malignity toward God and all good. By his successful deception of our first parents he got a footing in this world,

and has here planted and organized a vast Satanic kingdom, over which he reigns, and which he inspires and directs, impiously setting himself up as another god over against the true and only God, and particularly against Christ as the rightful Heir and King of the earth. Hence the saying of the Apostle Paul, which is ever true of all God's people: "We wrestle not against flesh and blood, but against principalities, against powers, against the rulers of the darkness of this world, against wicked spirits in the air" (Eph. 6: 12).

During these six thousand years, which the Apostle calls "*man's day*" as distinguished from "*the Lord's day*" or the day of enforced heavenly rule, this subtle and snaky spirit has managed to worm himself into everything that goes to make up human life, corrupting and perverting it to his own base ends, seating himself in all the centres of influence and power, and making himself the very king and god of this world. From all these places he must be dislodged, his dominion broken, his works destroyed, and he and all his effectually rooted out and put down, before the heavenly kingdom can come in its fulness or the great redemption-work reach its intended consummation. In other words, the whole empire and influence of the Serpent must be rent to atoms, worked clean out of the whole realm of humanity, and so crushed as never to be able to lift up its head again. Toward this end all the dispensations and gifts of God, from the first promise to Adam until now, have been directed. Toward this end all the works and administrations of Christ to this present are framed. To this end He is to come again in power and great glory as the Lion of the tribe of Judah, to "put down all rule and all authority and power," and to trample "all enemies beneath His feet." And here, in the first Decan of Leo, is the grand picture of that consummation. Here is *Hydra*, that old Serpent, whose length stretches one-third the way around the whole sphere, completely expelled from the places into which he had obtruded, fleeing now for his life, and the great Lion, with claws and jaws extended, bounding in terrific fury and seizing the foul monster's neck.

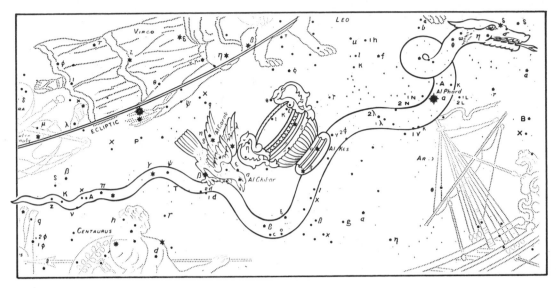

HYDRA, THE SERPENT
CRATER, THE CUP
CORVUS, THE RAVEN

Myths and Names

According to the myths, this *Hydra* was the terrible monster which infested the Lernæan lake—image of this corrupt world. It was said to have a hundred heads, neither of which could be killed simply by cutting off, for unless the wound was burned with fire two immediately grew out where there was only one before. The poets describe him as

> " Raising a hundred hissing heads in air;
> When one was lopped, up sprang a dreadful pair."

All this answers wonderfully well to the history of evil in the world, and the impossibility of effectually overcoming it in any one of its manifestations except by the fires of judgment.

The myths further say that it was one of the great labors imposed on Herakles to destroy this dreadful monster, in which he also succeeded, helped by his faithful companion and charioteer, Iolaus. But his success was only by means of fire and burning, by applying a red-hot iron to the wound as head after head was severed from the horrid form. Herakles was the deliverer sent to free the world of its great pests. He was the mythologic symbol of the Seed of the woman who was to come to make an end of all ill powers. Mythology thus answers to Revelation, and well bears out the interpretation of Hydra as a picture of Satan finally vanquished, rent, burned, destroyed by the fury of Judah's Lion.

In the Dendera sphere the Lion stands directly on the Serpent, whilst underneath is the hieroglyphic name *Knem*, which means vanquished, conquered. The plain idea is that here is the end of the Serpent-dominion.

The name *Hydra* means *the Abhorred.* The principal star, *Al Phard*, means *the Separated, the Excluded, the Put out of the way.* Another name in the constellation is *Minchir al Sugia*, which means *the punishing*, or *tearing to pieces, of the Deceiver.*

Everything thus falls in with the one idea, and adds its share to prove that we here have, by the intent of those who framed these signs, a direct and graphic picture of the glorious triumph of the Seed of the woman crushing the Serpent's head and putting him out of the way for ever.

And if further evidence is needed, it is furnished in the two remaining Decans of this final sign.

CRATER, OR THE CUP OF WRATH

The Psalmist (75 : 8) says : "In the hand of the Lord there is *a cup*, and the wine is red ; it is full of mixture ; and He poureth out of the same : but the dregs thereof all the wicked of the earth shall wring out, and drink ;" "Upon the wicked He shall rain burning coals, fire and brimstone, and a fiery tempest : this shall be the portion of *their cup*" (11 : 6). Concerning every worshipper of the Beast John heard the angel proclaim, " The same shall drink of the wine of the wrath of God, which is poured out without mixture into *the cup of His indignation ;* and he shall be tormented with fire and brimstone in the presence of the holy angels, and in the presence of the Lamb ; and the smoke of their torment ascendeth up for ever and ever : and they have no rest day nor night" (Rev. 14 : 10, 11). The portion of the worshippers of the son of perdition is "the lake of fire," and the same is likewise dealt out to the Beast and the False Prophet, and ultimately to the Devil himself : for John saw him " cast into the lake of fire and brimstone, where the Beast and the False Prophet are," and where he " shall be tormented day and night for ever and ever" (Rev. 20 : 10). In other words, he and all his are to drink of the wine of the wrath of God which is poured out without adulteration or dilution into the cup of the divine indignation.

And lo ! here, as the second Decan of Leo, we have the very picture of that *Cup*, broad, deep, full to the brim, and placed directly on the body of this writhing Serpent ! Nay, the same is sunk into his very substance, for the same stars which mark the bottom of the Cup are part of the body of the accursed monster, so that the curse is fastened down on him and in him as an element of all his after being ! Dreadful beyond all thought is the picture John gives of this Cup of unmingled and eternal wrath, but not a whit more dreadful than the picture of it which the primeval prophets have thus inscribed upon the stars.

CORVUS, OR THE RAVEN

But this is not all. The wise man says, " The eye that mocketh at his father, and despiseth to obey his mother, the ravens of the valley shall pick it out, and the young eagles shall eat it" (Prov. 30 : 17). When David, the first great impersonation of Judah's Lion, met the terrible Goliath of Gath, he cursed him in the name of the Lord God of Israel, and said : "I will smite thee, and take thy head from thee ; and I will give the carcasses of the host of the Philistines this day unto the fowls of the air and to the wild beasts of the earth" (1 Sam. 17 : 46). So, when the Lord of lords and King of kings dashes forth on the white horse, with the armies of heaven following Him on white horses, to tread the winepress of the fierceness and wrath of Almighty God, an angel stands in the sun, calling with a great voice to all the fowls and birds of prey to come and feast themselves on the flesh of the enemy (Rev. 19 : 17, 18). And here, in the third Decan of Leo, we have the pictorial sign of the same thing. Here is *Corvus*, the Raven, the bird of punishment and final destruction, grasping the body of Hydra with its feet and tearing him with its beak.

The myths have but little sensible or consistent to say of this Raven, except in making it the symbol of punished treachery. The Greeks and Romans had for the most part lost its meaning. The Egyptians called it *Her-na, the Enemy broken.* The star in the eye of this ill-omened bird is called *Al Chiba, the Curse inflicted.* Another name in the constellation is *Minchir al Gorab, the Raven tearing to pieces.* It is the sign of the absolute discomfiture and destruction of the Serpent and all his power ; for when the birds once begin to tear and gorge the flesh of fallen foes, no further power to resist, harm, or annoy remains in them. Their course is run.

Thus, then, and thus completely, does Judah's Lion dispose of that old Serpent-enemy, with all his Hydra heads, when once the day of final settlement comes.

The Career of the Serpent

Great and marvellous is the part which this arch-enemy has played in the history of our race, is still playing, and will yet play before the end is reached. Like a dark and chilling shadow he came up upon the new-born world, insinuated his slime into the garden of human innocence, deceived and disinherited the race at its very spring, and so spun his webs around the souls of the earlier generations as to drag almost the entire population of the earth to one common ruin. Hardly had that great calamity passed when he began again with new schemes to get men in his power and sway them to his will. Before the Flood he won them through their carnal passions. Now he set himself to taint their holy worship, perverting it into idolatries which have held and debased the great body of mankind for these forty centuries, and still holds great portions of the world in darkness and in death. Then he plied them with visions of empire and dominion, and thus filled the earth and the ages with murderous tyrannies, misrule, oppressions, wars, and political abominations. Then he began to corrupt the thinking and philosophies of men, thereby making them willing slaves to damning error. And even to-day he is *the very god of this world*, to whose lies the vast majority of the race render homage, whose rule is in living sway over at least two-thirds of the population of the earth, which is full of misery from his power.

Nor is there the slightest solid ground for hope that it will be essentially otherwise till the great Lion of the tribe of Judah comes forth in the fury of his almightiness to make an utter end of him and his infernal domination. But his doom is sealed. On the face of these lovely stars it has been written from the beginning, the same as in the Book. Though Satan's grasp upon our world should hold through the long succession of two-thirds of the signs, there is at last a Lion in the way, alive, awake, and mighty, even that Seed of the woman whom he has all these ages been wounding in the heel and trying to defeat and destroy. That Lion he cannot pass. Cunningly as the subtle Deceiver has wound himself about everything, injecting his poison and making firm his hellish dominion, he will soon be dragged forth to judgment, seized by almighty power, crushed, torn, pierced, put under the bowl of eternal wrath, whilst the hundred-headed body in which he has operated through all these ages is given to the black birds of uncleanness to be devoured.

The End

And when the Serpent thus falls the circle of time is complete, and it is eternity. There is no continuity of the way of time beyond the victorious triumphs of Judah's Lion. Death, and Hell, and all the wild beasts, with all their children, and the old Serpent, their father, with them, thenceforward have their place in the everlasting prison burning with fire and brimstone, which is the second death. And outside of that dread place "there shall be no more death, neither sorrow, nor crying, neither shall there be any more pain: for the former things are passed away." Then the great voices in heaven sing: "Behold, the tabernacle of God is with men, and He will dwell with them, and they shall be His people, and God himself shall be with them, and be their God;" for they "*shall inherit all things*" (Rev. 21).

Blessed consummation! How should we look and long and pray for it, as Jesus has directed where He tells us to say, "*Thy kingdom come—Thy will be done on earth as it is in heaven*"! Well might one of England's greatest poets cry: "Come forth out of Thy royal chambers, O Prince of all the kings of the earth! Put on the visible robes of Thy imperial Majesty! Take up the unlimited sceptre which Thy almighty Father hath bequeathed Thee! For now the voice of Thy bride calls Thee, and all creatures sigh to be renewed." How cheering the hope, amidst the clash of conflicting beliefs, the strife of words, the din of war, the shouts of false joy, the yells of idolatry, the sneers of unbelief, the agonies of a dying race, and the groans of a whole creation travailing in pain together in consequence of the Serpent's malignity, that a period is coming when eternal death shall be that Serpent's portion ; when peace and order and heavenliness shall stretch their bright wings over the happy sons of men ; when rivers of joy proceeding from the throne of God and of the Lamb shall water all this vale of tears ; when cherubim to cherubim shall cry, " Holy, holy, holy, is the Lord God of hosts ; the whole earth is full of His glory ;" when myriads of myriads and thousands of thousands of angels round about the throne shall join in the acclaim of " Worthy is the Lamb which hath been slain, to receive the Power, and Riches, and Wisdom, and Might, and Honor, and Glory, and Blessing ;" and when every creature which is in heaven, and on the earth, and under the earth, and upon the sea, and all things in them, shall sing, " To Him that sitteth upon the throne, and to the Lamb, be the Blessing, and the Honor, and the Glory, and the Dominion, for the ages of the ages " ! Yet such is our hope

given us as an anchor for our souls, both sure and steadfast, entering into that within the veil, and linking us even now to those solid shores of the world to come. We have it in the written word of Prophets and Apostles, and the same is certified to us by these everlasting stars in their ceaseless journeyings around the pathway of the circling year. God be thanked for such a hope ! God be thanked for the full and wide-sounding testimony to its certainty ! God be thanked that it has come to us, and that ours is the privilege of taking it to our souls in the confidence and comfort that it shall be fulfilled !

> " Not the light that leaves us darker,
> Not the gleams that come and go,
> Not the mirth whose end is madness,
> Not the joy whose fruit is woe ;
> Not the notes that die at sunset,
> Not the fashion of a day ;
> But the everlasting beauty
> And the endless melody,
> Heir of glory !
> That shall be for thee and me."

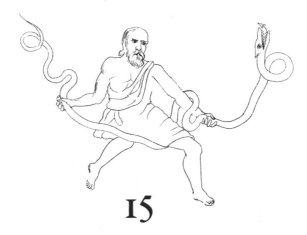

15

THE SECRETS OF WISDOM

He would show thee the secrets of wisdom, that they are double to that which is. —Job 11:6

THINGS are more than they seem. They are not only more in themselves than we can know or understand, but they are related to other and hidden spheres beyond the reach of our natural reason. "They are double" in their expression, so that what is external and natural at the same time includes something recondite and spiritual. The Scriptures everywhere recognize this, and constantly proceed upon it in what we call symbols, types, parables, allegories, and tropes. And the true "secrets of wisdom," as well as the characteristics of divine teaching, according to Zophar, lie in this double of what we naturally observe and experience.

In so far, then, as this doubleness of showing is a mark of divine teaching, the primeval astronomy is pre-eminently a part of God's own revelation; for here we find not only a superhuman knowledge of the natural economy of the starry heavens, but a doubleness of expression by which we may also read the whole system of Messianic truths, predictions, and hopes.

To human observation there is nothing grander than this universe of heavenly worlds. The study of them is justly regarded as the sublimest of the sciences. But, on the basis of these natural facts and presentations, there is a duplicate of meaning touching another department of the divine manifestations which is vastly sublimer and more precious than all the knowledge of astronomy.

The Ground thus Far

In our endeavors to trace this double of the starry expressions we have been occupied entirely with the Solar Zodiac and its thirty-six Decans. In this we have indeed the main stellar presentations. Following this Way through its various steps or stations, with their explanatory Faces, we necessarily have before us all the most conspicuous markings of the heavens. And if there really is a legible record of the Gospel in the stars, it must be found, above all, in what we have thus gone over. Whether the findings have in fact been such as to warrant us in concluding that Christ and His fore-announced achievements are there symbolized, must be decided by those who will candidly consider what has been brought out. For my own part, I have not the slightest doubt or question on the subject. Taking the facts, figures, and names as our common, every-day astronomy gives them, I find such clear and evident marks of connection and design, such thorough consistency in the elaboration of all the details, such distinct and orderly progress of thought in the arrangements of beginning, continuity, and end, such a universal and multitudinous array of myths and legends founded on the constellations and running parallel with their meaning as thus interpreted, such a complete identity of images and terms with the scriptural presentations of the same things, and such a self-evidencing and exhaustive outlining of all the great features of the Gospel story, along with such a profound and accurate penetration into the whole organization of the visible universe,—that I should have to go against all laws of evidence and principles of logic not to accept it as very truth that these heavens do declare "the glory of God" as embodied in the person, mission, work, and redemptive achievements of His Son Jesus Christ.

THE LUNAR ZODIAC

But the markings of the heavens are not exhausted by what pertains to the Solar Zodiac and its Decans. There is also a *Lunar* Zodiac. It consists of the same belt as the Solar Zodiac, but divides that belt into twenty-eight in place of twelve parts or steps; and these twenty-eight are called *the Mansions of the Moon*. To each of these twenty-eight steps a particular name is given. In the Indian astronomy each of these steps or Mansions also had a particular figure additional to the name; but the figures are not invariably the same. In China and Arabia the names are more uniform, but are given without figures or emblems. The Parsis also had the Lunar Zodiac, and made much of it. Astronomers agree in regarding this Lunar Zodiac as containing the most ancient remains

of the science of the stars. The Romans, Greeks, and Egyptians knew little or nothing about it, but it is a matter of record in China that it was known and understood in that country as early as the reign of Yao, about twenty-three hundred years before the Christian era, which was before the time of Abraham.* In the Chinese astronomy it begins with Virgo, which would seem to indicate that the Chinese table came from the antediluvian times.

The Lunar Zodiac is manifestly from the same source as the Solar, and great importance was attached to it wherever the knowledge of it was preserved in living observance. In Arabia and in India from time immemorial these Mansions of the Moon held place and rank equal, if not superior, to the Solar Zodiac, and are found interwoven with all poetry and science, and incorporated not only into the worship and mythology, but also into various customs of private life. Children there are still frequently named according to the Lunar Mansions under which they were born.

They are preserved in Scandinavia and Burmah, and traces of them have been found in the ruins of ancient Mexico. Al Fergani in Bagdad, Albumazer in Spain, and Ulugh Beigh, the Tartar prince and astronomer, grandson of Tamerlane, have transmitted to us the names and enumerations of these Mansions of the Moon, and preserved to the world the evidences of their corresponding antiquity with the twelve signs of the Solar Zodiac.**

There is, therefore, every reason to expect, if it was meant that the stars should carry a prophetic record of the Gospel, that we would find it also in the arrangement and naming of these Lunar Mansions. And, as we would anticipate, so it really is.

NAMES OF THE LUNAR MANSIONS

Christ was predicted as "the Desire of

* This point is scientifically presented in Max Müller's *Sacred Books of the East*, vol. iii., by James Legge, where it is said that "the most common, and what was the earliest, division of the Ecliptic in China is that of the twenty-eight Lunar Mansions, forming what we may call the Chinese Zodiac."

** See Hyde's *Syntagma*, vol. i.; Freytag's *Arabic Lexicon;* and Le Gentil, *Voy. dans les Indes.*

nations," "the Desire of women;" and so the first of these Mansions is named *Al Awa, the Desired*. Christ was foretold as "the Branch," God's "servant the Branch," "the Branch of Righteousness who shall execute judgment," and the like; and the second of these Mansions is called *Simak al Azel, Branch of the power of God*. It was predicted of Christ that His soul should be made an offering for sin (Isa. 53:10): "He is the propitiation for our sins and for the sins of the whole world." And so the third of these Mansions bears the name of *Caphir, the Atonement, the Propitiation by sacrifice*.

These three Mansions correspond to Virgo.

Christ was everywhere promised as the Redeemer, the Saviour, He who should bring redemption; and the fourth of these Mansions is named *Al Zubena, the redeeming, the regaining by purchase, the buying back*. When Christ died he said, "It is finished;" and the fifth of these Mansions is named *Al Iclil, the complete submission*.

These two names answer to Libra

And so the list proceeds in strict accord with the scriptural prophecies and descriptions of the Seed of the woman. Thus:

CORRESPONDING TO SCORPIO

Al Kalb, the cleaving or wounding; *Al Shaula*, the sting, the deadly wound.

CORRESPONDING TO SAGITTARIUS

Al Naim, the gracious, the delighted in; *Al Beldah*, hastily coming, as to judgment.

So far, the reference plainly is to the person and work of Christ as respects himself, as in the first quaternary of the Solar Zodiac.

The succeeding series runs thus:

CORRESPONDING TO CAPRICORNUS

Al Dibah, the sacrifice slain.

CORRESPONDING TO AQUARIUS

Sa'ad al Bula, witness of the rising or drinking in; *Sa'ad al Su'ud*, witness of the swimming or outpouring; *Al Achbiya*, the fountain of pouring.

CORRESPONDING TO PISCES

Al Pherg al Muchaddem, the progeny of the ancient times; *Al Pherg al Muachher*, the progeny of the latter times; *Al Risha*, the band, the joined together.

CORRESPONDING TO ARIES

Al Sheratan, the wounded, that was cut off; *Al Botein*, the treading under foot; *Al Thuraiya*, the enemy punished.

These names thus run in remarkable parallel of meaning with the signs and more ample showings in the second quaternary of the Solar Zodiac. It is the same also with regard to the rest of these names as compared with the last four signs.

CORRESPONDING TO TAURUS

Al Debaran, the Leader, the Governor, the Subduer; *Al Heka*, the driving away.

CORRESPONDING TO GEMINI

Al Henah, the wounded in the foot; *Al Dirah*, the ill-treated.

CORRESPONDING TO CANCER

Al Nethra, the treasure, the possession; *Al Terpha*, the healed, the delivered, the saved.

CORRESPONDING TO LEO

Al Gieba, the exaltation, the Prince; *Al Zubra*, the heaped-up, as sin and delayed punishment; *Al Serpha*, the burning, the funeral-pyre.

The whole series of these names thus runs parallel with the signs of the Solar Zodiac, and ends up precisely in the same way, proving that they are of a piece with it.

THE MILKY WAY

Another distinct marking of the heavens is a snowy belt, from four to twenty degrees or more in width, which stretches obliquely over the sky from south-west to north-east, thus cutting the Ecliptic, and extending entirely around the whole circuit of the heavens in another direction. It is best seen in the months from June to November, and looks like a great river of hazy brightness. It is called the Galaxy, the Milky Way, the Galactic Circle. It was once supposed to be a vast collection of nebulous matter consisting of yet forming or unformed stars, but later investigations have demonstrated that the whole Milky Way is made up of myriads on myriads of suns like ours, which is itself one of them. Milton refers to this great belt as

> " A broad and ample road, whose dust is gold,
> And pavement stars, as stars to thee appear—
> A circling zone, powdered with stars."

The ancient heathen poets and philosophers spoke of this Way as the path which their deities used in the heavens, and claimed that it led directly to the throne and " the Thunderer's abode." And if the primeval prophets had wished to mark on the sky the steps and stages in the life and work of the promised Seed of the woman, and the results of the same, this marvellous " pathway of the gods" was well suited to their purpose. And so we also find it employed.

Twelve of the constellations are situated in or on this Milky Way ; six of which relate to the first advent, and six to the second. They start at the lowest point with the Cross and the Altar of sacrifice, the burning penalty of sin ; as Christ humbled himself and became obedient unto death, even the death of the cross, and laid the foundations of salvation in becoming a curse for us. Then comes the cleft of Scorpio, the sting of death and the power of hell, seeming to split asunder the Milky Way itself. Then comes the Eagle pierced; then the Swan on outspread wings, going and returning with the bright cross displayed upon its breast for all the world to see ; and then the royal Cepheus swaying the sceptre of empire, with his foot upon the pole of dominion, high over all authority and power; all of which epitomizes with great exactness the biblical portraiture of Christ's history up to the time when He is to come again.

The first thing to occur when the time of Christ's second coming arrives is the seizing away of His true people, dead and alive, to himself in the sky ; and so the next sign on this Way is that of *Cassiopeia*, the enthroned woman, the Church set free from its bonds and crowned with heavenly glory.

The next picture is that of *Perseus*, the illustrious Breaker, full-armed and winged, the savior of Andromeda, whom he has engaged to make his bride, and the slayer of the Gorgon, whose head, writhing with matted snakes, he bears away in triumph.

The next is *Auriga*, the mighty Shepherd, ruling the nations with a rod of iron, but having the glorified Church in His bosom, and holding the alarmed little kids all safe on His mighty hand.

The next succeeding picture is that of *Gemini*, the heavenly union of Christ and His Church, the marriage of the Lamb.

The fifth picture is that of the doubly-glorious Orion, the mighty Hunter of all the wild beasts of apostate power in all their lurking-places, going forth in His princely and all-conquering energy, treading down the Serpent beneath His feet, and slaying even Death and Hell.

And then comes the last of the series, *Argo*, the anchored ship of the heroes returned from their perilous expedition to recover the Golden Fleece, securely landed now on the home-shores, with their imperishable treasure secured for ever. This completes the circle of the Snowy Way, which even the heathen recognized and celebrated as the path to glory and to God.

Could this arrangement, so clear, so consistent, and so thoroughly conformed to all that the Scriptures teach us on the subject of our salvation, have come about by mere accident ? Fitted in as it is with the Zodiacal showings, on a circle so different, and yet, in its own path, exhibiting the same story so vividly and so fully, how can we otherwise conclude but that here is proof of a purpose, and of the operation of some great master mind at once familiar with the whole Gospel scheme and with the whole system of the starry economies ?

But if we take the conclusion which thus presses upon our acceptance, then we might also reasonably expect to find other recognitions of it, and to be able to trace the same in the ancient symbolisms of the earthly economies also. And here too we only need to look to find many remarkable facts.

THE PRIMEVAL PATRIARCHS.

Take, for example, the names of the ante diluvian patriarchs as given in the fifth chapter of Genesis. From early Christian antiquity these have been held to contain a synopsis of the whole Gospel story. These names all have meanings; and those meanings, taken in their historic order, indicate the main things in the history of our redemption. But who would anticipate, without being told it, that these names and their meanings equally correspond with the Zodiac in the senses in which I have been explaining them?

Adam means the bright, the excellent, the godlike, and also to suffer death. And who is the fountain and soul of our salvation but another Adam, the brightness of the Father's glory and the express image of His person, given to die for our sins? But this is the picture of the Seed of the woman in *Virgo*, glorious as Spica, blessed as the Branch, precious as the Desired One, like God as Son of God, and the sufferer as Centaur and the Victim!

Seth means appointed in the place of another, a substitute, a compensation, a price. So Christ is our *Seth*, appointed to take our place as our substitute, making compensation for our sins, and paying the price by which we are redeemed. But this is the precise representation given in the sign of *Libra!*

Enos means mortal, suffering, afflicted. So Christ was the appointed bearer of our griefs, the carrier of our sorrows, stricken, smitten of God, and afflicted, by whose stripes healing comes to us. But this again is the exact showing we had in the sign of *Scorpio!*

Cainan means acquisition, forcible gaining of possession. So Christ's mission is to bruise the Serpent's head, to ride forth hereafter in joyous majesty as a warrior, whose right hand shows terrible things, and whose arrows are sharp in the heart of the King's enemies. But this is the precise exhibit in the sign of *Sagittarius!*

Mahalaleel means the display or praise of God. And so it is everywhere set forth as the particular outshining of God's glory and the special topic of His praise that Christ was "delivered for our offences and raised

again for our justification," thus begetting unto himself a peculiar people to "make known the riches of His glory," "to the intent that unto the principalities and powers in the heavenlies might be known by the Church the manifold wisdom of God," "to the praise of His glory." But this again is what we had in the sign of *Capricornus!*

Jared means the descending, the coming down, as the Holy Ghost shed forth to quicken and energize humanity, according to the promise. But this was the showing which we had in *Aquarius!*

Enoch means consecrated, initiated, taught, trained, and this is what characterizes the Church of all ages. To that of old time and to that of our dispensation it could equally be said: "Ye are a chosen generation, a royal priesthood, an holy nation, a peculiar people, that ye should show forth the praises of Him who hath called you out of darkness into His marvellous light" (1 Pet. 2: 9). But this is the very subject of the sign of *Pisces!*

Methuselah means released from death. So Christ appeared to John in the visions of the Apocalypse as the Lamb standing in the midst of the throne, marked as having been slain, but invested with the perfection of power, wisdom, and divine endowment, and having also the keys of Death and of Hades to release and bring forth all His people to the same heavenly life. But this, again, is the very presentation made in the sign of *Aries!*

Lamech means the strong, the mighty, the wild and invincible overthrower. And so Christ is to come "travelling in the greatness of His strength," "with power and great glory," to execute judgment upon the Enemy, to make the apostate nations drink the cup of His indignation, and to tread the winepress of the wrath of Almighty God, till the mountains are melted with blood. But this is the exact presentation which we had in the sign of *Taurus!*

Noah means *rest*. And so there remaineth a rest for the people of God after the wicked are destroyed—a calm repose with our Redeemer when we reach the farther shore of the boisterous sea of this world—an everlasting union with the Lord as His bride and wife.

But this is the very theme of the sign of *Gemini !*

This exhausts ten signs of the Zodiac in their order; and if we would have names similarly answering to the remaining two, Shem and Arphaxad, in whom the line of the promised Messiah was continued after Noah, may serve to furnish them.

Shem means *name, renown,* the standard of empire, the symbol of an established kingdom; just as is predicted of the glorious kingdom to be given to the saints. But this is the subject given in the sign of *Cancer !* And *Arphaxad* means the strength, the stronghold of the assembly; which again is the import of the sign of *Leo !*

It is marvellous that things should be so; but here are the facts, and they could by no possibility have been what they are by mere accident. There must needs have been great intelligence thus to fit what we might call accidents of earth with such elaborations of signs in the heavens, to utter and record in both the full-length evangelic story. Nor could that intelligence have achieved such a work unhelped by the Spirit of Him who alone knows the end of all things from the beginning.

The Twelve Tribes of Israel

Likewise in the names of Jacob's sons in his prophetic blessings on them (Gen. 49), in the corresponding song of Moses on the several tribes of Israel (Deut. 33), on the banners borne by these tribes in their march through the wilderness from Egypt to Canaan, and in the jewels of the breastplate of their officiating high priest, do we again find distinct correspondence to the celestial signs, just as I have been identifying and describing them. I may not enter now upon the full showing in these instances. I state only a few elements of the presentation.

Zebulon means *dwelling,* the choosing and entering upon a home. Jacob blessed Zebulon as to dwell at the seas as a haven for the ships. Moses sung of his joyful going forth. His jewel representative was *Bareketh, glittering, bright.* So Christ is the brightness of the Father's glory, who, when He entered upon His ministry of light and salvation, selected Zebulon as its home-centre, and on those shores opened out His brightness, so that the land of Zebulon beheld a great light come to dwell there as Lord and Saviour. But all this is in thorough correspondence with what hung prophetic in the sky in the sign of *Virgo.*

The next succeeding sign did not appear on any of the standards of Israel, for Levi had no separate banner. The sanctuary itself was Levi's ensign. His business was to take care of that, and there to offer sacrifices for the people's sins. But all the more expressively did he thus bear aloft the showing of redemption's price, just as we found it signalized in *Libra.* He kept the balances of the sanctuary.

Dan means *judge,* administering as a judge. Jacob describes him as judging and punishing, and as a serpent and adder by the way that biteth the horses' heels. Moses refers to him as a lion's whelp, leaping from Bashan. His emblem was the serpent, and the whole description concerning him answers to *Scorpio,* which was the place assigned him in the Jewish Zodiac.

In the same way Asher answers to *Sagittarius.* His jewel representative is called *Shoham,* the lively, the strong, and his name means the blessed, the happy, the triumphant going forth. Moses speaks of him as approved and prospered, dipping his foot in oil, wearing shoes of iron and brass, and riding forth in the strength of the God of Jeshurun, precisely as the picture is in *Sagittarius.*

Naphtali is "a hind," a wrestler with death, let go to drop and die, but filled with favor and blessing nevertheless; falling, yet joyfully bringing forth abundant new life and gladness by his "goodly words;" which is the showing in *Capricornus.*

Reuben in like manner corresponds to *Aquarius.* His name means *Behold a son,* new being. Jacob speaks of him as the beginning of strength and excellence, going on to excel as water flows. His jewel was *Nophek, the pouring forth,* as water and light.

Simeon means *hearing and obeying.* Jacob associates Levi with him, signifying the united, joined together, bound; and Moses assigns them the blessing of the prophetic lights and perfections; all of which answers to the Church as pictured in the sign of *Pisces*.

So Gad is *Aries*. The name means *the seer*, as the Lamb has "seven eyes." He is pierced, but overcomes at the last. He is blessed, seated as a lawgiver, dwelling as a lion. His jewel was the *diamond*, cutting and breaking, as well as shining. With the heads of the people he executes the justice and judgments of the Lord with Israel—that is, with the Church. All of which is precisely the showing in the sign of *Aries*.

Joseph is *Taurus*, the reem. Ephraim and Manasseh are his two great horns, pushing the people to the ends of the earth. The arms of his hands are made strong by the mighty God of Jacob. His glory is like the firstlings of the herd. His jewel-sign signifies *tongues of fire*. The two pictures are exactly identical.

Benjamin is *Gemini*. He had two names, as Gemini has two figures—Benjamin, *son of the right hand*, and Benoni, *son of my sorrow*, which together describe Christ and the Church He has "begotten by His sorrows.' Both are the beloved of the Lord, the latter dwelling between the shoulders of the other, sheltered and blessed by Jehovah all the day long, in the morning devouring the prey like a ravening wolf, and in the evening dividing the spoils.

Issachar means *recompense*. His jewel representative is *Pitdah, reward*. Jacob speaks of him as a strong ass resting between the burdens of treasure. He sees his resting-place that it is good. Moses describes him as rejoicing in his tents, to whose mountains the people come with sacrifices of righteousness, and to suck the abundance of the seas and the yet hidden treasures on the shore. All these presentations answer throughout to *Cancer*.

And in all the given particulars Judah is *Leo*. His name means the praise and glory and majesty of God. His banner bore the sign of the rampant lion. His jewel representative was the *ruby*, the symbol of blood-shedding unto victory. And Jacob describes him as the *lion*, the tearer in pieces, the glo-rious victor, the same as exhibited in the sign of *Leo*.

THE NEW JERUSALEM

And when we come to the New Testament we not only find the images of the constellations repeatedly employed in the same sense and application as in our interpretations of the signs, but also systematically placed together, if not in the twelve Apostles of the Lamb, yet in the twelve jewels which make up the foundations of the New Jerusalem, in which are the names of those Apostles. I am not sufficient master of the lore respecting precious stones to verify all the particulars involved, but, availing myself of several lists which claim to give the facts, I find the reading here just as distinct and marvellous as anywhere else.

The Apostle says, "The first foundation was *jasper*," which he describes as "a stone most precious," bright and clear. This reminds us at once of *Spica*, the bright and precious Seed of the woman. The meaning of *jasper* is said to be *coming to bruise and be bruised*—the same story of the coming of the precious Seed of the woman as set forth in Virgo.

"The second, *sapphire*," which means *number*, the count of price and weight; which is Libra.

"The third, *chalcedony*," which means *affliction, torture*; and this is the showing in Scorpio.

"The fourth, *emerald*," which means *defending*, keeping as a mighty protector; and this is the picture in Sagittarius.

"The fifth, *sardonyx*," which means *the Prince smitten*; the same as in Capricornus.

"The sixth, *sardius*," which means *the power issuing forth*; and so is the parallel of Aquarius.

"The seventh, *chrysolite*," which means *He who binds, who holds with bands*, the bound together; and this answers to Pisces.

"The eighth, *beryl*," which means *the Son, the first-born, the exalted Head*; corresponding precisely with the sign of Aries.

"The ninth, *topaz*," the distinguished gem

of Ethiopia, which signifies *dashing in pieces;* as we saw in Taurus.

"The tenth, *chrysoprasus,*" nearly the same as chrysolite, meaning *they who are united;* which is Gemini.

"The eleventh, *jacinth,*" which means *possessing,* He shall possess; just as we saw in Cancer.

"The twelfth, *amethyst,*" which means *He that destroys,* destroyer of the destroyer; which is Leo.

Now, if we should set ourselves with all the genius and thought we can by any means command, could we possibly express more clearly or fully by twelve stones the characteristics of the twelve signs of the Zodiac, as I have explained them in these *Lectures,* than we thus find them set forth by these twelve jewels of the foundation of the New Jerusalem? Nay, upon what else could the golden and eternal home of God's redeemed ones be built but on these precious jewels of the person, the character, the offices, the work, and the achievements of that illustrious Seed of the woman in whom standeth our salvation? It is wonder on wonder that these precious stones are there, with just this significance; but, having this significance, and epitomizing as they do the whole redemption-history from first to last, I should wonder all the more if this architectural picture of the eternal home and blessedness of the saints did not contain them as its foundation. And being there, in the precise order, and in full recognition of the precise imagery and symbolic import, of the twelve signs of the circling year of time, they give the stamp and seal of the final revelation of the sublime and finished result of all that fills the perturbed ages of this world to the reality of what I have been seeking to show; to wit, that the mystic garniture of these heavens, which modern science in its vanity has chosen to regard as crude and grotesque scribbling, is verily a writing of God, indited by His Spirit from the beginning to hold up to the whole race of man, in all its branches and generations, what He has also caused to be recorded in the Word deposited with His own particular people touching the course and outcome of all His grand purposes in Jesus Christ our Lord.

Thus, then, has the great Almighty inscribed the works of Nature with the symbols and signs of His more precious works of grace, and shown us "the secrets of wisdom, that they are double to that which is."

" Wisdom ! that bright intelligence, which sat
    Supreme when, with His golden compasses,
    Th' Eternal planned the fabric of the world,
    Produced His fair idea into light,
    And said that all was good ! Wisdom, blest beam !
    The brightness of the everlasting light !
    The spotless mirror of the power of God !
    The reflex image of the all-perfect Mind !
    A stream translucent, flowing from the source
    Of glory infinite—a cloudless light !"

16

PRIMEVAL MAN

With the ancient is wisdom.
—Job 12:12

AFTER what we have now seen of the presentations and connections of the ancient astronomy, the question of its origin becomes one of great interest and importance. Who framed this system? Who first so accurately observed these features of Nature's celestial economies, and so sublimely wove them together into one great scheme, at once so true to fact and so full of prophetic and evangelic significance? Whence has all this wisdom come? Our investigations would be left incomplete if we did not now endeavor to gather together what information exists touching these inquiries.

Astronomy is unquestionably one of the most ancient of the sciences. Its history runs back into an antiquity so remote and dim that the greatest of astronomers are unable to tell its source or beginning. Its existence is traceable in all known ages and among all nations, with all its main features settled and fixed from the most distant periods. Learned antiquarians of modern times have searched every page of heathen mythology, ransacked all the legends of poetry and fable, traversed all the religions, sciences, customs, and traditions of every nation, tribe, and people, and used the best sources of historic information the earth affords, with a view to rescue the matter from the heavy mists hanging over it; but with no further success than to trace it back to certain Chaldean shepherds who lived in a very early period of the world; but everything else concerning it and them is left undiscovered and untold. Had they first grasped the real meaning and intent of these primeval inventions of astronomic science, or entertained an idea of its true connections, they doubtless would have been able to reach much more definite knowledge on the subject.

THE FACTS STATED

We now have monumental evidence, in the Great Pyramid of Gizeh, that a very complete and sublime knowledge of the structure and economy of the visible universe, inclusive of a very exact astronomy, was by some means known to the great architect of that unrivalled edifice, built twenty-one hundred and seventy years before the birth of Christ. It is also a matter of accredited record that when Alexander took Babylon, Calisthenes, the philosopher who accompanied the expedition, found there certain astronomical observations made by the Chaldeans over nineteen hundred years before that time, which was over twenty-two hundred years before our era, and near to the great dispersion of mankind by the confusion of tongues. Cassini refers to Philo for the assertion that "Terah, the father of Abraham, who lived more than a hundred years with Noah, had much studied astronomy, and taught it to Abraham," who, according to Josephus and others, taught it to the Egyptians during his sojourn in that country. It is well known that the religion of the ancient Babylonians and contiguous peoples, which consisted of the worship of the heavenly bodies, was based throughout on astronomy, astrology, and the starry configurations—so much so that one was an essential part of the other, and the two were really one. But it is now demonstrated, from the recovered remains of these ancient peoples, that the Chaldean religion and mythology were already wrought out in a complete and finished system as early as two thousand years before the beginning of our era, so that a settled astronomical science must necessarily have existed a considerable period prior to that date.

The book of Job, so far as we can ascertain, is the oldest book now in the world; and it is a book which, more than all other books of Holy Scripture, abounds in astronomical allusions. Distinct and unmistakable references are contained in it to the constellations as we still have them. We there read of "*Arcturus* with his sons," "the sweet influences of *Pleiades*," "the bands of *Orion*," and "the fleeing *Serpent*." We there likewise read of "*Mazzaroth*," with its "seasons"—*stations, stopping-places*—which, according to the margin of our English Bible, the Jewish Targum, and the ablest Christian interpreters, is nothing more nor less than the Solar Zodiac. Astronomy, even as we now have it, was therefore established and well understood in Job's day. Nay, from the various astronomical references in the book different astronomers claim to be able to calculate the time in which Job lived, which they give as from B.C. 2100–2200. (See *Miracle in Stone*, pp. 203–206.)

On the faith of the Thebaic astronomers Ptolemy records an observation of the heliacal rising of Sirius on the fourth day after the summer solstice twenty-two hundred and fifty years before Christ, which could not have been made if there had not been among men a high degree of astronomical knowledge preceding that date.

Dr. Seyffarth claims it as solid truth that in the distribution of the letters in the primitive alphabet, which was essentially the same in all nations, there is a record of the celestial presentations which can occur but once in millions of years, and which designates the year, month, and day when Noah came out of the ark. Our astronomy must therefore have existed in and before Noah's time.

From internal evidences in the particular framework and order of the Solar and Lunar Zodiacs, Bailly was thoroughly convinced of a state of the heavens at the time these Zodiacs were formed which can occur only at intervals of more than twenty-five thousand years, but which really did exist in and about four thousand years before the Christian era. Nouet, on similar grounds, came to the same conclusion. (See also *Miracle in Stone*, pp. 140 seq.)

On the basis of astronomy's own records, apart from all other testimony, we are thus inevitably carried back to a period within the lifetime of Adam and his sons for the original of the Zodiac, and, with it, of the whole system of our astronomy.

THE TRADITIONS.

And to this agree the ancient sayings and worthiest traditions of the race. The best philosophers, the most honored poets, and the historians who have penetrated the deepest into the beginnings of humanity unite in commencing man with God and in close and happy fellowship and communion with the Divine Intelligence. Everywhere throughout the world of primitive nations the first of men were the greatest of men, the wisest, the divinest, and the most worshipped; and the first age was the Golden Age.

Plato says: "Our first parent was the greatest philosopher that ever existed." Baleus says: "From Adam all good arts and human wisdom flowed, as from their fountain. *He was the first that discovered the motions of the celestial bodies,* and all other creatures. From his school proceeded whatever good arts and wisdom were afterward propagated by our fathers unto mankind; so that whatever astronomy, geometry, and other arts contain in them, he knew the whole thereof." Keckerman doubts not that "our first parents delivered over to their posterity, together with other sciences, even logic also; specially seeing they who were nearest the origin of all things had an intellect so much the more excellent than ours by how much the more they excelled us in length of life, firmitude of health, and in air and food."

We learn from Medhurst that "in the early Chinese histories the first man, named *Pwanroo,* is said to have been produced soon after the period of emptiness and confusion, and that he knew intuitively the relative proportions of heaven and earth, with the principles of creation and transmutation." The Vendidad of the Parsis affirms that God conversed with Yima, the great shepherd, the first man, and taught him all the law of Nature and religion. Moreri gives it as the settled tradition that "Adam had a perfect knowledge of sciences, and chiefly of what related to the stars, which he taught his children."

The Jews hold it among their traditions that Adam wrote a book concerning the creation of the world, and another on the Deity. Kissæus, an Arabian writer, gives it as among the teachings of his people that Abraham had in his possession certain sacred writings of Adam, Seth, and Enoch, in which were "laws and promises, threatenings from God, and predictions of many events;" and it is affirmed of Abraham that he taught astronomy to the Egyptian priests at Heliopolis.

From the ancient fragments of Berosus, Polyhistor, and Sanchoniathon, as well as from the lately-recovered Assyrian tablets, we learn of the existence of sacred records which had descended from knowing men of the earliest times, who taught the world all the wisdom it had, and on whose instructions and institutes none were able to improve, but from which there was a constant tendency to apostatize.

The ancient Egyptians called all their kings *Pharaoh, the Sun,* but their traditions make Menes, the first of their kings, the greatest sun, from whom all wisdom and illumination came to them. And Menes was a very near descendant of Noah, through whom the primeval wisdom was brought over from beyond the Flood, and hence from the first fathers of the race.

From Adam sprang Seth, who, according to Josephus and more ancient records, followed his father in the pursuit of wisdom, as did also his own descendants. It is said in so many words that "they were the inventors of that peculiar sort of wisdom which is concerned with the heavenly bodies and their πάθη καὶ συμπτώματα—*condition and indications.*" Hornius says: "The first mention of letters falls upon Seth's times; who, being mindful of his father's prophecy foretelling the universal dissolution of things, the one by the Deluge, and the other by fire, being not unwilling to extinguish his famous inventions concerning the stars, he thought of some monument to which he might concredit these mysteries."

Enoch is also specially credited with special wisdom and writing, particularly as relating to astronomy and prophecy. Bochart writes: "I cannot but add what is found concerning the same Enoch in Eusebius, out of Eupolemus, of the Jews. He says that Abraham, when he taught astrology [astronomy] and other sciences at Heliopolis, affirmed that the Babylonians attributed the invention of the same to Enoch; and that the Grecians attribute the invention to *Atlas,* the same with Enoch." Macinus, Abulfaragius, and other Arab writers say that Enoch was called *Edris,* the sage, the illustrious, and that he was skilled in astronomy and other sciences. Baleus tells us that he was famous for prophecy, and is reported as having written books on divine matters. The Jews call him the Great Scribe, and say that he wrote books on sacred wisdom, especially on astronomy. That he did record certain prophecies is attested by the Epistle of Jude, which gives a quotation from him. Origen also tells us that it was asserted in the book of Enoch that in the time of that patriarch the constellations were already named and divided. Arab and Egyptian authors make him the same as the older Hermes—Hermes Trismegistus, the triply-great Shepherd—through whom the wisdom of the stars and other sciences were handed down to his posterity.

It was the remark of Gale on these and such-like traditions and fragments : " We need no way doubt but that Noah had been fully instructed by Church-tradition from his godly predecessors, Methuselah, Enoch, and Seth, touching the creation of the world by God, and particularly touching the excellent fabric of the heavens, the nature of those celestial bodies, their harmonious motion and order— that these celestial had a mighty influence on all sublunary bodies, etc. These and such like considerations, which greatly conduced to the enhancing of the wisdom, power, and goodness of God, we may not doubt were very frequent in the mouths of those sons of God before and after the Flood. And it is the opinion of some that the whole story of the creation written by Moses was conveyed down even from Adam to his time by a constant, uninterrupted tradition to the holy seed and Church in all ages."

Eugubinus, treating of the succession of doctrine from the world's beginning, says : " As there is one Principle of things, so also there has been one and the same science of Him at all times amongst all, as both reason and monuments of many nations and letters testify. This science, springing partly from the first origin of men, has been devolved through all ages unto posterity. The most true supputation of times proves that Methuselah lived and might converse with Adam, as Noah with Methuselah. Therefore Noah saw and heard things before the Flood. Moreover, before Noah died Abraham was fifty

years old. Neither may we conceive that this most pious man and his holy seed would conceal things of so great moment and so worthy to be known and remembered. Therefore from this most true cause it is most equal that the great science of divine and human affairs should be deduced unto following ages, though greatly overcome by barbarism, etc. . . . Therefore, that there has been one and the same wisdom always in all men we endeavor to persuade, not only by these reasons, but also by those many and great examples whereby we behold some vestiges of the truth scattered throughout all nations. Abraham was a Chaldean in whose family the ancient theology and the traditions of the fathers, whereof he was heir, remained. All these things being retained by Noah and his sons —whence also flowed the piety and wisdom of Job—were seen and heard by Abraham, and so passed unto his posterity" (quoted by Gale).

BIBLE REPRESENTATIONS

According to the Scriptures, Adam lived about seven hundred years contemporaneously with his son Seth, and about three hundred years contemporaneously with Enoch, and died only about one hundred years before Noah was born. All these were holy prophets. From Luke (1 : 69, 70) and Acts (3 : 21) we learn that there were inspired divine teachers " from the foundation of the world "—" since the world began." Whoever may be included in the list, Adam, Seth, and Enoch were by far the greatest and the most illustrious of them.

Adam from the first was in perfect fellowship with the Divine Intelligence, and knew all things that came before him by an intuitive divine insight into their whole nature and intention. He needed no instructors, for the light of God shone clear and unclouded upon his soul. His whole being was in most thorough accord with God and with the mind of God, for he was the complete image of God. His wisdom and knowledge were necessarily higher by far than that of any other mere man that ever lived. Even Peter Bayle agrees that it is not contrary to the analogy of faith nor to probability, and very proper to the narrative in Genesis, to believe that Adam came out of the hands of his Creator indued with innate science, and that he did not lose it by sin ; as the bad angels are not less knowing since their fall, and as crimes of learned persons do not deprive them of that knowledge they enjoyed before.   He also passes it as determined that the speculative understanding of the first man was endowed with all the philosophical and mathematical knowledge of which human nature is naturally capable.

Gale gives it as made out from the Mosaic record that Adam without all peradventure was the greatest amongst mere mortals that ever the world possessed, exactly prying into the very natures of things, and there contemplating those glorious ideas and characters of created light and order which the increated Light and Divine Wisdom had impressed thereon ; and thence he could immediately collect and form the same into a complete system and body of philosophy, as also most methodically branch forth the same into the particular sciences.   Hornius argues that "Adam, being constituted in this theatre of the universe, was ignorant of nothing that pertained to the mystery of Nature."

It is also a matter of inspired record that God gave to Adam special revelations.   After his fall Jehovah made known to him His purposes concerning the Serpent and its seed and the woman and her Seed.   The whole Gospel revelation and promise was therein included, and was given to him, not for himself alone, but to be made known to all his posterity as the great and only hope of man.

What Adam knew, Seth would thus also know, and so would Enoch.   And living contemporaneously together for more than two, three, or five ordinary lifetimes, there was the sublimest opportunity for them to observe, construct, and mature just such a system as astronomy presents, inwoven as it is with all the great facts, features, and hopes embraced in the promised redemption by the Seed of the woman.   In fact, it was the one great and only opportunity in the history of our race for such an accomplishment.

We know from Luke and Acts that every one of these primeval prophets did speak and prophesy of the raising up of "an Horn of salvation for us," the coming of Christ to suffer, to bring times of refreshing from the presence of the Lord, and eventually to work "the restitution of all things."   (Compare Luke 1 : 67–79; Acts 3 : 18–26; Jude 15.) The Bible tells us especially of Enoch's preeminent intimacy and life-communion with God, and recites certain of his predictions which run on the precise theme we have been reading from the constellations.

And what Adam and his believing children did not know simply as men, they would still know as prophets, which they certainly were

REASONABLENESS OF THE CASE

Going back, then, to that period of the world to which we must needs go for the origin of astronomy and the first fixing of its great foundation-elements, we find there the men duly capacitated for the work, duly supplied with motive and opportunity to do it, and such real prophets of God that in entering upon it from sacred impulse they would not fail of divine help in the matter, or of preservation from all mistake.   Under God, they were the great founders of the world, and were fully alive to the fact.   They were the great appointed teachers of the world from the very nature of the case.   They were the first great prophets of the world, the original recipients of the revelation of God's purposes of redemption through the promised Seed of the woman, and as such were under bonds to make known the facts, explain their import, and use every means of recording and transmitting to all men the knowledge of them.   They lived nearly a thousand years, and so had ample time for observation, study, and thorough elaboration to bring the work to finished perfection before being required to leave it.   And over them were the virgin stars, only waiting to be named and grouped, and hung with the records and symbols of the precious treasures of promise and prophecy on which the world's hopes depended, that they might become the everlasting witnesses to men of the God-given faith and hopes which shone in the serene imaginations of these great grand fathers of all sacred prophets. Nor can I see why a single shade of doubt should linger in our minds that these verily were the men who drew these celestial hieroglyphics, named and grouped the stars, laid out the Zodiacs and their signs, and made the heavens a picture-gallery for all the world, the first and greatest that ever was made, that there mankind might gaze and read the wondrous story of the promised Redeemer, the redemption, and the redeemed.

And this, and this only, will account for the sacred reverence in which all the ancient peoples held these starry emblems, and even fell to worshipping them and ascribing to them all sorts of divine and prophetic virtues. If put there by inspired prophets, and explained by them as the symbols of the divinest things of God's revelation and promises, then can we understand why they were so much made of in the sacred mysteries, why they were so seriously consulted as horoscopes, and why the early nations lapsed into the idolatry of worshipping them as gods. They are of holiest origin, and relate to the dearest hopes and anticipations of man; therefore have they been so prized in all the ages, and therefore the Perverter of all good set himself to turn them to evil, for which he could have found neither hold nor leverage had not some great and commanding sacredness gone before to seat them in the esteem of men.

Claimed to be from God

It was also the common and accepted doctrine of antiquity that the constellations were divine in origin and sacred in character. They are woven in with all the old ethnic religions. Much as heathenism has perverted them to false worship, it has ever held to the belief that they are from God—manifestations of the one supreme and eternal Deity. Even Pluche agrees that all heathenism is "nothing but the religion of the patriarchs corrupted by extravagant additions, transforming the signs, or the symbolic men and animals, into so many gods, with which their imagination peopled the heaven." But this assumes and implies that these signs in the hands of the patriarchs themselves were connected with their relig-

ion; and their religion being divine, so must these signs connected with it have been.

The Greek Sallustius treats of the myths and the constellations as undoubtedly of divine origin, and represents the chief poets through whom they came as *prophets*—persons to whom Deity was propitious, and who were really θεοληπτοι—*divinely-inspired men.*

The Roman Cicero affirms that these things were explained in the sacred mysteries as part of a divine instruction how to live in peace and die in hope, and hence as from God himself.

Maimonides states that the old Jewish fathers considered and held these signs in the heavens to be of divine original.

Josephus and the Arabian authors give it as a matter of historic truth that the primeval prophets invented these signs.

Gale lays it down as quite certain that " the first human institutors or authors of philosophy were indeed divinely illuminated; so that the wisdom we find scattered up and down among the pagan philosophers was but borrowed and derived from those divine lights who were enlightened by the Divine Word—that Life and Light of men which shined in the darkness." He also adds that "both Albertus and Sixtus Senensis collect that our Saviour was in some manner adumbrated in the Gentile fables and figures," implying that they certainly were originally from the Spirit of prophecy.

The sacred Bundahis of the Parsis gives an account of the formation of the Solar and Lunar Zodiacs, and mentions by name the twelve signs of the one, almost entirely as we now have them, and the twenty-eight divisions of the other, together with their Zend names, and asserts and claims that both, together with the assignment of the stars to each, were the work of *Auharmazd*, the Creator, "supreme in omniscience and goodness and unrivalled in glory;" and says that such was the teaching of Zorathost, the great traditional prophet of God.

The same is asserted and claimed in the Chaldean tablets of late recovered from the ruins of ancient Assyria and Babylon. Fragments of a whole library of books written on tiles or tablets of pottery, now in the British Museum, have been brought to light, and their cuneiform records deciphered. Among them is a poetic legend of *Izdubar*, supposed to be the same as Nimrod, which is framed throughout to the twelve signs of the Zodiac, proving that the Zodiac existed and was most highly prized when that legend was written, certainly not less than two thousand years before Christ.

But more important than this is a series on the six days of the Creation, called " the Chaldean Genesis," almost the same in substance with the Mosaic account, and certainly dating beyond two thousand years before the Christian era. Smith and Sayce state concerning this series that " the fifth tablet relates how GOD *created the constellations of the stars, the signs of the Zodiac*, the planets and other stars, the moon and the sun." The whole record runs thus:

" *Anu* [the supreme and ever-living God] made suitable the mansions of the (seven) great gods. [The signs of the Zodiac were always considered by the heathen nations the Mansions, stations, or resting-places of the seven planets, deemed the great gods.] The stars He placed in them. The *lumasi, their animal appearance* [figures], *He fixed*. He arranged the year according to the bounds, the limits [of the Zodiac], *which He defined*. For each of the twelve months three stars, or rows of stars [Decans], *He fixed*. From the day when the year issues forth unto the close *He marked the mansions* [Zodiacal stations] of the wandering stars (planets), to know their courses, that they might not err or deflect at all."

There can be no question of the reference in this extract to the Zodiac, its twelve signs, and the system of the constellations in general, including their figures. It answers to the declaration in Genesis that God placed the starry lights in the firmament, and said, " *Let them be for signs.*" And the remarkable point in the case is, that it was the sacred opinion and settled belief of those who originally composed what these tablets record that the Zodiac, with its twelve signs, and the three extra rows of the constellations and the

pictures designating them, were all the work of Almighty God himself by inspiration, impulse, and direction of His Spirit. It is indeed nothing more than we read out of Job, who wrote about the same period or a little earlier; but it is as if old Babylonia had risen up from its grave of ages to corroborate and attest the meaning which we took from the patriarch of Uz, where he gives it as part of Jehovah's glory that " by His Spirit *He* garnished the heavens," and that " *His hand* hath formed the fleeing Serpent," and hence all these celestial emblems (Job 26 : 13).*

* The ordinary explanations of the origin of these ancient pictures extend very little further than the Zodiac; but even as to that our men of science have nothing to give save a few jejune imaginings, lame and absurd in themselves, and without the slightest show of fact on which to lean.

It is said that herdsmen used to take great delight in their sheep and cattle as they led them forth in spring-time, and in the mating and nesting of the birds as the summer drew on, and so they gave the signs of a Ram, a Bull, and two entwined youths to the months of March, April, and May ! Men saw, we are told, that toward the end of June the sun began to come down from the north toward the south, which for some unknown reason they likened to a backward movement, and so gave that month the sign of the Crab, because the crab is apt to move backward ! The heat in July became fierce, and then, we are assured, the lions used to come to the river to quench their thirst, and so that month obtained the sign of the Lion ! Then in August, it is supposed, the people began to harvest or to sow their fields, and so they gave that month the sign of a prostrate young woman with sprigs of wheat in one hand and a branch in the other ! In September, it is said, they found the days and nights nearly equal, so they drew for that month the sign of the Scales, though the same thing in March had no sign, and these equal balances, unfortunately for the myth, have one side up and the other down ! October, it is said, was plentiful in fruits, and many people got sick, so they marked that month with the sign of the Scorpion ! November, it is said, was the month for hunting, and so they marked it with the sign of a Horseman with bow and arrow. In December, we are told, people noticed the sun again ascending toward the north, and so they marked that month with the sign of a Goat, because goats like to climb rocks ! January was found to be a wet and dreary month, so they gave it the sign of the Waterman ! And in February we are told that people went a-fishing, and so that month received the sign of the two Fishes ! This is the philosophy of the twelve signs as given in our books of science.

But then how came these signs to be the same in all parts of the earth in all the ages through ? And how comes it that there is not a country under the sun where these interpretations all fit ? And how did men know to name these months or to place these figures if the sphere had not been previously defined and fixed ? And what of the thirty-six remaining constellations and their equally conspicuous figures ? Where did they all come from, and what do they mean ? The Greek myths on the subject are out of the question here. These extra-Zodiacal constellations are as old as the Zodiac itself, and everywhere, in the earliest records as in the latest, appear along with it. And what of the names of the stars, which, for the most part, are as old as the signs, but tell quite another story from anything that men have thus given as the *rationale* of these celestial hieroglyphics ? And then, again, how did it happen that the people who thus fancifully characterized the months immediately wheeled about and began to consult as oracles and to worship as great divinities the very figures which they had themselves hung up ? Such philosophy will not hold together. It is simply amazing that learned men should have the face to put it forth for rational acceptance. It is so purely

THE STAR-RECORD ITSELF.

And the story which these astronomic signs and pictures tell is in all respects so worthy of a divine origin, and so much above man's science, that we may well consider the whole thing divine. It is precisely the same that we find in the Word, about whose divine source we have no question. And if it was a fitting thing for the great Lord of all to employ His Spirit to cause these matters of salvation to be authentically recorded in the books committed to His later peoples, why was it not equally befitting His gracious almightiness to do the same in the case of His primeval prophets, that all mankind in all the ages might ever have before their eyes the abiding testimony of His pristine revelations concerning that same Messiah "of whom Moses in the Law and the Prophets did write"?

And what if the key to the showings was afterward lost, and men only misread and perverted what was so sublimely recorded? The same has occurred again and again with the scriptural records; and why should the apostasies in the one case argue differently from what they do in the other? The failures and sins of men do not unmake the truth of God, neither do their misuses and perversions of His gifts disprove their divine source or good intent. The turning of Israel's calling and sacred institutes into a hypocritical, murderous, and depraved Pharisaism, which killed the Son of God and slew His holy Apostles, did not unmake the divine legation of Moses nor the heavenly inspiration of the holy prophets who spent their lives building Israel into a kingdom for the Lord. The perversion of Christianity into an imperial popedom, an Antichrist, and a tyrannous persecution of the saints of God by His own alleged vicegerent did not prove Jesus of Nazareth an impostor nor the testimony of His Apostles undivine or untrue. And if men in like manner have perverted these primeval records in the stars, and turned the showings of promised salvation into an instrument of damning superstition, and twisted a divine astronomy into a devilish astrology, and de-

veloped a bloody paganism out of a primitive evangelism, what is it else than the depravity of man and the trick of the great Deceiver belying God, but by no means discrediting or unmaking the divinity, the mercifulness, or the gracious ampleness of good intent in the sublime original?

Volney insists, and with good reason, that everywhere in antiquity there was a cherished tradition of an expected Conqueror of the Serpent, who was to come as a divine person, born of a woman; and that this tradition is most clearly reflected in the constellations and in all the heathen mythologies throughout the world. Dupuis has collected numerous ancient authorities, abundantly proving that in all nations this tradition, with singular particularity of details, always prevailed; that this divine Person, born of a woman, was to be a great sufferer in His conflict with the Serpent, but would triumph gloriously at the last; and that this tradition is represented and recorded in the constellations.

By a world-wide testimony we are thus assured that this is verily the inwoven mystic essence of the primeval astronomy, the same that constitutes the essence of all that is written by inspiration in the books of the Bible.

And to the external testimony the internal substance and conditions correspond. In three grand parts or books, each with four grand chapters, and each chapter divided into four distinct sections, is this record given. Set out in brief, the contents would run thus:

BOOK FIRST—THE REDEEMER PROMISED

CHAPTER FIRST—VIRGO:

1. The Seed of the woman
2. The Desire of nations
3. The Man of double nature in humiliation
4. The exalted Shepherd and Harvester

CHAPTER SECOND—LIBRA:

1. Price to be paid
2. The Cross endured
3. The Victim slain
4. The Crown purchased

CHAPTER THIRD—SCORPIO:

1. Cleft in the conflict
2. The Serpent's coils
3. The struggle with the Enemy
4. The toiling Vanquisher of evil

CHAPTER FOURTH—SAGITTARIUS:

1. The double-natured One triumphing as a Warrior
2. He gladdens the heavens
3. He builds the fires of punishment
4. He casts down the Dragon

BOOK SECOND—THE REDEEMER'S PEOPLE

CHAPTER FIRST—CAPRICORNUS:

1. Life out of Death
2. The Arrow of God
3. Pierced and falling
4. Springing up again in abundant life

CHAPTER SECOND—AQUARIUS:

1. Life-waters from on high
2. Drinking in the heavenly flood
3. Carrying and speeding the Good News
4. Bearing aloft the Cross over all the earth

CHAPTER THIRD—PISCES:

1. Swimming in the heavenly waters
2. Upheld and governed by the Lamb
3. Head over all things to the Church
4. The intended Bride bound and exposed on earth

CHAPTER FOURTH—ARIES:

1. The Lamb entered on dominion
2. The Bride released and making ready
3. Satan bound
4. The Breaker triumphing

BOOK THIRD—REDEMPTION COMPLETED

CHAPTER FIRST—TAURUS:

1. The invincible Ruler come
2. The sublime Vanquisher
3. The River of Judgment
4. The all-ruling Shepherd

CHAPTER SECOND—GEMINI:

1. The Marriage of the Lamb
2. The Enemy trodden down
3. The Prince coming in glory
4. His princely following

CHAPTER THIRD—CANCER:

1. The Possession secured
2. Lesser Fold, the first-born, the rulers
3. Greater Fold, the after-born
4. The Heroes landed from their expedition, their toils and trials over

CHAPTER FOURTH—LEO:

1. The King aroused for the rending
2. The Serpent fleeing
3. The Bowl of Wrath upon him
4. His carcass devoured

Here is a marked order and symmetry of construction, a thoroughness of digestion, an assortment of elements, an evenness of balance, and an exhaustive comprehensiveness, not excelled by the highest inspired genius whose writings have come to us—an order befitting the God of order, and bearing in itself, in its three and fours, the expression of eternal Godhead moving and doing with reference to earth and man; whilst every topic in the twelve and twelve times three is a genuine Gospel topic, handled exactly as we find it in the writings of the Prophets and Apostles. There is nothing added and there is nothing left out. The whole story is complete—more complete than half the ministers in Christendom can tell it to-day with the whole volume of both Testaments before them, and after all the prophesying and preaching and fulfilling that has occurred in the five thousand years and more since these star-pictures were made.

INEVITABLE INFERENCES

"What shall we say, then, to these things?" Was primeval man a gorilla, a troglodyte, a brutish savage, a wild man without knowledge? The Zodiac and the constellations as arranged upon the ancient sphere furnish the foundations of all astronomy. No man since they were made has been able to improve upon them. All subsequent touches of them have been bungles and absurdities. They stand to-day securely planted among the profoundest stabilities contained in human science. And yet the evidences are that they have come down to us from that selfsame primeval man. Then primeval man knew the visible starry heavens as well as any other man since. Then primeval man could draw maps, and make pictures, and write books, and teach wisdom, and transmit thought and intelligence, just as successfully as the remoter progeny sprung from his blood. Then the doctrine that modern man is a mere evolution from savageism, the result of a self-moved activity to become, his makership his own, his intelligence a mere self-efflorescence, *is a lie.*

Our particular ancestors of two thousand years ago may have been but semi-civilized, having been long and remotely separated from the chief centres of population and enlightenment, and so it may have been in part with the progenitors of the Greeks and Romans; but the agencies and influences by which they were lifted, and their descendants brought to the heights of which we boast too much, were not originated and evolved from among themselves, apart from what they got from the more knowing world outside. Egypt, Phœnicia, Arabia, Assyria, Chaldea, India, and China of the olden times never were savage or uncivilized. Government, society, law, arts, and sciences go back to the beginnings of their history, and from them all later peoples have learned. As far as we have any traces of man's existence—and those traces go back as far as Adam—we have evidences of enlightenment as high and as true to Nature and fact as anything we know, and which is to this day the very backbone of much of the world's best and highest wisdom. The weight of the showing is, that primeval man was the truest model and representative of man, and that all human progress since, though upward in some things, has been in the main an unceasing deterioration.

All the world that came next after primeval man honored, and even worshipped, their first fathers as very gods of light, knowledge, and greatness. They pushed their veneration to a base idolatry indeed, but there was reason and deserved gratitude at the bottom of it. The world now-a-days regards such reverence as a weakness and a fault, and has swung off into a far meaner and baser idolatry of self, glorying in its earth-born gaslight as the superlative illumination, and floundering like the dazed moth around the flickering smoke-flame, as if the sun in the heavens were not half so bright and beautiful. Could Adam and Seth and Enoch and Noah appear among us, and take an inventory of our prevailing philosophies, the ways in which modern thinking practically runs, and the atheistic stuff which many would baptize with the name of wisdom, how would those venerable patriarchs sigh and lament and sicken over the degeneration of their posterity! What if we have found out that a wire magnetized at one end is instantly magnetized at the other end also? What if we have discovered that there is power in boiling water to push against confinement, and so to drive pistons and turn wheels? What if we have made up short-hand ways of putting lettering on paper and of multiplying impressions like autumn leaves? What if we have succeeded in making war-guns and implements of death such as they never saw and never wished to see? From the high standpoint of those primeval sages Noah would have to write again: "Behold, the earth is corrupt, for all flesh hath corrupted its ways." Intenser than ever would Enoch fulmine his ancient commination: "Behold, the Lord cometh with ten thousand of His saints to execute judgment upon this convict population, full of ungodly deeds and ungodly speeches, traducing the things which it knows not, and following only what it knows naturally as brute beasts." Whilst Adam's thoughts would needs turn inward with all the deeper self-reproach for having with open eyes started the spring whence has come all this earthiness and apostasy.

"What shall we say, then, to these things?" God certainly did not make man without at the same time beaming into him all the light and intelligence to equip him fully for all the requirements of the highest perfection of his being in his sphere, and for the intellectual and physical mastery of the whole earthly creation at the head of which he stood. That first man fell, but that fall did not obliterate from his intellect the knowledge which his Maker had previously shined into it. An apostate from Christianity does not thereby lose the knowledge he possessed. Judgment came upon Adam, and hard necessities, by reason of his transgression, but there was no obliteration of his intellectual treasures or his intellectual powers. Much as they have depreciated in transmission to his posterity, they were not blotted out of Adam himself. Neither did God cease to speak to him, or refuse to open up to him new and richer fields of wisdom to meet his condition as a sinner. Fallen Adam was still capable of redemption, and that redemption God meant to accomplish in the course of the ongoing ages and generations of the race. To save Adam it was necessary that Adam should know of it, and to save his posterity it was necessary that the same knowledge should be transmitted to them also. And as from him human life was multiplied, so to him it pertained as the great father to teach and transmit his sacred and saving wisdom with the multiplication of himself. In the nature and necessities of the case he was God's prophet to those born of him. Of all knowledge, the knowledge of the promised Redeemer was the most important and essential. Therefore God would not leave him in any ignorance as to that promised Redeemer, the nature of His work, and the results of His administrations. The whole Gospel, or none, he needed to know. The whole Gospel, if any, he would be most anxious to comprehend. The whole Gospel, as he got it from God and

hoped and rejoiced in it himself, he would be most concerned to teach to his children and to have securely recorded for all coming generations. Such devout and active fidelity was his interest and duty as a man and a prophet, and what God, according to all His word and promises, would certainly approve and bless and help. It would be in the line and spirit of all His subsequent inspirations vouchsafed to men that He should do for Adam in such a case even more than He did for Moses and Samuel and Isaiah and Daniel. And here, in the records and emblems of the stars, demonstrably dating back to Adam's time, and linked in with a true and admirable astronomy, we have what in every particular best resolves itself into a pictorial memorial of that promised Redeemer's character and achievements as then looked for and believed in. The things thus symbolized could never have become known from natural reason, neither could unaided man ever have made for them so perfect and sublime a record even after they were known. Then certainly God's hand was in it. Then divine revelation is a demonstrated reality. Then inspiration is an indestructible fact. And then these glorious stars take on the holier brightness as the sublime underwriters of our Scriptures, and as God's witnesses from beyond the gulf of ages to assure us there is no mistake in building on Jesus of Nazareth as our hope and our salvation. Well, then, might Zacharias sing:

"Blessed be the Lord God of Israel; for He hath visited and redeemed His people, and hath raised up an Horn of salvation for us in the house of His servant David; *as He spake by the mouth of His holy prophets, which have been since the world began!*" Luke 1: 68–70.

17

THE STAR OF BETHLEHEM

We have seen His star in the east, and are come to worship Him.
—Matthew 2:2

A LEARNED Christian antiquarian has expressed his belief " that far more conclusive proofs of the promise of a Redeemer can be found in the primeval traditions of our race than even in the Hebrew Scriptures." He may perhaps have expressed himself a little too strongly, for the Old Testament, rightly read, is very full of the Messianic hope. But it is a great mistake to consign to the Evil One the whole human family outside of Judaism prior to the time of Christ, and thus to brand almost the entire race with the mark of Cain. It may have the guise of orthodoxy, but it lacks the element of truth. The case which comes before us in connection with the text effectually confutes it.

It must also go very far toward establishing the doctrines which I have been propounding respecting the source and intent of the primeval astronomy to be able to find a case so clear and well authenticated in which the study and observation of the stars, in connection with the primitive traditions,

have served to fix in Gentile minds a living belief in a Virgin-born Redeemer—a knowledge so complete as to embrace the time and place of His advent and to bring them in humble adoration around His infant cradle. Nor can we do better, in bringing these studies to a close, than by devoting a final Lecture to the consideration of this case.

THE VISIT OF THE MAGI

For a thousand years and more Christendom has been inquiring and wondering, Who were "the wise men from the East" that came to Jerusalem asking about a new-born Jewish Prince? How came they to know about Him? What were those starry indications to which they referred as having induced them to make such costly and laborious search for Him? What were the sources of illumination by which they were thus brought to honor and worship Him in His lowly infant couch? For fourteen hundred years and more the Church has been observing a festival in commemoration of their visit, and made it the initiation of a season of her calendar scarcely inferior in prominence to the greatest of her sacred festivals and seasons. All Christian literature from the earliest centuries is full of comments and homilies and songs and liturgical prescriptions relating to the same. The first book of the New Testament places it close to the beginning of its account of the Saviour as a special testimony to His dignity as the King of the Jews and His worshipfulness as the Son of God. The apocryphal Gospels of the Infancy set it forth with great zest and circumstantiality as one of the divinest gems in the testimonies to the glory of Jesus of Nazareth. And neither in sermon nor in song is there any one thing, save and except the Cross and the Resurrection, which is more joyously contemplated than this so-called "Star of Bethlehem."

Diverse Opinions.

But when it comes to the explanation of particulars, Christians have not been so clear nor so well agreed as we would expect in a matter of so much prominence and interest. The diversities of opinion are almost endless, and the Christian world as yet has not settled itself down upon any one theory as certainly the truth or of sufficient clearness to be free from serious difficulties and objections on the one hand or the other.

As to the starry leading spoken of, some think it was a meteor or a comet. Others think it was the bright light which shone upon the shepherds when the angel made known to them Christ's birth, assuming that to men afar off that remarkable light may have been mistaken for a star. Some think it was some unidentified supernatural light in the sky which appeared to certain devout men in some remote region, and which they could no better describe than to liken it to a star. Some think it was a true star among the stars, brought into being, or at least brought into view, for the particular purpose of giving token of the Saviour's nativity, and then made to disappear, never more to be seen. Some think there was no real external manifestation at all, that no star was ever seen by any

one, and that the whole thing was only a vision vouchsafed to these men alone.

Of later years it is more generally supposed to have been a conjunction of the planets Jupiter and Saturn, such as did actually occur about that time, and which may have entered somewhat into the case, although the conjunctions referred to were not close enough to create the appearance of a single star, and were not in any respect what could with propriety be called Christ's Star. Admitting all that Jewish rabbis as well as the Gentile astrologists and prognosticators have claimed for such conjunctions, there still would be a great lack to account adequately for the very definite and powerful convictions respecting Christ's birth which these men showed, and for their reference to an individual star, which they described as the star of the new-born Prince they were seeking. True, Tacitus, Suetonius, Josephus, and others testify that there was at that time a widespread expectation of some great and triumphing Prince to arise in the East; but said expectation was so indefinite, and was actually applied in directions so unaccordant with the true Messiah and His predicted character, that it cannot be taken as at all up to what was in the mind of these Magi and implied in their inquiry. They expected to find a divine and worshipful being, by birth a Jewish Prince, and by character and right entitled to the homage of all the children of men. They had no question or doubt upon the subject. They knew that a great and wonderful personage was born. They knew and believed that He was worthy of the sacred worship of all men, and that it was their holiest interest and duty to come and greet Him with their best gifts, acknowledgments, and adoration. This was more than the prevailing expectation anywhere showed.

Whence, then, came this clear and definite knowledge on the subject, exceeding even that of the sacred scribes and priests of Judea itself, with all the records and foreshowings of Moses and the prophets before them? The prophecy of Balaam touching the Star that was to arise out of Jacob may have had some remote connection with it, but it will scarcely begin to account for the clear, un-doubting, and living faith touching the new-born Saviour which glowed in the hearts of these wise men. Prophecies of Daniel and influences of the Jewish teachings in general may also have floated down among these people from the great Captivity times ; but, at the best, it would still not account for what we see exhibited in these Magi. A special revelation to them alone, without any further record of it on earth, would be so unlike what we know of God's methods and purposes in the giving of His revelations that it is un-warranted to suppose it.

How, then, did these Magi come to know so much about Christ as an adorable King and Saviour? How came they to such full conviction that His birth had occurred in Ju-dea? The true answer is: *By the signs and constellations of the primeval astronomy, and the legends connected with them, interpreted as we have been contemplating them in these Lectures.*

Astronomic Facts

It is an astronomic fact, independent of all hypotheses, that at the precise hour of mid-night, at the winter solstice, or the last week of December, in the period in which Christ was born, the sign of *Virgo*, everywhere and always regarded as the sign of the virgin-mother from whom the divine-human Re-deemer-King was to be born, was just rising on the eastern horizon.

It is a further astronomical fact, independent of all hypotheses, that at the spring equinox of the same period, just nine months earlier, this sign of the Virgin at midnight was on the meridian, with the line running precisely across her bosom.

It is a further independent astronomical fact that at the same date, at midnight, the stars of the little constellation of *Coma*, the special sign of the infant Seed of the woman, the Desire of nations, was likewise, along with the Virgin, directly on the meridian.

Now, if our interpretation of these ancient astronomical signs be the true one, we have here some remarkable indications in which the facts and the signs singularly coincide. Taken by themselves, they might not mean much ; but if other particulars, to be named, duly fill out the picture, they would help to fix the heavenly tokens that the time had in very truth come in which the great Virgin-born Deliverer was to appear. They are im-portant factors in the case.

A Primeval Tradition

It is also a matter of record, among both Gentile and Jewish peoples, that the patriarch Seth, in whose day these heavenly signs were arranged and completed, gave out a prophecy in connection with them, that in the period in which the great promised One should be born there would appear a very bright star in the heavens. This was perhaps the very proph-ecy traditional among the ancient Magi and Parsis, that there should come a heavenly Child to command the homage and obedience of mankind, the sign of whose birth would be the appearance of a new and peculiar star in the sign of Virgo. Likewise, the Jews also have always held and taught that Messiah's advent would be heralded by a new and pecu-liar star. Hence the great impostor who gave himself out as their Messiah called himself *Barcokheba*, "the Son of the Star."

A New Star

Now, it is a matter of record that a new and peculiar star *did* make its appearance in the first Decan of Virgo in the period imme-diately preceding Christ's birth, and that it was so bright as to be visible even in the day-time. Ignatius says it "sparkled brilliantly above all stars." The same continued in the sky during the whole period of Christ's lifetime, and for a time thereafter. Hip-parchus, about one hundred and twenty-five years before Christ, observed it as a new star, and was led by it to draw up his catalogue of the stars. Ptolemy, about one hundred and fifty years after Christ, refers to it as having been observed by Hipparchus, but as having become so faint as hardly to be any longer distinguishable. The Chinese records also make mention of this new bright star at a time corresponding to the period of our Sa-viour's birth. Since the time of Ptolemy we have no record of any observation of it. This star was in *Coma*, the sign of the Infant accompanying Virgo, and it marked the very head of that Infant. It was on the meridian at midnight at the spring equinox, just nine months before Christ was born, as again three months thereafter. Its brightness would necessarily arrest the attention of observers of the heavens, and awaken special interest in *Coma* and the Virgin-born Infant which that constellation signified both in figure and name. Believers in the sacred meaning of these signs, especially in connection with the traditional prophecy of the new star, which seems also to have been in Balaam's mind, could not help but be convinced from these showings that the coming of the Desired One was surely approaching. It was a sort of midnight cry, "Behold, He cometh!" The star itself would thus also be just what these Magi called the star by which they were led—namely, Christ's Star, emphatically "*His* star;" for it was a star of His particular constellation as the Desire of nations, and the peculiar star of His infancy, as it marked the Infant's head, and was at the time by far the brightest in the constellation, as well as in all the heavens around.

To believers in the import of these signs as I have given them there could be no question about the meaning of these indications. But still, the time would remain far more indefinite than it seems to have been in the minds of these distinguished visitors. There needed to be some further and more sharply-narrowed indications to account for the whole case in this line of explanation. But such more definite indications were not wanting.

Conjunctions of Jupiter and Saturn

In the rabbinical commentaries of Abarbanel, Eliezer, and others great stress is laid on conjunctions of the planets Jupiter and Saturn. It is there also affirmed that about three years before the birth of Moses a conjunction between Jupiter and Saturn occurred in the sign of Pisces. By astronomical calculations we know that such a conjunction of these particular planets in that particular sign did take place about that period. According to Josephus and the rabbis, this sign was interpreted by the Egyptian astronomers and wise men as very favorable to the Jews and very unfavorable to the Egyptians. Their sacred scribes, noted for their skill and sagacity in these things, came to the king insisting that it foretokened the birth of a child among the Jews who, if allowed to live, would bring the Egyptian dominion very low, excel in virtue and glory, exalt the children of Israel to power and honor, and be remembered throughout all ages. (See Josephus, *Ant.* ii. 9, §§ 2 and 27.)

Three things here come out with great clearness and conspicuity which deserve to be particularly noted: *first*, that the star-reading of a conjunction between Jupiter and Saturn betokened the birth of a great, virtuous, princely, and glorious operator among men, and the beginning or starting of a new order of things;* *second*, that the sign in which the conjunction occurred indicated the people among whom the child was to be born; and *third*, that the children of Israel were already at that early period associated with the sign of Pisces.

Josephus says that it was in consequence of what the scribes augured from these indications that the decree went forth from Pharaoh to slay every male child that should be born during the time impending.

We thus have the Jewish rabbis and the Gentile Egyptian scribes most seriously, on both sides, concurring in the interpretation of some very important points in astronomic indications, and may well conclude that their views and teachings with regard to these particulars were the same that held on the subject among the learned in such lore throughout the world in general, including the wise men who asked the question of the text. Abarbanel, in his Commentary on Daniel, affirms it as a settled thing that the conjunction of Jupiter and Saturn always betokens some great event or beginning in human affairs, and because such a conjunction occurred

---

* Kepler, on consulting the periods of the conjunctions between Jupiter and Saturn, gave it as his opinion that such conjunctions astronomically coincided with the approach of each climacteric in human affairs; to wit, the revelation to Adam, the birth of Enoch, the Deluge, the birth of Moses, the birth of Cyrus, the birth of Christ, the birth of Charlemagne, and the birth of Luther.

in his day (about A. D. 1480), he expected the speedy birth of the Messiah, as still expected by the Jews.

Now, if an individual and isolated conjunction of these two planets presaged the birth of one so illustrious as Moses, and always indicates the coming of some great one on earth, what would be the dignity and glory of a Child whose birth is heralded by three successive conjunctions of these same planets in one and the same year? And yet this is what, in fact, did occur just before the birth of Jesus of Nazareth.

In the year of Rome 747, within the two years preceding the Nativity, during the last days of May, there was one such conjunction. In the same year, during the last days of October there was another such conjunction. And again in the same year, during the first days of December, there was a third conjunction— all three being conjunctions of Jupiter and Saturn, as on the occasion of the birth of Moses. It was Kepler, the great German astronomer, who first pointed out these remarkable incidents of the heavens, and gave the opinion that they were most likely the starry phenomena which influenced the wise men in the case before us. The calculations on the subject have been repeatedly re-examined, and latest by the astronomer-royal at Greenwich, and pronounced to be correct. Independent of all theories or interpretations, the facts thus stand attested by the best science, and, as Farrar says, "do not seem to admit of denial."

And as the star in the head of the Virgin-born Infant was at the time shining with a peculiar brilliancy new to it and brighter than all other fixed stars in the firmament, those who took the conjunctions of Jupiter and Saturn as indicating the near birth of a lordly and illustrious operator in human affairs could by no means help themselves from the conclusion that here was the astronomic showing of the pending birth of a triply-illustrious One, who could be none other than that divine-human Seed of the woman everywhere set forth in the constellations, and promised and hoped for among all nations from the foundations of the world. These

wise men would thus know, and be assured beyond all doubt or misgiving, that the particular time had come in which the worshipful One they were seeking was to make His advent. Such portentous conjunctions, along with the new star in *Coma*, and the Virgin herself on the meridian at the same time, would seal the whole matter. The signs were full, definite, and complete.

THE SIGN OF THE FISHES

And as to His being born in Judea as a Jewish Prince, that they would know from the same signs, just as well as the Egyptian priests knew from the conjunction of the same planets many centuries before that the illustrious one they held to be presaged at that time was to arise from among the seed of Jacob. The conjunction occurred in *Pisces*, the sign of *the Fishes;* and the sign of the Fishes, by Jews and Gentiles alike, was assigned to the Israel-itish people as to the Sethites and Shemites, who held to the worship of one only God and His holy promises over against apostates and unbelievers. Abarbanel argues five reasons for the reference of the sign of Pisces to Israel. In our explanations the sign of the Fishes means the earthly Church, and the seed of Jacob at that time constituted God's chosen and acknowledged people. And, as a matter of astronomic fact, all three of the conjunctions between Jupiter and Saturn which immediately preceded Christ's birth were *in the sign of the Fishes*—the first in the twentieth degree, the second in the sixteenth degree, and the third in the fifteenth degree. With the same clearness and loudness, therefore, with which these planetary conjunctions and stellar indications announced the immediate birth of the glorious divine-human Seed of the woman, did they also announce that He was to arise out of Jacob and to be a Jewish Prince.

THE FOLLOWING OF THE STAR

It was in December, at the winter solstice, then the twenty-fifth day of the month, that Christ was born. It was most likely in the following March, about the time of the spring equinox, at the first anniversary of the angel's annunciation to Mary, that these wise men reached Jerusalem. The Church mostly puts it a little earlier, but without very solid chronological reasons. It was at this time that the bright star in *Coma* was vertical at Jerusalem at midnight. The record plainly implies that these men were following the star they spoke of as Christ's Star. The following of the star in Coma, so emphatically the star of the infant Seed of the woman, could be no other following than the going to the place at which it would be thus vertical over them at that hour. We cannot conceive of any other sort of following of a fixed star. And it was at Jerusalem, and only there or close on that particular line of latitude at that particular time of the year, that this star was vertical at exact midnight. This would also allow the required time for their journey after the third conjunction.

The further item in the narrative, to the effect that "the star went before them till it came and stood over where the young child was," is explainable in the same way. The short distance of some six miles between Jerusalem and Bethlehem would make so little difference in the observation of a vertical star that it would be impossible to note it without special astronomical appliances. Hence, when these followers of the star came to Jerusalem, they had gone as near to the spot they were searching for as their natural observation could serve to bring them. Accordingly, the record implies that there they somehow lost the benefit of the star's leading, so that they applied to Herod for further information. Their light from the observance of the stars being in this way exhausted, they would naturally betake themselves to the reigning sovereign there to learn the specific locality in which this sublime Prince was born, being assured by their starry guidance that it must needs be somewhere in that immediate vicinity. And having obtained answer that *Bethlehem* was the exact place indicated by sacred prophecy, they set out for Bethlehem.

But on their way to Bethlehem, by some means or other, to their great joy, their star began to serve them again the same as it did before. How this came about is explained by a well-preserved and beautiful old tradition which we have no reason to discredit.

Though Bethlehem is only about six miles from Jerusalem, it is said that these distinguished visitors stopped on the way, and tarried by the side of a deep well. What they halted for in so short a journey it would be hard to tell, except it was to take another midnight observation of their star. For this purpose the well, with its perpendicular walls, would serve them the same as a fixed observatory. It was by means of such a well, and the reflection of the sun in it, at Syene in Egypt, that the line of the tropic was determined, and the extent of its declination in the time that had elapsed since that well was dug. So these wise men, by looking down the well, and observing the reflection of their bright star in the still water at the bottom, could find with great accuracy whether it was exactly vertical over them, or in what respect, if any, it was not. And so the tradition is, that they looked into the well and saw their star, and perceived that it "stood over"—was exactly vertical at—not Jerusalem, but *Bethlehem*, "where the young child was." Making it designate *the house* is not in the record.

JUNCTION OF PROPHECY AND ASTRONOMY

The result of the acquisition of this new light by means of their own star-guide tradition and the Scriptures both describe. They both say that "when they saw the star" and realized its relation to Bethlehem, "*they rejoiced with exceeding great joy.*" And well they might, for it was a conjunction like that of Jupiter and Saturn themselves—the perfect conjunction and coincidence of the primeval astronomy and the revelations given by Israel's prophets touching the great Messiah. These men, indeed, had not yet reached the object of their search, but they were now doubly sure of finding and seeing the illustrious Virgin-born Saviour of the world, of whom the heavens and all sacred story had been telling and prophesying from remotest antiquity, and in whom they felt more interest than in all the earth besides. It was the *Eureka! Eureka!* of Gentile faith and hope on the threshold of embracing the adorable infant Seed of the woman, of whose glorious advent they had now no longer the least shadow of a doubt. Nor need we be surprised if it should turn out that this was the very well of Bethlehem of which David had such fond remembrance, and from which he so longed to drink.

And when we come to consider who these "wise men" were, whence they came, and what their character, position, relations, and main occupations, our explanation of the case is doubly strengthened.

Who the Magi were

There has been about as much uncertainty, debate, and diversity of opinion touching the identity of these people as about the star of which they spake. It would be a waste of time to describe the wide-ranging imaginings upon the subject. We only need to know the solid facts in the case.

It is settled by Matthew's narrative that these people on their mission of homage to the infant Christ were *Magi*, and that they came from a country far eastward from Palestine. Whether from due east is not involved in the statement. According to all the elements of the showing, and by the general consent of the Church in all ages, they were *Gentiles* — the first-fruits unto Christ from the Gentile world. All classic writers, from Herodotus down to Ammianus, agree in pointing to *Media* as their home-country — the country of the illustrious Cyrus, who is noted in sacred prophecy and was announced by inspiration as God's anointed for the deliverance of Israel from Babylon long before he was born.

The *Magi* are specially named in the list of the Median tribes, just as Matthew names them. Anciently they were mostly a pastoral people greatly occupied with religion, astronomy, and other sacred sciences. They were the great teachers of kings and people in the divine wisdom. They were a priestly or sacerdotal tribe, after the style of Levi among the tribes of Israel. It was their hereditary privilege to provide their country with priests and religious instructors. They were the ministers and prophets of their day. Their religion was the noblest and the least corrupted of all the ancient world. They lived mostly in towns without walls, observing their own laws and trusting to God alone for protection. It was from among them that Zoroaster sprung, if indeed such a man ever lived, and that Confucius, more remotely perhaps, obtained his better knowledge. It was from among them that Cyrus selected his priests for Persia. They believed in one God, original Creator, supreme in omniscience and goodness, unrivalled in splendor, and dwelling in light eternal. They believed in a great and powerful spirit of evil in constant antagonism to God, the spoiler of the divine works and the author of all mischief. The history of the world to them was the history of the conflict of the good originating with God and the evil originating with the Devil. All men they considered active in this conflict on the one side or the other. They held that God by His prophets gave a revelation and a law by which men might know their duty, fashion their hopes, and direct their conduct, and which it was their business to preserve and expound. They possessed both the Solar and Lunar Zodiacs, and claimed that they were given of God to teach man wisdom, forecast the future, and give hope to the good. According to the showings of the constellations, they looked for a time when a Son of the eternal Lawgiver would be born, who should be a great Saviour and Deliverer, by whom the spirit of evil and the powers of hell would be destroyed, the dead raised up to life again, and a kingdom of everlasting life and happiness established over all the earth.

So I find it written in the best accounts of them and in those fragments of their sacred books which are still preserved and of late years published in our tongue.

And, as before Abraham's time and outside of his chosen family-line, there were men like Job and his friends, like Melchisedec, king of Salem, like Jethro, priest of Midian and father-in-law of Moses, like Balaam before his fall — men of faith in the traditional revelations that came forth out of the ark — men whom the Spirit of God and saving wisdom had not entirely abandoned—so in the time of Christ's birth there were some noble spirits among the descendants of these ancient Magi who still eagerly clung to the hope of the sure fulfilment of the primeval promise, and hence continued to observe the heavens, and to consult what they considered the inspired lore of the skies, that they might not miss the signs and tokens noted in the hereditary prophecies of their caste as presages of the advent of the great Virgin-born Son of the eternal Sovereign.

And to men of such descent, culture, faith, hope, office, and pursuits, what more would be necessary than just the starry indications which I have named to thrill their souls with profoundest enthusiasm, fan the smouldering embers of their hereditary knowledge into a flame of intensest animation, and create just such an expedition to greet the new-born divine King, as that described in connection with the text? Had we been in their place, with their beliefs, feelings, and anticipations, with such signs and indications upon the face of the sky, where we and our fathers were taught to read the sacred foreshowings of what was to come to pass, I feel sure that we would have been moved, rejoiced, thrilled, and impelled just as they were.

And why, then, should we not accept the conclusion that so it was? There is not a particle of evidence on earth that this was not the true state of the case as respects the Magi. All the conditions and known facts and presumable likelihoods point in this one direction. Everything in the record thus explains to the full as it will not explain in any other way known to men. And the whole result in this view takes on that dignity, importance, and far-reaching instructiveness which best befit its place in the New Testament. It is a view which silences and sweeps away the unworthy suspicions, perplexities, and cavils which have so long hung about it in the minds and estimates of many, clearing it up into definite and comprehensible shape, and vindicating the action of the Church in putting it forward as the subject of a special festival, the opening theme of a prominent season in her calendar, and the keynote of the earthly

Epiphany of the sublime Redeemer of the world.

THE SUM OF THE WHOLE

Here, then, is a magnificent instance, accredited by the Holy Ghost, which stands as an everlasting testimony to the fact of a primeval revelation to all men, to the existence of a record of that revelation in the primeval astronomy, and to the preservation of the same in sufficient incorruptness to inform those who clung to it of the time and place of the nativity of the long-promised Seed of the woman, and to move them to go and greet Him in His cradle with their devoutest homage and adoration. Surely, this ought to be enough to put the matter beyond dispute, and to settle for ever that there is such a thing as THE GOSPEL IN THE STARS—even that very Gospel of God which holds forth Jesus of Nazareth as the promised Seed of the woman, the divine-human Son of the Virgin, who was to come, to suffer, and to toil and die for the deliverance of man from darkness, sin, death, and the power of the Devil, to bruise the head of the Serpent, to destroy the works and dominion of the great Enemy, and to bring in everlasting redemption to our fallen race. It was to Jesus of Nazareth, even in His cradle, that the primeval astronomy conducted these remote Gentile believers; and to that same Jesus, amid vivid and glowing illustrations of the truth respecting His nature, person, mission and work, past, present, and future, the primeval astronomy is still capable of conducting even Christians themselves.

To those who have entered into the induction of facts and showings which I have given, though imperfectly, in these Lectures, I am sure no further evidence is needed to work conviction of the merit and worth of the subject, and of the evangelic illuminations which it furnishes. We have considered these heavens, and, behold, we have found them flaming from end to end, from centre to circumference, with that superlative "glory of God" which shines "in the face of Jesus Christ." We have taken our stand beneath the shining archway, and looked at the grand procession of the celestial scenery as inscribed by God's primeval prophets, and have listened to the story as it unfolded; and, lo! it is the same blessed story of the fall and redemption—of Jesus and "the restitution of all things"—which we have in the writings of the Prophets and Apostles. Our experience has been akin to that of those on Jordan's banks, who saw the heavens opened, and beheld the Spirit alighting on the Virgin's Child, and heard a voice from the depths of eternity saying, "*This is My beloved Son, in whom I am well pleased.*" On that great Virgin-born our eyes were fixed from the very starting-point. On Him our attention has been kept and riveted at every step of the way through the whole circuit of the skies, with the Ecliptic and across it. And ever sharper, clearer, gladder, and fuller grew the glorious testimony as we advanced, till all the morning stars seemed to resume their ancient songs and all the sons of light their primeval shouts, whilst these far-spanning heavens through all their constellations rang out, "*Hosannah! Blessed is He that cometh in the Name of the Lord! Hosannah in the highest!*"

On such sublime heights, amid such scenes of song and brightness, we would fain linger. Like Peter on the mount, we would here build tabernacles and abide. But, though to other scenes and duties called, like him we still may bear away with us the memory of what we have witnessed, and think of it in our humble toils and sad solitudes, and be all the firmer in our faith and the more hopeful in our outlook toward the nearing eternity. And happy they, and wise indeed, to whom it is given through these contemplations to say in truth and soul-earnestness of Him to whom the heavens thus testify, "*We have seen His star, and are come to worship Him.*"

Thus, then, my long task is done. And may the God of heaven and earth, who bringeth forth Mazzaroth in his seasons and guides Arcturus with his sons, bless the humble contribution to the confirmation of His Word, the honor of His Name, and the vindication of the claims of Jesus Christ to the undoubting faith and everlasting adoration of all that live and move beneath His genial skies!

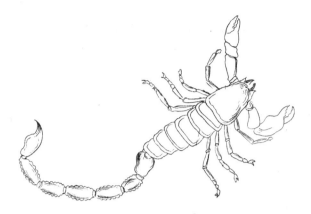

SUPPLEMENT

CRITICISMS

THE adverse notices of this book have mainly come from three classes of minds. The first class consists of those who have no idea of a personal God, treat all religion as superstition, reject inspiration in the sense of divine revelation, and see no need of an atoning Redeemer. A reviewer expresses the belief that " one of the uses of this book possibly will be to tend to destroy much of the force of that kind of infidelity which pretends to find all the germs of Christianity in precedent religions and mythologies." The author has learned of an instance in which the consideration of these presentations was the means of reclaiming a pronounced infidel to faith in the Gospel. The book, therefore, is very much in conflict with infidelity, and has done anything but please skeptics and those skeptically inclined.

The second class consists of professed Christians, of the so-called liberal and rationalistic school, the bent of whose philosophy is to contemplate man as a creature of cultivation from a troglodite or savage, and destined to rise by self-development, perhaps with a little adventitious aid, into ultimate perfection, and who are accordingly very devoted to what they are pleased to call Progress. The whole showing and doctrine of this book is much of a stumbling-block in the way of such thinking, and hence, to minds of this class, it is " wild," " imaginary," " a fanciful endeavor to make a pro-

phetic purpose out of the names (?) of the constellations," " absurd."

The third class consists of certain self-complacent believers, jealous of everything that happens to go beyond the range of their treadmill paths. These are stirred with pious alarm at any attempt to show that the same prophetic Word of God may possibly have another record of its glorious contents in another place and form from the Bible. They cannot favor this book, lest they should encourage a style of reasoning that may bring discredit on the very cause it seeks to advocate.

A striking example of such cowardly trembling for the Ark of the Lord is presented in one who deploringly says, " The purpose is so praiseworthy, and the zeal and eloquence brought to bear upon it are so great, that some will doubtless be carried away by the reasoning of the author to a conviction that the heavenly constellations are indeed a previous revelation of vital importance "!

There is, of course, but one Revelation, one Christ, one Gospel, one plan and purpose of Redemption for fallen man, even that which is written in the Old and New Testaments; but why may it not be given in a thousand different modes of presentation, to as many prophets, in different ages, symbolically here and didactically there, in high poetry or in simple parable? And where is the harm or loss to sacred truth, the calamity to souls, the disadvantage to faith, if it should appear that God verily caused His glorious Gospel to be pictorially inscribed on the everlasting stars from the beginning, as well as afterward written in divers forms and languages on perishable parchment? The early world certainly had a revelation of Gospel truth, whether they hung it on the stars or not.

Of course, nothing contrary to the written Word is to be admitted as matter of faith, whether from the pictures in the starry heavens or from any other source. We cannot so much as know that these pictures set forth the Gospel, except as they accord with the written Word. But when men deny the inspiration of the written record, and seek to empty it of its sublimest substance by their miserable rationalizing, it is a transcendent gain and advantage, in which every genuine believer should rejoice with thankfulness, to be able to point to a duplicate record of precisely the same glorious things, in quite another form, and in place and time where nothing but the special inspiration and illumination of God could have produced it. Whether we really have such an earlier duplicate of the grand substance of the Gospel in the primeval astronomy can only be decided on the evidences in the case; but it is a super-devotion and a very stupid pietism to deplore the finding of grounds for such a conviction.

No Champion for Current Theories

A NOTEWORTHY fact with regard to the adverse notices of this book is, that not one of the writers has ventured in any degree to champion or defend the current theories respecting the origin and meaning of the constellations. Those who have had the field and the sway hitherto when put on trial have nothing to say. They thus show that they secretly feel they have no case against the showings of this book. They are in the unpleasant plight of having sanctioned a line of thinking which they are at a loss to maintain, and of being confronted with a great, heaven-wide, universal system, as old as the oldest records of the race, and handled every day by all peoples on earth, which they are not at all able rationally, historically, or scientifically to explain; whilst their former thinking is assailed and pressed with a new method of contemplation so reasonable, so dignified, so true to the worthiest records and traditions, so consistent, harmonious, and exhaustive in its explanations of all the multitudinous facts entering into the case, that they do not know where or how to attack it, or how to dispose of it without a radical revolution in their ways of looking at things, to which they are by no means willing to submit.

One writer so feels this embarrassment that he has sought a way out by declaiming against "taking the ignorance of everybody as a basis of knowledge." But that will not help him. This book does not assert that the constellations are inspired prophetic symbols of the promised redemption by "the Seed of the woman," *because* nobody can tell whence else or for what else they came into being. The whole field is diligently surveyed. The entire system as originally constituted is searched out and exhibited. The principal myths connected with each constellation, as well as the figures which mark them, both in themselves and in relation to one another, are carefully analyzed. The names of the chief stars belonging to each group are sought out and interpreted by the light of the best linguistic guides. The whole is closely compared, section by section, with the statements, imagery, and diction of the Holy Scriptures touching the Author and Work of human redemption. A clear and complete correspondence—as clear and complete as that between the parables of Christ and the spiritual truths they were meant to illustrate—is traced out in detail. A vast body of historical, scriptural, traditional, and mythical facts is presented, which not only accord with the theory, but largely demand it as the only right conclusion from them. And there is thus fairly made out a full, legitimate, and independent case, which must, in all just logic, go through, unless the facts on which it rests can be solidly refuted or some equally adequate and verifiable explanation of them can be given. Not on men's ignorance is the doctrine of this book built, but on evidences which demand to be handled as all other testimony when in honest search for the truth. Nevertheless, when people avow ignorance and inability to make any showing to the contrary, their sneers and jeers are to their own discredit and shame, and their plea against the presentation is itself a disqualification for the giving of any judgment in the matter.

The Southern Cross

BUT the writer last referred to makes one point of legitimate attack which, if it could be maintained, would be of some weight against the presentations of this book. The following is the statement in full in which this point is made:

"Dr. Seiss is not consistent with himself. His theory requires him to stick to the ancient signs. It is only those that issue from the deep antiquity back of the Theban Tables, about which our ignorance is vast enough, to give room to unfold the wings of his spacious argument. The unknown-prophet theory will not work for constellations whose recent origin discloses the fact that there was no prophet of any kind in the case. The Southern

Cross is one of these. The stars that form it are in the heavens, but there is nothing said about the constellation in Ptolemy or in the Theban Tables. But it is too inviting a constellation for Dr. S. to resist the temptation to use it. Accordingly, he shifts his ground from the map to the heavens, lets the unknown astronomer prophet who impressed the eternal record on the Zodiac go, and proceeds to interpolate the Southern Cross into the record on its own merits."—*N. Y. Independent*, Sept. 7, 1882.

The author of the above extract also wrote and published an attack on *The Gospel in the Stars* some months before it was in print—before he had seen a line of it except the statement on the publisher's prospectus. This is mentioned to show with what sincerity and earnestness he is concerned to get at and set forth the truth on this subject. Still, if he finds a fair objection, it is due that it should have a fair hearing and be fairly met.

Now, it is true that the constellation of the Southern Cross is designated and used in this book (pp. 37–39) as the first Decan of *Libra*, just as the Northern Crown is given as the third Decan of the same sign; but it is not true that either the one or the other, or any constellation used in this attempted reading of the stars, belongs to those fabrications of conceit, flattery, and self-will which, in more recent times, have been thrust into the celestial charts.

It is also true that the Southern Cross, as a separate constellation, does not appear in the list of Hipparchus repeated in the Almagest of Ptolemy, and that it came for the first time into modern atlases in Royer's *Celestial Chart*, published in 1679, whence it has been erroneously ascribed to him as his own invention. These facts had not been overlooked, and it is a very superficial acquaintance with the history of the matter which would take them as proving this constellation one of those which have been obtruded into the celestial maps in modern times.

The reason why it does not appear in the list of Hipparchus and Ptolemy is obvious. That list was intended to give only what was verified by practical observation, and none of the constellations are included but such as the makers of it could see and identify in the heavens. But the Southern Cross in their day had sunk by the precession of the equinox so far into the south as to be scarcely visible any more from the latitudes in which their observations were made. Some of the stars of the Southern Cross are embraced in the list, as they could then be seen hanging low down on the southern horizon; but the constellation, as such, was invisible, and so its higher stars, which could be seen, were assigned to the constellation *Centaurus*, immediately over the Southern Cross, while the

Southern *Crown* was put in to fill out the traditional number in place of the Cross, which these observers could not find.

It is plain, however, that the Southern Crown—*Corona Australis*—was not one of the great old original forty-eight signs. It is far inferior to any one of them, having no star above the fifth magnitude, and no meaning anywhere to be discovered. It is totally destitute of all mythological place, history, or tradition. It is situated near where the Southern Cross was expected to be, and because that could not be found and identified, this seeming Crown was substituted for it, and the Cross dropped out as mythic and having no real existence. None of the authorities on the primeval constellations mention it, and Aspin says it is an invention of the later times.

Ptolemy himself also confesses that in the tables and charts presented by him liberties were taken to change figures and the places of stars in them. He says:

" Multis ego in locus accommodatiora ipsis figuris attribuentes vocabula, priscorum usum immutavimus, sicut, verbi gratia, figuras quas Hipparchus in humeris Virginis locat, nos in costis ejus sitas esse dicimus, quoniam distantia earum ad stellas quæ in capite sunt major apparet, quam ad eas quæ in extrematibus manuum collocantur, hoc autem sicut et costis accomodatur."

Two things appear from this statement. The one is that, for æsthetic reasons, changes were made in the figures, etc. of the constellations, and hence that we are not to look to these charts as faithfully presenting in full all the old forms of the astronomical signs. The other is of still more consequence touching the point in question, and that is, the clear and distinct acknowledgment that neither he nor Hipparchus were the inventors of these signs, and that a system of them, covering the whole visible heavens, existed, and was held to be of unquestioned authority, unknown origin, and unsearchable antiquity in his day. Whether, therefore, the Southern Cross belongs to the ancient forty-eight constellations or not cannot be determined from its absence from the Ptolemaic tables, as that can argue nothing for or against the assertion that it does so belong, apart from other showings.

THE CROSS ONE OF THE ANCIENT SIGNS

OTHER and more decisive showings, however, are not wanting. Ulugh Beigh, about two centuries before Royer, Aben Ezra, about four centuries before Royer, and Albumazer, about eight centuries before Royer, all three give this south polar constellation as named and designated in the most ancient astronomy as one of the Decans of *Libra*. Albumazer and Aben Ezra give it with the accompanying statement that, according to the old traditions and accounts, it was in the form of a cross. They likewise give its name as *Adom*, which means *cutting off, the boundary, the lowest limit*, as the last letter of the old Oriental alphabets was *tau*, and always written in the form of the cross. Ulugh Beigh also gives its name in the old Coptic, where he says it was called *Sera*, which Birch says means *victory, triumph by a great conflict*. All this quite agrees with the death of "the Seed of the woman" on the cross.

Unlike Hipparchus and Ptolemy, these men were not giving the constellations as then to be seen and identified on the heavens, but as handed down in the most ancient astronomical traditions. If they had been describing from their own observations, they would also have had to omit the Southern Cross from their charts, for it was not visible in their days in their latitudes, and will not be again for thousands of years, until it comes around to its ancient place by the completion of the precessional cycle. They spoke from the ancient records and traditions, which it was their aim to present, and they all claim to give faithfully and truly what had thus been transmitted from the earliest times. Christians they were not, neither had they any liking for Christianity, and there is nothing whatever to induce suspicion that they did not report the facts as they found them.

These authorities ought to be sufficient upon the point; but it is not all to indicate that the constellation of the Southern Cross has come down "from the deep antiquity back of the Theban Tables."

Calculating back on the precessional cycle for the position of this sign in the period when these signs were invented, we find that it was then conspicuously visible in all the north temperate zone at a considerable elevation, rendering it nearly as conspicuous as Orion now. It is made up of four of the most brilliant stars in the south polar heavens. Another so lustrous a group is not to be found in all that field of sky. The pre-eminent glory and remarkable lustre of this group, as then visible from the banks of the Euphrates and that region, put it out of the question that it could or would have been overlooked or left out in the making up of any complete system, intended for any purpose, embracing all the most illustrious stars then and there visible. And yet it must have been thus overlooked and left out if we are to discredit the clear traditional record of its having been one of the original forty-eight constellations.

Standing as it then did at about sixteen degrees above the horizon at meridian, it gradually sunk toward the south pole, until its highest star was last visible in the latitude of Jerusalem about the time the Saviour reached the lowest limit of His passion and yielded up His life upon the cross. It cannot be seen now except in latitudes far down to the southward.

When Americus Vespucius was on his southern voyages, more than a hundred years before Royer's chart was made, and his eyes beheld the brilliant stars of the Southern Cross, he congratulated himself on having rediscovered what had been for so many ages lost except to mythic fable, and boasted of having seen what had not been seen by civilized man till then except by the first of the human race. He it was who pointed out in Dante's *Purgatorio* that remarkable passage, which he claimed to be a description of the Southern Cross:

> " To the right I turned, and fixed my mind
> On the other pole attentive, when I saw
> Four stars ne'er seen before save by the ken
> Of our first parents. Heaven of their rays
> Seemed joyous. O thou northern site ! bereft
> Indeed, and widowed, since of these deprived !"
> Cary's *Dante*, Purg., canto i.

Ventura wonders at this description, particularly as the Southern Cross, to which the words and allusions so admirably fit, had not yet been rediscovered in Dante's time. But Cary very properly suggests that "*from long tradition* the real truth might not have been unknown to our poet;" and adds that M. Artaud mentions a globe constructed by an Arabian in Egypt, with the date of the year 622 of the Hegira (corresponding to 1225 of our era), *in which the Southern Cross is positively marked.*" Von Humboldt thinks he also saw this constellation on Arabian globes. It certainly was not transferred from Royer's chart to these globes, though Royer may have incorporated it from some Oriental source or tradition, confirmed as it had become in his day by various navigators and travellers who had looked upon it and found it to be a reality and not a mere myth.

Dupuis also gives it as an ancient tradition that this south polar constellation was lost, and that whensoever it would again be found it would be found to be in the form of a cross.

Albumazer, in his enumeration of the Decans, including the Southern Cross, says, " They were known all over the world," and considered of sacred prophetic significance.

Humboldt refers to the fact that the ancient Persians celebrated a feast of the cross a few days before the sun entered *Aries*, which was the time of year when the Southern Cross was highest and most brilliant in their skies. He also speaks of the modern Persians, Kaswini, and Mohammedan astronomers as searching for crosses in the signs of the Dolphin and the Dragon (the Southern Cross having disappeared below the southern horizon), in order to account for this ancient sacred festival. Restore that constellation to its ancient position and all is adequately explained, as well as the uses made of the sign of the cross and its associations and significations in the mythologies of ancient Egypt, India, Mexico, and of other primitive peoples.

According to Albumazer, the Persians called this Decan of *Libra* by the name of *Arbedi*, which carries with it the sense of *covering*, and so would wonderfully well coincide with the purpose of the death upon the cross accomplished in the fulness of time by the Virgin-born Redeemer predicted and promised from the foundation of the world.

From all this it is made amply evident that the author of this book does not at all " shift his ground " when taking in the Southern Cross as part of the grand evangelic record inscribed upon the heavens, and that he does not " interpolate " the primeval constellations, but gives them in their unmutilated intergrity, when he gives the Southern Cross as one of them.

Dr. Seyffarth

ONE writer speaks disparagingly of the author of this book for " taking Seyffarth as his guide in Egyptology." The assertion, however, has not the slightest foundation in fact. Dr. Seyffarth's astronomically-founded opinion on the age of the Zodiac (p. 22), and his curious presentation of the astronomical reference in the placement and order of the letters in the alphabet (p. 23), are referred to, but these particulars are no essential part of the argument. They are only coincident with it. Dr. Seyffarth is not the basis or " guide " for any Egyptological facts or doctrines cited, or for anything else vitally entering into the presentations of this book, although he is no mean authority in matters of archæological science and astronomical calculations. He has done more solid work perhaps than three-fourths of the men of whom more general notice is taken. Here is an extract from the London *Times* (Dec. 31, 1859) which may serve to show that he is no fool in these things :

" Professor Mitchell in his lectures on astronomy said that not long since he had met in the city of St. Louis, in Missouri, a man of great scientific attainments who for forty years had been engaged in Egypt deciphering the hieroglyphics of the ancients. This gentleman stated to him that he had lately unravelled the inscriptions on the coffin of a mummy now in the British Museum, and that by the aid of previous observation he had discovered

the key to all the astronomical knowledge of the Egyptians. The Zodiac, with the exact position of the planets, was delineated on the coffin, and the date to which they pointed was the autumnal equinox in the year B. C. 1722, or nearly four thousand years ago. Professor Mitchell employed his assistants to ascertain the exact position of the heavenly bodies belonging to our solar system on the equinox of that year, 1722 B. C., without having communicated his object in so doing ; the calculations were made, and, to his astonishment, on comparing the work with the statements of his friend already referred to, it was found that on the 7th of October, 1722 B. C., the moon and planets had occupied the exact positions in the heavens marked upon the coffin in the British Museum."

This gentleman, so tested and complimented by Professor Mitchell, was none other than G. Seyffarth, Ph. D., D. D., quoted in this book, and so unwarrantably sneered at by the Boston *Literary World*.

The Origin of Language and Writing

ANOTHER writer argues that the author of this book is quite innocent of " recent researches in philology and palæontology," and shows " a very primitive faith " in coolly asserting that language and writing are as old as the human family. It is hard to tell what this assailant means, unless he be a believer in what Carlyle calls " the Gospel of dirt," which considers man a sort of natural evolution from slime and slimy things through all stages of reptilian, animal, and savage life in successive unknown and unknowable ages. If so, the great difference between him and this book is, that it appeals to positive facts, records, and memorials (see Lect. xvi., on " Primeval Man "), whilst he rests on a conceit of agnosticism which has not one positive fact to which to appeal that can at all be admitted as legitimate proof of what he avers and accepts.

The Bible and all records and traditions of primitive man attest the beginning of our race with Adam, and show that he was the most divinely favored and the most perfect, intelligent, and divine man that ever did live, save the second Adam, the glorious " Seed of the woman," the great Redeemer of the world.

There is evidence that Adam spoke and was spoken to, and that things he said and that were said to him were preserved and made matters of transmission to subsequent generations. Then certainly there was language from the beginning— language fixed and comprehensible to others besides himself, the same as language now. To deny this is to contradict the whole record. He did not learn this language from parents or contemporaries, for they did not exist. It necessarily was the gift of God, immediate and direct. Fix it as we will, it was a miracle, the same as his own being. And if God gave Adam the use of spoken language, it was a mere fraction of the wonderful endowment to give also the idea and means of writing what he could speak and so well understood. The very supernatural enlightenment which gave him the intelligent use of language was itself sufficient to suggest to him the writing of it and the making of records of it—the representation of it to the eye as well as to the ear.

We know that Adam called things by names, and those names described the true nature and qualities of the things to which they were applied. What he called them they were and were called. Here was at once the highest science, and the fixed linguistic embodiment of that science. The heavenly bodies came before him the same as creatures and objects on the earth. He must therefore have named them also, and named them as truly as he named other things. Something of astronomy would thus necessarily be born of him. And the evidence now amounts next thing to demonstration that the Zodiac, the constellations, and the naming and designations of the principal objects displayed in the heavens date back to Adam's time. In this we have recorded pictorial and vocable language, and connected with a perfection of astronomic science which remains as the true and indestructible basis of all that we possess in that department even to this present. How, then, can it be questioned that both language and writing existed in Adam's time?

All "the recent researches in philology and palæontology" go to confirm the Bible doctrine on this subject; and that doctrine, as old John Weemes has drawn it out (in the second part of his *Christian Synagogue*, 1633), is, that "God made Adam to have perfect knowledge, both of God and His creatures;" "Man in his first estate had the first principles created in him of all sciences and liberal arts, whereby he might understand the nature of the creatures here below, and so learn by them. As he was the father of all living, so he was the father of all science; for as he was able to beget children, so he was able to teach his posterity;" "He had the knowledge of all things that might be known;" "Adam knew as much as was in the creatures;" "Man in his innocent estate excelled all that ever were in the knowledge of natural things;" "He had the knowledge of all the liberal sciences;" "Adam knew all arts and sciences; therefore Philosophy is not an invention of the heathen, for it came first from Adam to the Patriarchs, and so hath continued still" (pp. 91–96).

All this necessarily involved the use of language —how to speak it, how to embody thought in it, how to represent it to the eye as well as to the ear, and hence how to make records of it. We know positively, from the inscriptions on stones, tiles, cylinders, and seals recently exhumed in Chaldea and Assyria, that alphabetic writing, engraving, and the preservation of knowledge in phonetic signs not only existed, but were in a high state of cultivation and common use, full two thousand years before Christ, and date back close to, if not within, the lifetime of Noah. Some of these exhumations are parts of dictionaries, grammars, and presentations with regard to the science of language, as well as accounts of the Creation, of the facts in the earliest history of the race, of the Zodiac and its accompanying circles of other constellations, of the Flood and the Babel disaster, of the forms of agreement and contract respecting lands and chattels, and the recording of them as well as elaborate poems. And with this demonstration before our eyes, and these records in tangible and readable form in our possession from such indisputable antiquity, there is no escape from the conclusion that alphabetic writing dates back to the lifetime of Noah, and that, existing and employed in his day, it must have come with him from the other side of the Flood. Noah lived and conversed with Methuselah, and Methuselah lived and conversed with Adam; so that there was but one lifetime between Noah and Adam. And if Noah used alphabetic writing, as we may be sure he did, then there is every reason to believe that he brought it from the time of Methuselah, who lived before the death of Adam, from whom all the race has most likely received it, as he, through his pre-eminent illumination, from God.

The learned George Stanley Faber, in the second volume of his *Origin of Pagan Idolatry*, devotes a chapter (v.) to the many, widespread, and almost universal early traditions of certain sacred books and writings made by the antediluvian Patriarchs, and one way and another preserved during the Flood for the instruction of the descendants of those elected to survive it. He thinks these traditions certainly traceable to a period anterior to the building of the Tower of Babel, and that they attest a common belief at that time in the existence of writings as old as, or even older than, the Deluge— a belief which could hardly have found entrance into men's minds if there had been no basis of truth at the bottom of it. There must have been writing then, or there could have been no thought of writing done before the Flood; and if there was writing *then*, there is every reason to conclude that there was writing from the beginning, and that it came to the first man from God among the rest of his equipments for the commencement of a high, civilized, and perfect human society and life.

And with all this before us we ought to be prepared to have some respect to Dr. Seyffarth's summation of the results of modern archæological investigations when he says : " It is currently maintained that our alphabet was not invented until 1500 B. C. by the Phœnicians ; now, *it has been clearly proved that there have existed an alphabet and books since the time of Seth, more that a thousand years before the Deluge ;* that all the alphabets in the world had their origin from one and the same primitive alphabet ; that our alphabet was transmitted through Noah, and so arranged as to express the places of the seven planets in the Zodiac at the termination of the Deluge.—According to a very generally received opinion, the hieroglyphics of the Egyptians or the cuneiform characters of the Persians, Medes, and Assyrians were the first of all written characters ; now it is ascertained that all these and similar written characters have the Noachian alphabet of twenty-five letters for their basis.—Hitherto a great number of Indo-maniacs have maintained that the original language had been the Indo-Germanic, a sort of Sanskrit ; now it is known that all the languages in the world are derived from the old Hebrew original language, as the very names of the antediluvian letters among the different nations, and the language of the ancient Egyptians, prove.—According to Letronne and others, our Zodiac had its origin only five hundred years before Christ ; now we know that *it is as old as the human race*, and that it passed through Noah to all the nations of his posterity.—Hitherto it has been supposed that the earliest and innumerable astronomical observations of the ancient Egyptians, referred to already by Diodorus Siculus, had utterly disappeared from the sphere of human knowledge ; now we know that several hundreds of them, extending down to the Roman emperors and back to Menes, 2781 B. C., have been preserved upon the Pyramids, in temples, on sarcophagi, stellæ, and papyrus-scrolls." (See his *Summary of Recent Discoveries,* New York, 1857.)

It may also be added, in passing, that an enormous ship, greater than the Great Eastern, was built before the Flood. It was one hundred and twenty years in building. It served to weather the turbulence of an ocean world. But how was it possible practically to carry out the work of constructing such a vessel without the use of a fixed system of measures, or without the use of figures, drawings, and an established and comprehensible order of notations which the workmen could read and refer to ? Will those who deny the existence of writing before the Flood give the solution of the problem ? The successful building of such a structure is itself a demonstration that Noah could write and that the antediluvians could read.

SCIENCE AND THE CONSTELLATIONS

THE question has been put : " If this theory be true, how is it that the inspiration does not fit in with the Copernican centre instead of the Ptolemaic ?" It has also been objected that " the indisputable facts of science are obstacles to such a belief as that of Dr. S.—obstacles which he has scarcely made an attempt to overcome, and to which he is very likely indifferent."

It may be laid down as an ethical axiom that no man has the right to be indifferent to " indisputable facts," whether of science, religion, or the common affairs of life. Nor is the author of this book indifferent to any " facts of science " having in them the element of settled truth. But no such facts are known to him to impose a bar to the acceptance of his explanation of the origin and meaning of the ancient constellations, or to negative the astronomy on which they are based. Any objection to be raised on the ground here indicated can be raised with equal force against the Scriptures and against the popular almanacs which modern science itself puts forth for the use of mankind, and which are accepted on all hands. The astronomy of the ancient constellations is all embraced in the astronomy of to-day, and belongs to the fixed verities of that noble science. There is nothing in the astronomy of the primitive constellations at variance with the truths of the so-called Copernican system, or else it would be impossible for the Copernicans of to-day to accept and embody it in their science, as they all do. Neither is there anything in this primitive record to identify it with the elaborate and exploded errors of the Ptolemaic system, or any other which failed to accept the present doctrine of centres of gravitation and that the earth and planets revolve around our sun. And if it notes the sun as one of the exalted travellers that seem to move across the face of the sky, and to connect notations with these apparent motions, it is in full accord with universal observation, with all the almanacs, with the diction of the Bible, and with the ordinary statements of astronomers themselves. We all accept the same in our common language every day. Although we know the scientific facts, that does not alter the appearances to the eye or our way of speaking, or furnish a basis for any better popular representation. Only for the sake of the manifestation to the eye of the beholder is the sun thus numbered with the other travellers in the pictorial readings attached to the heavenly orbs. And it is the only way, indeed, in which the sun can be used for such a purpose, no matter what the scientific facts may be.

Neither does such a notation of the apparent motions of the sun to an earthly beholder argue ignorance of the real astronomical truth. It is a great error to suppose that no true knowledge of the real structure of the solar system or of the universe existed before the time of Pythagoras, Copernicus, Kepler, Galileo, and Newton. On this point hear the testimony of Sir William Drummond.

"*The fact is certain*," says he, "that at some remote period there were mathematicians and astronomers *who knew that the sun is in the centre of our system*, and that the earth, itself a planet, revolves around the central fire; who attempted to calculate the return of comets; who indicated the number of solar years contained in the great cycle by multiplying a period (variously called in the Zend, the Sanskrit, and the Chinese, Ven, Van, and Phen) of one hundred and thirty years by another of one hundred and forty years; who took the parallax of the sun by a method superior to that of Hipparchus, and little inferior to our own; who fixed with considerable accuracy the distance of the moon and the circumference of the earth; who held that the face of the moon was diversified with vales and mountains; who asserted that there was a planet beyond Saturn; who reckoned the planets to be sixteen in number; and who calculated the length of the tropical year within three minutes of the true time. All the authorities for these assertions are stated in my *Essay on the Science of the Egyptians and Chaldeans.*

"There is nothing, then, improbable in the report of Josephus when he says that the descendants of Seth were skilful astronomers, and seems to ascribe to them the invention of the cycle of which Cassini has developed the excellence. The Jews, Assyrians, and Arabians have abundance of traditions concerning the antediluvian astronomical knowledge, especially of Adam, Seth, Enoch, and Ham. It was asserted in the book of Enoch, as Origen tells us, that the constellations in the time of that patriarch were already named and divided. The Arabians say that they have named Enoch *Edris*, on account of his learning.

"That the invention of the Zodiac ought to be attributed to the antediluvians may appear to some a rash and idle conjecture; but I shall not renounce this conjecture merely because it may startle those who never thought of it before. Tradition has told several of the Oriental nations that the antediluvians were eminently skilled in astronomy; and tradition has generally some foundation in truth. When

Bailly undertook to write the history of astronomy, he found at the outset certain fragments of science which proved to him the existence of a system in some remote age and anterior to all regular history, if we except the fragment in the book of Genesis. As all the emblems in the similarly divided Zodiacs of India, Chaldea, Bactria, Arabia, Egypt are nearly alike, it would seem they had followed some common model; and to whom should we attribute its invention but to their common ancestors?" (*On the Zodiacs of Esne and Denderah*, pp. 38–40.)

Drummond was once a skeptic. In his earlier work, *Œdipus Judaicus*, he treated the Scriptures with much disrespect. But when he came to search into the originals of human history and science, and to investigate the remains of early antiquity, he came to the convictions above expressed, and in the essay quoted gives full confidence to the biblical records. And the conclusions to which he came respecting the mathematical and astronomical knowledge of the ancients have since his time received abundant confirmation.

Goodsir, in his *Homilies on Ethnic Inspiration*, takes the ground that, as it is unnatural and rash to suppose that God never taught any of the human race, nor led any of them to see, during those early generations, the scientific truth respecting these wondrous creations of His own that shine in the heavens, so there is solid reason to believe that some were so led, and were taught *supra*-scientifically those things, and that there is proof of it now which all who are willing to investigate will find as clear as the noonday sun.

One part of this proof he finds in the great Pyramid of Egypt, the first, greatest, most perfect, and most scientific building now upon the face of the earth, and constructed certainly more than four thousand years ago. By the scientific labors of many within the last twenty years it has been ascertained and clearly demonstrated that there is in the measures, pointings, form, and features of that great primeval monument, whosoever built it and for whatever purpose, a massive and indestructible stone memorial of a complete and faultless knowledge of the structure of the universe, of the exact and physical sciences both terrestrial and cosmical, a determination of a perfect system of weights and measures scientifically conformed to what the Opifex Mundi fixed in things when he fetched a compass round the worlds and weighed the hills in balances. Scientific investigation on the part of different men competent to the task have made it clear that there is built into that edifice a record of the condition of the starry heavens at the time of its erection which gives its age by astronomy in full accord with all external indications and evidences; also a record of the size, form, and weight of the earth and its relation to and distance from the sun, the true length of the solar year, the number of years in the precessional cycle, the average temperature of the habitable world, together with multitudinous cosmical facts and mathematical formulas and proportions no better told by any science now existing among men. Nay, more, says this author: "The unquestionable and remarkable coincidences between the structure of the Great Pyramid and astronomical facts find an exact place amongst, and give consistency and form to, what may be called a collection of astronomical and physical traditions, the whole of which, in the result, corroborates the standard chronology and history of the race." (See my book, *A Miracle in Stone.*)

The demonstration is thus before our eyes, open to every one's examination, that there was a true scientific astronomy anterior to Herodotus, the father of modern history, and before Hesiod and Homer, which took the Zodiac and the constellations as an essential part of it, whose teachers and professors were no more Ptolemists or Jasperites than the Newtons and Herschels of modern times, and who possessed, and could architecturally embody for the reading of the long after ages, as pure and sound a knowledge of the heavens as any who have lived since our astronomy has cast off the swaddling-clothes of its babyhood. The evidence is here that those who invented the constellations and made the most of them, and noted the apparent motions of the sun with other travellers of the circuit of the heavens, were as good Copernicans as Copernicus himself thousands of years before Copernicus was born, and who were favored with a vastly broader and deeper insight into the economy of the universe than Copernicus ever dreamed of. No power or intelligence of man to-day can convict them of ignorance in any point as to any "indisputable facts of science." Their work has come down to us through long intervening ages of darkness, superstition, and apostasy, so superior to the after intelligence of the race that it was no longer in human power so much as to understand it until the advances made within the last few centuries. And just in proportion as solid science grows and comes to fixed results do these primeval lights loom up as the very kings of mind, whose sublime comprehension of Jehovah's works we are only beginning to approximate. In five thousand years the world has not been able to go beyond them in these matters. They knew "the indisputable facts of science," and with that science and to that science they framed the constellations, whatever else they meant to record by the names, figures, and explanations which they attached to them as they present themselves to human observation.

THE BIBLE AND THE CONSTELLATIONS.

ONE reviewer just quoted makes the further point: "If these constellations, in their names, etc., with all their mythological associations, mean what the author claims for them, how strange that we have no intimation of it in the Scriptures!"

This exclamation is meant to indicate an argument, but it is an argument which makes unwarranted assumptions, and rests on a *non sequitur* for its conclusions. If there were no mention at all of the constellations in the Bible, that silence might perhaps still admit of explanation, and, whether explainable or not, it still would not follow that inspired men had nothing to do with them. But it is not true that the Scriptures are totally silent touching the existence, origin, intent, and meaning of the constellations, as will presently be shown, although direct biblical allusions to the subject are not numerous.

Approaching the matter solely from the side of what we rest on as the record of all that God has revealed concerning His plan of grace, it is natural to feel a little surprise that the Bible does not more appeal to and rest on the older record of the same things in the constellations. But a closer contemplation of the peculiarities of the case shows that we should not be thus surprised even though the theory of this book be thoroughly and unmistakably true.

It must be remembered that all the books of the Bible, with the exception of the book of Job, were primarily and most immediately intended for the children of Israel, as the giving of these books was exclusively to and through that people. The entire calling and mission of Israel, its peculiar and emphatic segregation from all other peoples, and its special training and development for a particular purpose in the divine plan, thus necessarily come into the question and furnish an important element in reaching a correct answer to it. Whatever might tend to obscure or diminish the broad lines of separation between Israel and the other portions of the human family, was against the call of Abraham, and hence was to be avoided by all true Israelites. In every possible direction we observe the utmost precaution to keep Israel in complete isolation. Not only in religious observances, but in the entire law, ceremonial, civil, domestic, even to the minute details of dietetics, there was a studied fencing off of this people from all other inhabitants of the earth. The observance of these laws, the worth of which in some instances cannot otherwise be traced, was the test of their loyalty. Nothing in common with the rest of the world was regarded with favor or could lawfully be.

Now, it is a matter of scriptural record that there was a primeval revelation of the Gospel made to man immediately after the Fall. It must have been a very clear and full revelation, or it could not have sufficed for the comfort and saving of the early patriarchs. The New Testament is specific in telling us that there were inspired prophets from the very foundation of the world, and that what they taught and prophesied was precisely that which has been or is yet to be fulfilled in and through Christ. (See Luke 1 : 69, 70 and Acts 3 : 21.) This Gospel necessarily went abroad with the multiplication of the race, first through all the antediluvian generations, and then through and from Noah to all his descendants. Above all, if the first prophets—Adam, Seth, and Enoch—did connect the truths of the primitive revelation with astronomy, and hung the full record of the Gospel promise upon the stars by means of the pictures and names in the constellations, it necessarily was the common possession of all the early nations, as we find from the traditions and records which have been preserved that the constellations were. There was then what we might call the primitive Ethnic Revelation—the original divine Gospel —whose line went out through all the earth for all people alike.

Through the working of the depravity, perverseness, and consequent deterioration of the descendants of Noah that Gospel became greatly obscured and lost. Even the records and illustrations of it which the ancient prophets had inscribed upon the sky, through the evil genius of Nimrod and the seductions of the great enemy of souls had become almost universally prostituted to idolatry and degrading superstition, just as the brazen serpent, which Moses made by divine direction, was prostituted among the Israelites. Sabaism, the worship of the figures of the constellations, and the turning of these celestial signs into instruments of fortune-telling and an impious astrology, had arisen upon what holy hands by sacred impulse had connected with the stars as God's promise of salvation through the Seed of the woman. The very sacredness of the thing was a power to help on the accursed perversion. And thus in the wisdom and goodness of God it was ordained to select and train a separate and distinct people to be the depository of a re-enunciation of His plan and promises of grace, and out of whom to develop the chosen Servant of God who was to bring the great salvation. That people was Israel, and that Servant, the inmost centre of Israel, was the Christ.

In this new start of the kingdom of God it was needless—and would have really been a weakening of the whole procedure—to appeal to the old ethnic records, which had become so abused and perverted to that very state of things which the new start was meant to offset and remedy. It was enough to take the old promise as it had been given at the first, to recognize the prophetic character of those to whom it was given, and who found in it their hope and their salvation, and to reannounce and re-embody that promise in special forms among a people chosen and separated for the purpose. And just this is what was done, in which there was no occasion whatever to make appeal to what the heathen had, and had so terribly perverted, or to mix up the common possession of the world with the training of a people called to be separate in all things from all others. As we cannot conceive of Christ enforcing His teachings by appealing to the sayings and opinions of heathen sages who lived before Him, however true they may have been, and as we would feel it strange if Moses had sought to intensify faith in his laws and precepts by showing that they accorded with " all the wisdom of the Egyptians," so it would have been incongruous in the Israelitish prophets to appeal to the Chaldean astronomers to supplement or support their predictions of " the sufferings of Christ and the glory that should follow," however truly the same things may have been set forth in the constellations.

The Jewish people were, moreover, so prone to take up with the worst idolatries of the nations around them, even with all the precautions and stern laws to prevent it, that it would have increased and facilitated that proclivity had their sacred prophets mixed up with their instructions any prominent references to what was so deeply interwoven with all the living idolatries of the time. For this reason it perhaps was that, in the Jewish Zodiac, all the figures were expunged and the letters of the Hebrew alphabet substituted in their place. It was to guard against ethnic idolatries, all of which were more or less connected with the constellations, which the nations had utterly perverted from their true meaning and intent.

The whole condition of things in the general world, and the whole intention with regard to the Israelitish people, thus come in to show that, however truly the Gospel may have been set forth in the original invention of the constellations, it would have been a hazardous and very unfitting thing for the Hebrew prophets to make their appeal to the ancient astronomy, which, by the depravities of men, had become the chief foundation of the idolatries, false worships, auguries, and astrologies then so dreadfully debasing the entire world around them.

So far, then, as respects the sacred books issuing from the Jewish prophets, there is every reason to expect little or no reference to the ethnic records of the primeval revelations. The simple absence of any *condemnation* of the constellations, then held sacred by all the nations, and so much perverted by them, is more marvellous than the absence of appeals to them as records of the original promise of a Redeemer to come. It argues that in the mind of the Spirit there was still some reserve with regard to that system as not a thing of mere human invention or to be denounced with heathenism in general. The particular purpose of the call of Israel had no special use for that system, and too much regard to it would have so militated against that calling that the wonder is that the Jewish prophets never once assail it or speak one word against it, even while burdened with messages of the wrath and punishment of God upon heathenism and idolatry. Had that system been nothing but an outgrowth of the wild imaginations of man, incorporated as it was with the false religions then dominating over all the world, it is next thing to impossible to explain why it was not pre-eminently singled out for prophetic malediction; and any recognition of it at all in the prophetic books, as connected with a proper understanding of things, is a powerful consideration in favor of its prophetic origin and sacred intent.

THE BOOK OF JOB

THE book of Job, however, did not originate with the Jewish prophets. It was written before Israel's time and outside of the Israelitish race. Though by inspiration adopted into the list of the Hebrew canon prepared by the special inspiration of God, it belongs to the ethnic records of the primeval revelations, and embodies the sacred light and truth of those revelations as received, held, and exemplified in its time by the purest and truest of the ethnic believers. It is a sort of encyclopædia of the faith, life, thinking, worship, and wisdom of God's people before Moses and outside of Israel. As an ethnic book divinely inspired we would expect to find in it references to whatever belonged to the ethnic records and teachings respecting the true God and the Redeemer that was promised, including the system of the constellations, if indeed that system was of primitive prophetic origin and meant to record and illustrate the Gospel as first revealed to man. In such a book, from such a source and age, and with such an object, we would certainly expect to find allusions to these frescoes on the heavens if they be what is affirmed of them in these Lectures. Nay, the absence of such allusions here would necessarily argue either that no such system as that of the constellations existed in Job's time, or that, if existing, it had nothing whatever to to do with the revelations and promises of God.

In this particular instance the argument suggested by our reviewer would apply in full force, and would be next thing to conclusive against our theory, if there were no intimations in the book of Job as to its

reality. But what we hardly should expect in the Jewish prophets we do find here in this exhibit of the pure ethnic faith and piety. At least five of the principal constellations are referred to by name in the book of Job:

1. *"Arcturus" (Aish)*, which nearly all the best commentators, Jewish and Christian, take as denoting the north polar constellation now known under the name of *Ursa Major*, the Great Bear (chaps. 9 : 9 and 38 : 32).

2. *"Orion,"* so named by Homer hundreds of years before the time of the earliest Greek philosophers, and called *Kesil* in chaps. 9 : 9 and 38 : 31.

3. *Taurus*, by its centre and chief mark, *"The Pleiades" (Kimah)*, the Seven Stars (chaps. 9 : 9 and 38 : 32). The Arabians, according to Hafiz, considered the Pleiades the seal or seat of immortality. Maedler, in modern times, from observations of the motions of the so-called "fixed stars," has pointed out the centre of this group (Alcyone) as the great central Sun of the universe, around which all others revolve. In all the ancient myths and traditions this group of stars plays a most conspicuous part, and is ever associated with benignity and blessedness. And "the sweet influences of Pleiades" are here referred to after the same manner, as perhaps embodying the universal centre of gravitation as well as ushering in the genial spring.

4. *Scorpio*, the constellation directly opposite to *Taurus*, described in the English version as *"the chambers of the south"* (chap. 9:9). That the reference is to some asterism of the same sort as the three with which it is named it would be arbitrary to doubt. Some think it refers to such of the constellations as were hidden below the southern horizon in the time and latitude of Job; but the definiteness in the three preceding references would seem to require that we should take this as equally definite. The mention of a house to the south, over against the Pleiades, would call for a particular Zodiacal constellation, which would necessarily be *Scorpio*. Aben Ezra, E. S. Poole, and others translate it *Scorpio*, and so Dr. Hales, Dr. Brinkley, President Gouget, and M. Ducoutant take it, and calculate the age in which Job lived from these notations.

5. *Hydra*, "The Fleeing Serpent" (chap. 26 : 13). The best interpreters agree that the reference here must be to one of the constellations; and of all the stellar serpents there is no one to answer the description so completely as the vast constellation of *Hydra*.

This gives two signs of the Zodiac and three other constellations. But the *Zodiac* as a whole, with its succession of signs and seasons, is recognized and spoken of: "Canst thou bring forth *Mazzaroth* in his season?"—in the margin, *"The Twelve Signs."* Rosenmüller, Herder, Umbreit, Gesenius, and many others, with the Jewish authors at their head, understood by it nothing more nor less than *signa celestia*, the celestial signs—"*The Zodiac.*" The word means the separated, set apart, divided, apportioned, as the spaces given to the twelve signs in the circle of the Zodiac, and which mark the successive seasons in the year. Selden informs us that in later Jewish writings *Mazzalôth* are the signs of the Zodiac, and the singular, *Mazzal*, is used to denote signs singly. *Mazzalôth* is the same in later Hebrew that *Mazzaroth* was in the more ancient forms. Everything about it goes to confirm the rendering in the margin of our English Bibles, and to prove that the Zodiac with its twelve distinct spaces, signs, or houses, bringing forward the seasons in their succession, is what is meant.

And with the twelve signs of the Zodiac recognized, and three of the Decans besides, the whole system of the constellations is necessarily implied and included, while the entire showing is directly associated with the work, majesty, and glory of God.

Nay, the book speaks of a general *garnishing of the heavens*, which would imply that there was a dividing off of *the whole face of the sky* into groups and pictures, just as we find in the ancient constellations (see chap. 26 : 13). Barnes finds in this *garnishing* the "*pictures of the heavens*, with a somewhat fanciful resemblance to animals, etc., one of the most early devices of astronomy still continued as aiding in the description of the heavenly bodies." Nor is there any adequate reason for taking the reference in any other way.

Thus it clearly appears that the constellations were known and determined in Job's time, and that they were well understood and much in view in the sacred contemplations of the believers of that age.

But the record goes still farther. This *garnishing of the heavens*, this grouping of the stars in pictures on the face of the sky, is here affirmed and claimed to be *the work of God Himself* by His Spirit. The declaration concerning the Lord of Creation and Providence is: "*By His Spirit He garnished the heavens*; *His hand hath formed the crooked* [fleeing] *serpent*" (chap. 26 : 13). There is here the ancient poetic parallelism, giving the general statement in one line and the repetition of the same in particular in the next. The intimation is not that the forming of the fleeing serpent—*Hydra*—is a thing separate and distinct from the garnishing of the heavens, but that it is a specimen of that sacred garnishing, that we may determine and know from a specific part what is the true character of the whole. The subject is the formation and arrangement of the figures of the constellations; and that work is unqualifiedly ascribed to the Spirit of God, to prophetic inspira-

tion—the same as the biblical records are ascribed to the Holy Ghost.

This gives us scriptural evidence that the most approved and pious of the old ethnic believers considered and interpreted the constellations as from God, and as containing a sacred record of great consequence and worth in connection with their faith and hopes. And it is thus more than likely that from the stars, as much as from any other records and traditions, Job derived that triumphant evangelic confidence: "I know that my Redeemer liveth, and that He shall stand at the latter day upon the earth : and though after my skin worms destroy this body, yet in my flesh shall I see God : whom I shall see for myself, and my eyes shall behold, and not another; though my reins be consumed within me" (Job 19 : 25–27).

Now, this book of Job, with these presentations in it, has become a part of the canon of Holy Scripture, certainly not without inspired sanction. The same Spirit which moved the Hebrew prophets has thus recognized the ethnic inspiration, and hence also these claims with reference to the constellations. It is therefore a false assumption to say that "we have no intimation in the Scriptures" of what is sought to be shown in these Lectures.

THE HEBREW PROPHETS

BUT even the Hebrew prophets, being moved by the same Spirit which was in the ancient ethnic believers, have not been totally silent touching these uses of the stars. The book of Genesis is largely made up of early records held to be sacred, distorted fragments of which have come down through all the more ancient peoples; and the quotations of those records in the foundation-book of the volume of inspiration appear in the Bible with precisely the same allusions which attend them everywhere else.

Thus, in the very first chapter of Genesis, in the account of the creation of the celestial luminaries, there is a distinct statement of their appointment and uses, including and specifying one which can in no possible way be satisfactorily and adequately explained in fidelity to the divine Word without admitting what we claim for the ancient system of the constellations. It is there written that "*God* said, Let there be lights [luminaries, light-bearers] in the firmament of the heaven to divide the day from the night; *and let them be for* SIGNS, and for seasons, and for days, and for years: . . . *and it was so*" (Gen. 1 : 14, 15).

Whatever this being "*for signs*" may mean, it is here affirmed to be one of the intended uses of the heavenly luminaries. It is also included in the statement that God is the author of that use, that it was instituted and established by Himself, and, further still, that said use was a matter of fact at the time this record was made; for it is added, "*It was so.*"

It has been one of the standing perplexities of commentators to explain what this making of the heavenly orbs into "*signs*" can mean, apart from "seasons," "days," and "years" which depend upon their natural revolutions. Admit into the case the divine formation of the primeval constellations, and the whole statement takes on a grand meaning, worthy of so solemn and magnificent a record; but let that out, and our expositors are all at sea, without chart or compass, and without the possibility of suggesting anything worthy of the record or of themselves. In other words, they can do nothing with it deserving of serious respect, and the whole thing in this grandest of all narrations, in which every word is overflowing with the profoundest meaning, evaporates into a bundle of puerile, contradictory and unverifiable human conceits.

There is in the sacred statement an element of historic fact overlooked by our commentators, but presenting some clue to the real meaning. It is affirmed that at the time of the making of the statement the use of the heavenly orbs as "signs" existed. The record is plain: God said, "*Let them be for signs,* . . . AND IT WAS SO." The record itself dates far back beyond Moses, for the same, in almost the same terms, has been found in the cuneiform writings made more than two thousand years before Christ. The same is also found in some sort traditionally preserved among all the primitive peoples, who must have derived it from one common source antedating the Babel dispersion. It certainly belongs to the time of Noah, who perhaps was the prophet of God who originally wrote it, and from whom the world after him received it.

Was there anything, then, in Noah's time of such note and sacredness as to answer to the statement of the actual use of the heavenly bodies as a system of "signs"? Unquestionably there was, and that system was the system of the constellations. This is not a matter of guess or inference, but a matter of positive record dating back to Noah's time, and now brought to light in the exhumed remains of the ancient Assyrians and Chaldeans. Nay, among those remains there has been recovered a written account of the Creation answering in every vital particular to the account in Genesis, and furnishing what may be regarded as the primeval commentary on the biblical account of the creation of the heavenly orbs, especially with reference to the particular statement touching their divine appointment as "signs." A translation of this tablet-record is given at page 407, as furnished by Smith and Sayce, who add that it tells about "*the constellations of the stars, the signs of the Zodiac,*" etc., as God's creation, and that it

occupies the place of, and is equivalent to, the phrase in Genesis which speaks of the forming of the heavenly orbs into "*signs.*" Even the whole system of the constellations is given in detail in these tablets, and ascribed to the great God as His work at the beginning.

This is the oldest paraphrase of the words in Genesis known to man. It was made more than four thousand years ago. It agrees with all the old ethnic traditions and beliefs. There is nothing whatever to show that it is at all at variance with the truth. It harmonizes with the literal sense of the words of the Bible, and corresponds with every point they contain or suggest. And it must needs go very far to fix the meaning of the sacred record on this particular item to be, that in appointing the celestial orbs "*for signs*" God instituted a system of symbols and indications by means of them from which mankind might ever read the revelations of special divine importance, and that this system is nothing more nor less than the system of the constellations, everywhere and always called "*the signs.*"

Here, then, among the fundamental presentations of the Scriptures, we have not only "intimation," but something of a positive assertion, that the astronomic system of the constellations is of divine origin, and that it has in it the record of divine revelations. Delitzsch agrees that the statement, in part at least, refers to the astronomic signs, the constellations.

A less direct, but an equally striking, indication of the same thing appears in the vast range of vivid coincidences between the imagery, symbolism, and general diction, the doctrines and the prophecies, of Holy Scripture, and the pictures, names, and images which appear in these ancient "signs." So largely and so completely does the one answer to the other that infidels have seized upon this correspondence to prove that Christianity has been derived from the myths of the constellations. No one can look at the texts cited in this book in connection with the constellations, one after the other, without being struck with the marvellous analogy throughout. But how could all this have been, or hold good through so vast a system, except on the admission that the same God who has given us the Gospel was equally concerned in the making of the constellations as a grand prophetic record of what, in the fulness of time, should be accomplished by "the Seed of the woman"?

See also what is said (p. 12–13) on the nineteenth Psalm, which certainly cannot be fairly gone through with without finding intimation of a sacred voice and record on the starry heavens beyond what the celestial orbs can naturally tell apart from the system of the constellations.

THE NEW TESTAMENT

AND even in the histories of the New Testament St. Matthew narrates a case of practical demonstration that the sublimest elements of the Gospel revelation could be learned from the stars, and were so learned by the Wise Men in such clear and convincing perfection that they undertook a long and expensive journey to pay their adoration to the new-born King of grace and salvation. Commentators talk of the diffusion of what was written by the Hebrew prophets, and have racked their brains and exhausted their erudition to find out possibilities as to how these Wise Men came to the amount of evangelic knowledge and faith by which they were moved; but it is, after all, nothing but guesswork, and an obtrusion into the record of what it does not at all embrace or warrant. The account is that the Magi came to Jerusalem *led by astronomical indications;* hence the suggestion of anything else is impertinent and contrary to the inspired statements. It is possible that they may have had some extraordinary illuminations of the Spirit of God in connection with the matter of their coming, as they had in connection with the way of their returning; but the record says that they had their convictions and guidance *from the stars*, and we have no right to interpolate anything else. And if the stars could so evangelically enlighten and lead them as to the coming of the Saviour, His birth as a child, His worshipful nature, the time and neighborhood of His advent, and His claims upon the faith of mankind, then the stars must have upon them an evangelic record capable of being read, and of conducting men to faith in Him who was born at Bethlehem, crucified on Calvary, and ordained Captain of salvation to bring many sons to glory. *How* the stars were made to fulfil such an office is shown in detail in this book; and that they actually did it in the case of these Magi we have from the pen of an inspired apostle of the Church.

There is, then, no such silence of the Scriptures touching the origin and meaning of the constellations, or of the connection of evangelic prophecy with astronomy, as to make us wonder at the doctrine set forth in this book or to raise a reasonable suspicion against its truth.

THE STAR BIBLE

IT is a matter of interest to one who has entered an uncultivated field, and who has come to important conclusions which some, for want of better information, regard as wild and foolish, to find serious thinkers entering the same field and boldly enunciating similar convictions. No man can advance far in the study of the mystery of the constellations without being convinced of the richness and important of the subject, or without a feeling of wonder that so little attention has been bestowed upon it. But antiquarian research has been showing such brilliant results within the present generation that it is impossible for this territory to be left uncultivated much longer. To show that it is worthy of exploration, and to enlist Christian thinking and scholarship in the grand possibilities which its proper investigation is likely to develop, have been among the chief objects of this book; and the author has been gratified to find that a venerable German pastor was engaged in a like effort contemporaneously with himself.

There has very recently come to hand a volume, published in 1883, entitled *The Chaldean Star-Bible; or, The Starry Heavens according to the Seven Stages of the Mithras-Mysteries in Seven Spheres as the Way to Completion for Time and Eternity, again after centuries presented anew, by Rev. George Karch.* * The method adopted by this writer differs materially from that pursued in *The Gospel in the Stars*, and is quite too indirect to produce satisfactory results; but it nevertheless develops much the same conclusions. Believing that the constellations stand in vital connection with the primitive divine revelations, and with the purest worship of the ancients anterior to and outside of Israel, he endeavors to trace some of the vital elements of the old Iranian or Mithras religion among various ancient peoples—Aryans, Bactrians, Indians, Medes, Persians, Magi, etc.—and deduces from the connection between this ancient cult and the stellar signs many elements of the true biblical faith and hope of the ethnic believers. In this line of inquiry he would naturally reach general conclusions quite agreeing with those more directly developed in *The Gospel in the Stars*. The book embraces forty-five pages of introduction and two hundred and twenty-six additional pages of particular discussion, to which is appended a chart of the constellations. There is some lack of thorough elaboration in the way the argument is conducted, but there is in it a grasping after the truth, with serious conviction that there is something in this ancient system of star-pictures of infinitely more significance and worth than the modern world has even remotely suspected.

To show the beliefs and conclusions of this writer, and how they conform to and sustain what we have endeavored to set forth, a few extracts from different parts of the book are here translated, which will be of interest to those who are disposed to entertain the subject:

* DIE CHALDAISCHE STERNENBIBEL, oder der Sternenhimmel nach den 7 Stufen der Mithras-Mysterien in 7 Gebieten als der Weg zur Vollendung für Zeit und Ewigkeit wieder nach Jahrhunderten neu dargestellt, von George Karch, Pfarrer. Würzburg, Druch von J. B. Fleischmann, 1883.

"Closer examination with regard to the constellations which make up the Ecliptic," he says, "gives assurance that there must be an intentional symbolization in the selection and combination of the ancient pictures of the star-groups. The very fact that many of these figures are so remotely and vaguely traceable in the stars themselves bespeaks design in the choice and formation of them, especially when we take in the pious fancy of the old Orientals and their fondness for emblems and likenesses. I am persuaded that the starry heavens, according to the religious contemplations of the oldest astronomers, present a picture-gallery of doctrinal and rich spiritual significance."

"Albertus Magnus has written (*De Universo*) that all the mysteries of the Incarnation, from the Conception on to the Ascension into heaven, are shown us on the face of the sky and are signified by the stars."

"Not from the ruins of Nineveh, not from the Rosetta Stone, but there in the heights above us—there where the holy Magi beheld the Saviour's star—we find the primordial record and testimony of the way of God to us, and of our way back to God. It is there written on the heavens, to be seen and read of all men."

"The old Persian sphere, as Aben Ezra found it, and as may be read, according to Scaliger, in Petavius and Dupuis, has for each of the Twelve Signs three separate figures or constellations—three Decans. The foundation (fundamental idea) of these three Decans is given in general in the regular zodiacal sign to which they belong; but they give that general idea in different and special pictures."

"These old forty-eight constellations all belong to one great hieroglyphical system, and all cohere as one original casting. They have an enigmatic meaning. They are sacred monuments. Rightly understood, they are a kind of Holy Scriptures in symbolic form, given as a witness to all nations, to aid and enlighten reason and to testify of higher divine truth."

"As these star-pictures have a symbolic meaning of their own, it also follows that many of the heathen myths will be found to correspond with them, along with other analogies. The classic myths incontrovertibly connect with these appearances and movements of the heavenly bodies, and, certainly in their most inward meaning, stand related to these star-signs and what they were meant to express, since they are the same, with only a few local modifications, among all peoples."

"Likewise, the alphabet of the Holy Scriptures embodies a record and expression of the glory of God, the same as it is written on the heavens."

This author speaks of himself as advanced in life, and says that, being relieved from other engagements, he considered it most fitting for him to employ his declining years in endeavoring to become better acquainted with the heavens, and to do some work toward a better understanding of the symbolism portrayed in the ancient system of the constellations—"the beauty of heaven, the glory of the stars, an ornament giving light in the highest place of the Lord" (Ecclesiasticus 43 : 91).

INDEX

Besides the ordinary indication of subjects, this Index contains a Glossary of the names which occur in the constellations and by which particular stars were anciently called. The meanings of these names are largely determined by the ancient Hebrew or Noetic roots from which they are formed, and the significations are given according to the best lexicons and philological authorities.

STARS OF THE FIRST MAGNITUDE
.. .. SECOND ..
.. .. THIRD ..
.. .. FOURTH ..
.. .. FIFTH ..
.. .. SIXTH ..